Sheri Laizer is one of the most knowledgeable of contemporary writers about the Kurds. The passion and commitment she displays for their cause shines through this absorbing and rich book. Anyone wanting to understand why the Kurds continue to fight for their legitimate rights need read no further.

Andrew Whitley, Lecturer in Middle East Politics at New York University; former Executive Director of Middle East Watch

If you care about the Kurds, please read this book. It is the most vivid, detailed, up-to-date and passionate account of their struggle for nationhood.

Michael Ignatieff

Where the book excels is in charting the close and often deadly relationship between Turkey's war against the Kurds and the fratricidal conflicts which have weakened the Kurdish cause in Iraq. A comprehensive account of the troubles of the Kurds since the end of the Gulf War, it is enlivened by much vivid description, fruit of the author's many visits to both Iraqi and Turkish Kurdistan.

Martin Woolacott, Assistant Editor, The Guardian

Sheri Laizer's skilful and sensitive discussion of the question of the role of women in Kurdish society is particularly welcome. She gives a perspective that seldom appears in print.

David McDowall, author of A Modern History of the Kurds

OTHER BOOKS BY SHERI LAIZER

Into Kurdistan: Frontiers Under Fire

Poetry
Maelstrom
Love-letters to a Brigand

Martyrs, Traitors and Patriots: Kurdistan after the Gulf War

SHERI LAIZER

Zed Books Ltd
LONDON & NEW JERSEY

Martyrs, Traitors and Patriots was first published by
Zed Books Ltd, 7 Cynthia Street, London N1 9JF,
UK, and 165 First Avenue, Atlantic Highlands,
New Jersey 07716, USA, in 1996.

Cover designed by Andrew Corbett
Photographs © Sheri Laizer
Top: Shrine to martyrs, Heran, Iraqi Kurdistan, 1991
Bottom: Saddam embraces Kurdish children, Sulaimania,
  Iraqi Kurdistan, 1989
Set in Monotype Ehrhardt by Ewan Smith
Printed and bound in the United Kingdom
by Biddles Ltd, Guildford and King's Lynn

A catalogue record for this book is available from the
British Library

US CIP data is available from the Library of Congress

ISBN 1 85649 395 4 cased
ISBN 1 85649 396 2 limp

Contents

pw

Acknowledgements

I would like to express my warm thanks to Michael Ignatieff for the perceptiveness and integrity with which he responded to the complex situations we met on our journeys in Kurdistan; Saman Jaff for exposing the realities of Kurdish social attitudes, politics and history; Mike Pallis and Anne Rodford, my editors, and Farouk Sohawon, sales manager, at Zed Books for their support; and the many sincere Kurdish friends who accompanied us in Kurdistan despite the risks to all concerned.

I would also like to thank a number of people active in the Kurdish question in the diaspora with whom I conferred on various issues relevant to this book: Ibrahim Ahmad, Mohammed Rasoul Hawar, Burhan Jaf, Ali Manaz, Mahmoud Othman, Andrew Penny, Latif Rashid, Estella Schmid, Mizgin Şen, Mouloud Suara and Parviz Zabihi.

Preface

Sheri Laizer is one of Kurdistan's best and most long-suffering friends. She is not of Kurdish origin herself, but she has chosen to ally herself with the Kurdish cause: writing books about Kurdish history, editing Kurdish poetry, leading fellow journalists in and out of the war-zones of the Kurdish struggle. That is how I met her, in 1993, when making a film on Kurdistan that formed part of *Blood and Belonging*, the BBC television series on nationalist struggles around the world after the end of the Cold War. For three weeks, we travelled throughout the Kurdish homeland in southern Turkey and northern Iraq. Sheri seemed to be on first-name terms with all the major Kurdish figures and was trusted by freedom fighters who no longer trusted each other. She had earned their trust, for, as she recounts in this book, she was in Kurdistan during the unforgettable days of March 1991, when Saddam Hussein's tanks and helicopter gunships re-took the territory won in the Kurdish uprising after the Gulf war. She was on the terrible march into the mountains on the Turkish border; she saw the Turkish troops turning the Kurdish people back to face Saddam's troops.

It is never easy being the friend of revolution; it is never obvious how to hold on to an independent position of your own in the midst of a struggle which is riven by division, in-fighting and factional intrigue. But Sheri Laizer has managed the difficult feat of maintaining solidarity with the Kurdish struggle, while retaining a degree of critical distance towards its failings and weaknesses. Sheri shows the price Kurds have paid for their divisions, and she is honest about the moral dilemmas that arise when a movement of national liberation feels itself obliged to risk innocent lives for the attainment of a just cause. As a woman, she is also able to cast a sharp and dispassionate eye over the cost to women of the cult of the fighter. Women have to struggle to be included in the national movement on their own terms, and this struggle is by no means over.

Through Sheri Laizer's work, and through my own travels in Kurd-istan, I learned to see just how important the Kurdish struggle is, both to the politics of the Middle East and to the understanding of modern nationalism. The Kurdish homeland lies across four national frontiers: Syria, Iraq, Iran and Turkey. The failure of the post-First World War mandates to grant the Kurds autonomy or statehood has brought instability to the region for 80 years. Now that the Palestine question is beginning to move towards a resolution, the Kurdish question becomes the next major item on the agenda of the region. But the obstacles to a settlement of Kurdish claims are formidable. The Kurds are opposed by four of the most virulent nationalisms in the world: the Kemalism of Turkey, the Islamic fundamentalist nationalism of Iran, and the Ba'athist nationalism of Iraq and Syria. Each of these nationalisms requires an enemy to mobilise against. If the Kurds did not exist, those regimes would have had to invent them to justify the rigid centralisation of power on which their survival depends. In repressing Kurdish claims, these states have been able to count on the implicit and explicit support of the major powers who, preferring the devil they know to the devil they don't know, have chosen to prop up the state order of the region at all costs, rather than explore the possibility of a Kurdish homeland.

Squeezed between four nationalisms, patronised or ignored by the major powers, the Kurdish movement struggles for just recognition. It is hardly surprising that it is divided. There are those who think limited autonomy within other states is the best that can be achieved; others believe that armed struggle will bring them a sovereign homeland of their own. These differences of principle are systematically exploited by their enemies.

For the moment, a precarious kind of Kurdistan does exist: a UN protection zone in the territory of northern Iraq, patrolled by Allied aircraft based in Turkey. The protection zone has accorded the Kurds precious little protection; both Iranian and Turkish forces have been able to enter the region at will. Still this experiment in protecting civilians from the attacks of their own state is unique in international affairs: if it works it may provide a model for UN attempts to protect civilians elsewhere who find themselves at the mercy of cannibalistic states. It may also provide the nucleus for a future Kurdish state, carved out of a post-Saddam Iraq. This is the most tantalising hope of all – but it may yet be dashed if Kurdish divisions overcome the common yearning for a home, and if the Allies, out of a desire to placate the Turks, or a desire to reingratiate themselves with oil-rich Iraq, decide to withdraw the air cover. Sheri Laizer has provided the best guide to a region and a struggle which should occupy everyone's attention.

Michael Ignatieff

Glossary

Amn (A) (Mudiriyat al-amn al-ameh) General Security Directorate.

Anfal (A) Military code name for the campaign of genocide against the Kurds in northern Iraq (1987-89), masterminded by the Revolutionary Command Council led by Saddam Hussein. The operations were headed by Saddam's cousin, Ali Hasan al-Majid.

Intifada (A) Uprising.

Istikhbarat (A) military intelligence.

Jash (K) Kurds working in the National Defence Batallions on the side of the Iraqi government.

Korucu (T) State-paid Kurdish militia in Turkey, known as 'village guards' or 'protectors' against the Kurdish guerrillas and pro-Kurdish parties, having a similar function to the *jash* in Iraqi Kurdistan.

Mujahadin Khalq Mixed ethnic Islamic revolutionary opposition party in Iran.

Mukhabarat (A) Foreign intelligence agency with decisive authority over public, internal and external affairs.

Newroz (K) Kurdish New Year (21 March) marking the spring equinox; a symbol of resistance and Kurdish identity for several centuries.

Peshmerga (K) Kurdish fighter – 'those who face death'. The term is mainly used of Iraqi Kurds. The Kurds of the PKK refer to themselves individually as guerrillas with the People's Liberation Army of Kurdistan (ARGK); in Iran, as partisans.

Raperîn (K) Uprising.

Rizgarî Liberation; one of the non-combatant Kurdish patriotic movements which arose in Turkey in the 1970s and continues today.

Shahid (A) Martyr.

Tudeh Mixed ethnic pro-Soviet opposition party based in Iran.

Zahmet Keshan Toilers' Party, led by Kadir Aziz; split from the Socialist Party of Iraqi Kurdistan. The party became strong after the internal clashes of 1994-95.

(A) *Arabic*, (K) *Kurdish*, (T) *Turkish*

Abbreviations

ANAP   Anavatan Partisi (Motherland Party) led by Turgut Özal prior to his death.

ARGK   Arteşa Rizgarîya Gelî Kurdistan (Kurdistan People's Liberation Army), the armed wing of the PKK; PKK guerrilla forces.

DEP   Demokrasi Partisi (Democratic Party) banned in Turkey in 1993; chair, Hatip Dicle.

DHKD   Devrimci Halk Kültür Dernekleri (Revolutionary People's Cultural Associations).

DYP   Doğru Yol Partisi (Right Path) led by Süleyman Demirel and fronted by PM Tansu Çiller since 1992.

ERNK   Enîya Rizgarîya Netewa Kurdistan (National Liberation Front of Kurdistan), the popular and political wing of the PKK.

HADEP   Halkin Demokrasi Partisi (People's Democratic Party), successor of the HEP and DEP formed in 1994; chair, Murat Bozlak.

HEP   Halkin Emek Partisi (People's Labour Party) banned in Turkey after 1992; chair, Fehmi Işiklar.

ICP   Iraqi Communist Party led by Hamid Majid Musa.

IMK   Islamic Movement of Kurdistan (Bizutnawayi Îslamî li Kurdistan) in Iraqi Kurdistan, led by Shaikh Osman until the internal war of 1994–95; thereafter led by Ali Bapir.

INC   Iraqi National Congress – Iraqi opposition coalition led by Ahmad Chelebi.

KCP   Kurdistan Communist Party (Iraq) led by Kerim Ahmad.

KCP   Kurdistan Communist Party – Turkey (Kurdistan Kominist Partisi).

KDP   Kurdistan Democratic Party (Partîya Demoqrata Kurdistan – PDK); first led by Mullah Mustafa Barzani and then by his son Massoud (Kak Massoud).

KDPI   Kurdistan Democratic Party of Iran, formerly led by the late Abdurrahman Qassemlou, and thereafter by Mustafa Hijiri.

KDPI–RL Kurdistan Democratic Party of Iran – Revolutionary Leadership; breakaway wing of the KDPI, led by Jalil Gardani.

KOMALA   Iran-based socialist party attracting broad ethnic membership in Iran.

KPDP	Kurdistan Popular Democratic Party, led by Sami Abdurrahman, disbanded in 1992.
KSP	Kurdistan Socialist Party led by Kemal Burkay, previously TKSP (Turkish Kurdistan Socialist Party).
MCC	Military Coordination Centre – office directing the Allied over-flights above the 36th parallel in northern Iraq, the area designated as the 'safe haven' for Iraqi Kurds.
MİT	Milli İstikhbarat Teşkilat (National Intelligence Organisation [of Turkey]).
MHP	Grey Wolves – Turkish Nationalist Party on the far right, led by Alparslan Türkeş.
PASOK	Partîya Sosyalist Kurd – Iraqi Kurdistan; led by the late Azad Mustafa; merged with the KDP after the 1992 elections.
PKK	Partîya Karkerên Kurdistan (Kurdistan Workers Party), led by Abdullah Öcalan (Apo).
PSK	Kurdistan Socialist Party led by Mahmoud Othman until 1981, in Iraqi Kurdistan, and thereafter by Rasoul Mamand until it merged with the KDP after the elections of 1992.
PUK	Yekîtî Nishtiman Kurdistan (Patriotic Union of Kurdistan), led by Jalal Talabani (Mam Jalal).
RP	Refah Partisi (Welfare Party); pro-Islamic party, led by Necmettin Erbakan, which became more prominent in Turkey after the regional elections of 1992 and the intimidation by the government of the pro-Kurdish legal parties.
SHP	Sosyalist Halkçi Partisi (People's Socialist Party), led by Ismet Inönü; one of the two coalition partners with the DYP in the Turkish government since 1992 .
TAJK	Tevgera Azadîa Jinen Kurdistan (United Women's Movement of Kurdistan), formerly known as Yekîtîya Jinen Welatparêzen Kurdistan (Women's Patriotic Union of Kurdistan); the women's branch of the PKK.
TKP	Türkiye Komünist Parti (Communist Party of Turkey).
TKP-ML	Türkiye Komünist Parti – Marxist Leninist (split from Communist Party of Turkey).
TL	Turkish lira.

© S.Jaff, KIC

Black Sea

Istanbul
Bursa

Ankara ★

TURKEY

Izmir

Maras

Antalya

Adana

Entap

Halab (A

★Nicosia

CYPRUS

S

Mediterranean Sea

Beirut
LEBANON ★

Damascus ★

Tel Aviv ★

Alexandria

Port Said

ISRAEL

EGYPT

Cairo ★

Suez

Beni Suef

Red Sea

Map 1 Area of Kurdish

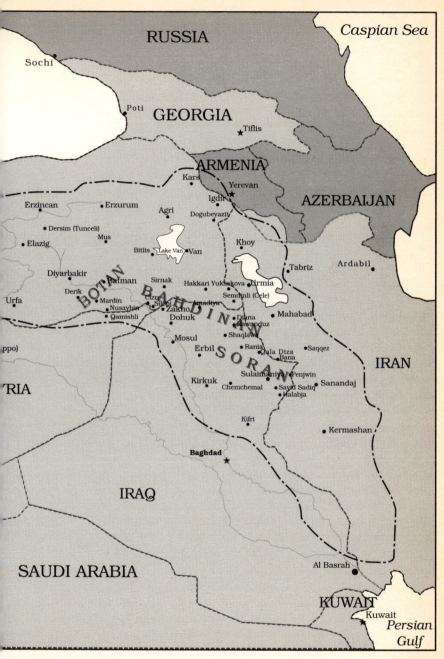

RUSSIA

Caspian Sea

Sochi

Poti

GEORGIA

Tiflis

ARMENIA

Kars

Yerevan

Igdir

AZERBAIJAN

Erzincan

Erzurum

Agri

Dogubeyazit

Dersim (Tunceli)

Khoy

Elazig

Mus

Bitlis

Lake Van

Van

Tabriz

Ardabil

Diyarbakir

BOTAN

Derik

Batman

Sirnak

Hakkari Yuksekova

Urmia

Urfa

Mardin

Cizre

Amadiya

Semdinli (Cele)

Nusaybin

Silopi

Zakho

Diana

Mahabad

Qamishli

BAHDINAN

Dohuk

Rawanduz

(ppo)

Mosul

Shaqlawa

RIA

Erbil

Rania

Qala Diza

Saqqez

SORAN

Bana

IRAN

Kirkuk

Chemchemal

Sulaimaniya

Penjwin

Sanandaj

Sayid Sadiq

Halabja

Kifri

Kermashan

Baghdad

IRAQ

SAUDI ARABIA

Al Basrah

KUWAIT

Kuwait

Persian Gulf

opulation prior to expulsions

For Sarbaz and Saman

In the Middle East, the past is rarely ever just that. In the shape of the motivation for and legitimation of the present, it hangs like a mill-stone around everyone's neck.

Kanan Makiya (Samir Al Khalil)

When there are too many cockerels in the village, the village wakes up late

Kurdish proverb (referring to Kurdish leaders)

I

The Kurdish uprising

Diyarbakir (Amed) – the *de facto* capital of North Kurdistan: a stench of stagnant waste water and garbage lying in the streets, traffic in chaos, shuffling masses. The quarter adjoining the airport is one of Diyarbakir's poorest; sheep graze near the terminal, donkeys and handcarts compete with taxis for the right of way along the rutted roads, and fruit vendors stack up their oranges and watermelons close to the rough kerb to ply their trade. It is here that most foreign journalists arrive *en route* to southern (Iraqi) Kurdistan, the last airport on the long journey by road and river. The border with northern Iraq has been closed since the coalition forces attacked Saddam's troops in January 1991.

I look for the KDP (Kurdistan Democratic Party) leaders of the refugee camps, here since the chemical attacks against the Kurds of Northern Iraq between 1987 and 1989 which had signified a new phase of the Anfal[1] campaign. Stalked by Turkish secret agents (MİT) through Diyarbakir's dangerous back streets, they generally stood out from the local Kurdish population because they continued to wear their national dress. Few of them are here now.

From 4 March 1991 onwards, since the beginning of the Kurdish uprising, most of the Kurds from Iraq have headed home across the border to take part in the defence of Iraqi Kurdistan against the remnants of Saddam's demoralised army. Those who remain behind are civilians hoping for lasting guarantees of peace in their homeland, devastated during the Anfal, before forsaking Diyarbakir for the tents and ruins yet again.

The Anfal was a special operation of genocide bureaucratically engin- eered from 1987 to 1989 by the Ba'ath Party against the Kurds of northern Iraq. Key areas of the Kurdish Autonomous Region were designated as targets of the Anfal. These vast areas comprising Kurdish towns and villages with populations of as many as 70,000 people per town were systematically destroyed by the military employing methods such as burning, bulldozing, and bombing. The inhabitants were subjected to mass evacuation, deportation, imprisonment, execution ('dis-appearance') and, in some cases, mass extermination by a combination of conventional and chemical warfare. In the course of the Anfal, an estimated 182,000 Kurds were murdered by the various agencies within the Ba'ath Party's command structure including the security forces, intelligence departments, special commandos, the army, police and chemical weapons units. Saddam Hussein invested his cousin Ali Hassan al-Majid (nicknamed *Ali Kimiya*, 'Chemical Ali', by the Kurds) with extraordinary powers to manage operations in the North. Under decree No. 160 passed 29 March 1987 by the Revolutionary Command Council (headed by Saddam), al-Majid, as the Ba'ath Party Northern Bureau's Secretary General was given absolute authority over all other agencies and supreme command of the Anfal. The entire Ba'ath party apparatus, army, *jash*, security and emergency committees went into operation under al-Majid, in a fully systematic way, to carry out the campaign aimed at eliminating the 'saboteurs', as the dissident Kurds were named. The Anfal operations against Iraq's Kurds were every bit as thorough and efficient in their stages of execution as had been the Nazi Holocaust against the Jews.

The heady days of the uprising: 'Free Kurdistan'

The Khabur Bridge, on the old TIR (Transport International Routier) trade route between Turkey and Iraq, has been blown up and there is no way into liberated Kurdistan except across the snowbound Turkish moun-tains, or by boat or raft across the Tigris river from Syria. Cameraman Mark Stucke and myself opt for the river.

Spring rains have swelled the Tigris to a muddy brown torrent and our two-person TV news crew has to wait in Qamishli until it subsides. Other foreign journalists eager to see Iraqi Kurdistan historically in Kurdish hands also watch the river, waiting for an opportunity to cross.

After two days of futile attempt, word arrives that a crossing may be possible today. Iraqi Kurds with Syrian contacts and Syrian Kurdish support assist travellers in reaching the fording point. They make ready their Land Rovers and tractors to take on the muddy fields lying between the villages and the torrent. Jalal Talabani, the head of the PUK (Patri-otic Union of Kurdistan), is also in Qamishli giving press conferences and waiting to return with his entourage of bodyguards. We leave shortly before him, on 26 March 1991, after obtaining a vehicle and peshmerga guides courtesy of the KDP which also has an operations base downtown. Qamishli is a rough oily frontier town with a mixed Kurdish and Arab population, half of whom seem to be wearing military uniform. Even schoolchildren are dressed like junior soldiers.

Crossing the waste land of muddy pastures, we halt midway in the path of an oncoming vehicle. It is a makeshift ambulance driven by Syrian Kurds and it carries wounded peshmergas out of the battle zone in northern Iraq for medical treatment in Qamishli. The excited Kurds report that fighting has become fierce during the night.

After a short briefing we wend our way on through the mud, down to the riverbank. Small fibreglass skiffs powered by outboard motor contend with the swift currents of the river to deliver a cargo of guns, food supplies, expatriate Kurds and foreign correspondents to Kurdistan. There are many armed Kurds waiting on the Syrian shore to cross and we join them in a loose group as they organise guns and baggage for loading. Only two boats are running. It is going to be slow.

Finally, six people, including ourselves, are taken on board one of these 'ferries' and looking back over the wake and flying spray of the noisy little boat we watch as the Syrian flag on the riverbank disappears behind the swirl of currents which convey us towards Iraq. There on the opposite shore, where the river laps the pebbled banks of Iraqi Kurdistan, we can now discern the white mushroom clouds of Iraqi bombs blooming above the tranquil green foothills of Khabur.

'Welcome to Kurdistan', our ferryman exhales as the boat grates against the pebbled shore. Among the new arrivals there is an air of excitement; many are exiles returning to 'Free Kurdistan' after decades away. There are many peshmergas here loading the supplies from the skiffs into Toyota Landcruisers and cramming Zakho-bound passengers in beside sacks of guns and flour.

The Zakho road curls around the green hills away from the river through Ibrahim Khalil, where the old Iraqi customs and quarantine buildings of border control now provide temporary housing for destitute Kurdish families. Clusters of anti-personnel mines and tank mines, both live and deactivated, pepper the fields and roadside all the way.

In the streets of Zakho the mood is jubilant. Patriotic Kurdish poems are being amplified from several buildings simultaneously, a cacophony like that of numerous mosques whose *muezzin*[2] never chant their call to prayer in unison.

Barzani's KDP officials whom we now meet in their Zakho head-quarters, a former primary school, seem to believe that this is the beginning of a new era of freedom in Kurdistan. They speak in glowing rhetoric of their *raperîn*, or *intifada* (uprising). Zakho fell to the Kurds on 15 March. The Kurds here have tasted freedom for nearly a fortnight.

Kurdish men, youths and young boys, almost all carrying guns, wave their weapons in the air over these scenes of conquest and speak of liberating the whole of Iraqi Kurdistan by the end of the week. The Kurdish irregular forces are facing the Iraqi army along the frontline of Iraqi Kurdish territory and have become confident of success; the Iraqi army has put up little resistance and more than 60,000 soldiers have fled to the Kurds or been captured by them, meeting few reprisals.

With the announcement of the Gulf War ceasefire on 27 February 1991 and the formal cessation of hostilities around daybreak on 28 February, it was only a matter of hours before popular ferment against Saddam turned to revolt in the southern Iraqi town of Basra. The tale widely told has it that one of Saddam's commanders, leading a tank column back from Kuwait into Sa'ad Square in downtown Basra, positioned his tank opposite a large portrait of Saddam in military uniform mounted beside the Ba'ath Party Headquarters. A crowd gathered. Cursing Saddam for the humiliation and hardship he had caused, the tank commander fired a first shot at the presidential image, thereby sparking off the uprising.[3] Four days later, on 4 March in the Kurdish north of the country, the Kurds of Raniya also turned against the government, triggering the uprising that then swept through the entire Kurdish region. On 7 March, the large city of Sulaimaniya arose in response to a fervent call to the Kurds to seize their freedom, broadcast from the PUK's *Denge Gele Kurdistan* mobile radio station (Voice of the People of Kurdistan).[4]

Indeed, within the week, 95 per cent of Kurdish territory was to be taken by the combined forces of the peshmergas and the armed Kurdish masses, their weapons seized from captured Iraqi bases. These numbers were swelled by former *jash*[5] (the Kurdish popular army which fought for Saddam) together with many experienced army officers who changed sides to join the Kurds. The Kurds commenced an attack on 12 March, on the oil city of Kirkuk, the location of Iraq's No. 2 military airport. It fell to the Kurds between 19–21 March. By the time I arrived in Kurdistan, Arbil and Dohuk were also in Kurdish hands.[6]

The atmosphere of fear and oppression had vanished, utterly unlike my visit to Iraqi Kurdistan in September 1989, when I was surrounded by minders from the Ba'ath Party's Ministry of Information. Gone were the army's gun emplacements which had dominated the main roads, the Ba'ath police checkpoints, and the shadow of fear which had darkened the faces of ordinary people at the sight of foreigners. Gone too was the listless way the people had of walking, as if they struggled to conceal some inner secret from the many malevolent eyes which kept constant surveillance over their lives.

In place of the old weight of oppression and constraint, one could feel the burgeoning of the Kurdish nation's confidence and its exhilaration in this uprising. But despite the popular enthusiasm and the early Kurdish victories, I could not help but wonder how these ragged Kurdish forces would contend with the full brunt of an Iraqi attack, should it eventually come. From radio reports broadcast from 27 March onwards, it appeared that Saddam's elite fighting force, the Republican Guards, had been able to escape the war zone in Kuwait to return to Baghdad and protect the regime before the Allies had occasion to attack. The president's army, a force of around 100,000 troops, had apparently remained intact and was at hand to take on the Kurds in the north and Shi'as in the south as soon as Saddam saw fit.

After a first night in liberated Zakho under blackout, we spend the morning filming around town: truckloads of Iraqi deserters are being assisted to leave the country (some appear to be prisoners, but others wave and make the V sign for Kurdistan); brightly dressed Kurdish women wash dishes in the river – water pipes have been destroyed and plumbing disrupted; peshmerga sentries up on the rooftops man anti-aircraft guns; daily life is apparently going on.

Our next stop is the hospital. The wards are choked with women clutching malnourished infants, yellow, wizened and desperately ill. There has been a shortage of milk powder and the babies of the poor are the first to suffer; many will not live out the day. The hospital is short of medicine and staff; most of the doctors are struggling to treat people with the few supplies remaining after the invasion. We decide to carry on south to Dohuk city, closer to the strategic front at Faida. The road to Dohuk is heavily littered with the debris of recent battles: burnt out and abandoned Iraqi tanks, stripped and mangled military vehicles disabled by the retreating army. As we leave Zakho, we see Kurds trying to repair several tanks by the roadside; others are being towed back to town.

Destruction is the keynote of the place – every building previously occupied by the hated Ba'ath party has been ransacked or torched. Although the retreating army and officials began this work of destruction with the aim of destroying anything useful to the Kurds, the ordinary people have continued to tear down, smash and defile anything that remains of Saddam, and to loot the rest. Given a kind of guided tour by the peshmergas, we stop at several buildings and pick our way through the rubble of *Amn* (Security) offices and Ba'ath Party headquarters. Saddam's life-sized portraits have been slashed or shot to pieces. Files and documents – records of interviews with the families of 'saboteurs' compiling their biographies; interrogations of Kurdish captives; numerous columns listing details of torture and executions – are scattered everywhere.

The Kurdish city of Dohuk

Dohuk's green valleys are awash with pink and white blossom. Small streams of melting snow flow through the hills. It is beautiful, fresh and new. I think to myself that this is a bright and hopeful Newroz (New Year) for Kurdistan. The weather has been fine since we left Syria and the rains appear to have stopped. The Kurds are outside in their gardens or visiting relatives and neighbours, wearing newly sewn Newroz clothes, as the custom goes. Downtown amidst the crowds, I happen upon a family I met two years before in Diyarbakir refugee camp,[7] now buoyant and relaxed in their home town. I accept their invitation home, and we leave the impoverished vegetable bazaar to share a midday meal of rice, cucumber and tomatoes. Conversation is animated and optimistic.

Bahjat tells me not all families in Dohuk have been as fortunate as themselves since the Allies attacked Iraq. During the war, this residential quarter of Dohuk, Old Jamiyah, and some other locations were hit in error by Allied bombs. There were no military targets in the area. On 9 February 1991, sixty-three people were injured and seven were killed. The casualties included the family of Rashid Mustafa, an English-speaking teacher whom I later visited with Bahjat. Rashid lost his wife and eldest daughter. His two teenage children, Shirin and Shivan, both lost an eye and two of his younger children were left scarred by flying shrapnel – all this from an American bomb which fell on three houses, leaving only flattened envelopes of concrete behind.

A month has passed since the end of the war and supplies in the town are almost down to nothing. The Kurds are living off the remains of the Iraqi army's stores. There is hardly any flour, little rice and almost no meat. There is no municipal electricity supply. Clean water is scarce. Communications have been cut. No telephones work and petrol too has almost entirely run out. The fighters of the Kurdistan Front hold the last fuel supplies, but even for them fuel and transport has become a critical problem.

None the less, morale is high: thousands of Kurdish men cheer and applaud as Jalal Talabani (leader of the PUK) and Sami Abdurrahman (leader of the Kurdistan Popular Democratic Party) make their first triumphal visits to Dohuk on 27 March, assuring the Kurdish people that their country is in their own hands and all Iraqi Kurdistan will soon be free – only Faida, Sheikhan and the Kurdish outskirts of Mosul remain to be liberated.

The setting sun cloaks Dohuk's barren grey mountains a brilliant amber. Frogs croak across the darkening valleys. The only electricity is that supplied by an occasional generator in the homes of the wealthy, or at the headquarters of the parties. This means getting off the road at nightfall to find a place to stay as we are advised not to be out after dark. Ba'ath party agents, *musteshar* (Kurdish commanders of *jash* units) and individual *jash* still loyal to Saddam have not abandoned their power here. So the peshmergas take us home to their families, share their food and even forsake their beds for us, such is the hospitality. As conversation dies down and darkness encroaches, the rumble of shells exploding on the nearby hills seems closer than it did by day and one begins to get a feeling of the real proximity of the enemy.

Our host on one such evening is Mohammad Rajib, now aged 84. Mohammad had been one of the companions of the late Mulla Mustafa Barzani; he trekked with the KDP leader on the historic exodus from south Kurdistan, up through the triangle of Turkey, Iraq and Iran, and north along the Turkish-Armenian border into the Soviet Union and a 16–year-long Russian exile, following the collapse of the Kurdish Republic of Mahabad in 1946.

Although Mohammad tries his fluent Russian on me, then Arabic, Kurdish, and Turkish, I am clearly not the linguist he is. Mohammad's wife, Ayshe, dressed in flowing green Kurdish skirts, watches us with amusement, sitting beside her son and his wife, with three of their four children. Framed black and white photographs of Mulla Mustafa Barzani and of his son and successor, Massoud Barzani, have recently been hung on the walls and positioned on top of the television. This in itself would have been unthinkable before the uprising when only portraits of Saddam were permitted. Mohammad deftly tunes into Radio Monte Carlo in time for the latest news report. Apparently there is fierce fighting in Kirkuk. Saddam's ground forces have massed 250 tanks along the front-line ready to recapture the city.

Sitting there by lamplight, listening to these grim reports, I wonder how long it will be before the fighting reaches us in Dohuk. Should we carry on south to film the next phases of the battle in Kirkuk, or should we remain where we are? That afternoon a minibus full of European journalists had gone off towards Kirkuk after our briefing from the Kurdistan Front. Another delegation vanished in pursuit of Massoud Barzani. Considering this, we decide to stay where we are. We realise we must be the only foreign journalists left in Dohuk. As the news bulletin ends and the shelling outside gets louder, conversation in the hot room thins. The men sit back to smoke. The tanks and rockets of the Iraqi army are already breaking through into Kirkuk.

By the following day, 28 March, after intense fighting, Kirkuk will have fallen into government hands once more. The Arabs, Turkomans and Assyrians brought into the city in the course of the Iraqi government's Arabization process had not taken part with the Kurds in the attempted liberation of Kirkuk. The Kurds could not match the Iraqi forces in strength, arms or numbers.

The close dark bedroom I've been garrisoned in feels like a vault. I listen to the sound of bombs echoing from the hills and wonder whether sleep will ever capture my consciousness. Despite myself, I manage to drift off, although I am constantly startled into wakefulness by the sheer impact of the explosions. Hour after hour, I raise myself up on my elbows to peer out of the upper window at the night sky and watch the bright trails of falling bombs, then fall back again realising it is futile to watch any longer.

The new day starts peacefully enough, and by 6 a.m. the household is up for breakfast and to listen to the first radio reports.

Although we have a specific agenda for filming, it is difficult to accomplish anything quickly as the peshmergas have become preoccupied by the general disorder which has developed overnight. From being a welcome sight, journalists now seem to be something of an irritant to them. The chiefs keep on putting us off, quite understandably, in accordance with their own priorities: there is no car, there is no petrol, there is no interpreter. They insist that the frontline near Faida is too dangerous for us to film and they refuse to take us there. We continue to petition the commanders as we must, and they keep holding us back. We suspect there may be something they don't want us to see, that things are already falling apart; that if only morale can be kept up and the population prevented from panicking, there may still be a chance. This is the only sense we can make of the change in their behaviour.

Convoys of jeeps carrying armed men begin to screech in and out of town. The peshmergas look anxious.

'Sheikhan has fallen!' they warn. 'We must hold Faida.'

The KDP's commander finally gives in to our requests; they will send us with some peshmergas to film the defences of Dohuk above Faida and then to interview Ba'ath Party *mukhabarat* and *istikhbarat* officers taken as prisoners of war by the fighters.

After first waiting for a car and then for petrol to make it work, Fehim Abdullah, our KDP liaison officer, takes us to film two sites manned by the Kurdish resistance. The first location boasts only a single long-range gun trained on a gap in the hills a few kilometres down the Zawita road outside town. All is quiet. We double back and take the Mosul turn-off which leads to Faida. The jeep is parked and we begin to climb the hillside. Here we find a small team of peshmergas with a rocket launcher and a Doshka (anti-aircraft gun) mounted on the summit overlooking the lush green plain which spreads out to Faida, and eventually to Mosul beyond. These defences look alarmingly inadequate. We climb up the hillside until we reach the site of a large crater. Fehim tells us two peshmergas were killed here last night by an Iraqi shell – it is very close to town.

As the sun slowly sets on another day in the nervous city, we film the peshmergas as they fire off rockets and a few long-range cartridges at the Iraqi army post just beyond a water-tower, on the Faida plain – little more than three kilometres distant.

The Ba'ath Party's legacy: prisons, forts and torture chambers

It is 29 March 1991. A small stone fort, now being used as a prison, squats atop a low hill above the forested resort of Zawita, just 15 minutes east of Dohuk. It now flies the yellow flag of the Kurdistan Democratic Party (KDP). Armed peshmergas stand guard at the entrance to the prison and patrol the high walls above an open grassy courtyard. Most of the small rooms flanking the grassy square are in use as cells. The cells have heavy metal doors and no windows save a small spy-hole. Once admitted within the enclosure, we present our request to interview the POWs on camera to the KDP official in charge of the place. He readily agrees.

A circle of prisoners sit out in the sunshine on the grass, guarded from above by peshmergas armed with Kalashnikovs and RPGs (rocket-propelled grenades). Some wear army uniform, others are dressed in *dishdasha* (loose cotton gowns traditionally worn by Arab men in hot countries). Some of the prisoners have dirty, bloodied bandages wrapped around recent wounds, festering and untreated.

One senior Ba'ath official, a military commander, has lost an eye in the fighting prior to his capture. When he surrendered to the peshmergas he was shot by his own people. The empty eye socket is raw and weeping. His legs too are swollen and he has strange bruises and burn marks around his neck. He wears a soiled, striped *dishdasha* full of holes. Like all these prisoners, he is in poor shape and his colour is bad. He calls Saddam *mujrim* (criminal or evildoer) and swears that he hated his cruelty. Under such circumstances he can say little else. He knows already what his fate will probably be.

The prisoners are given water during our visit. They appear to have been given little access to fresh air and light beforehand, as they squint at the sun and make the most of our presence to ask for additional refreshment. The KDP want us to see that they treat their prisoners well and oblige them, clearly enjoying the reversal of roles with their former tormentors.

For some time since our arrival in the fort, I have been conscious of the buzz of muffled voices issuing from behind an iron door. I ask the KDP commander if he will ask his guards to unlock the cell so we can look inside.

It is like opening an oven door. A wave of heat surges into our faces, so intense that Mark's glasses instantly steam over. Within the cell we find about forty prisoners all crushed tightly together in the dark heat. The commander explains that his prisoners are all security agents captured by the Kurds: murderers, torturers, and senior Ba'ath Party officials known individually for the crimes they carried out in the course of Anfal operations in Dohuk governorate. Now they have become the pathetic and terrified objects of Kurdish revenge.

Leaving Zawita, we stop off at the larger fort of Nizarkeh on the outskirts of Dohuk, one of the large Gothic-style citadels that the Ba'ath have constructed throughout Kurdistan. These stone forts, all of the same design, were purpose-built for the army in 1981. During the Anfal operations the buildings were no longer necessary for the army as the countryside had been cleared of 'traitors' through systematic mass deportations to Anfal camps. At this time, thousands of Kurds were rounded up *en masse*, transported from the 'prohibited areas' and expelled from the region, or lodged in forts such as these. The empty forts subsequently became holding centres, or prisons, for hundreds of Kurdish families.

No unauthorised persons were ever permitted access to the forts, either when they were in use by the armed forces, or later when they became detention centres. The entire surrounding area was also off limits and the perimeters were planted with landmines and patrolled by helicopters. Any 'trespassers' were shot on sight. Local Kurds believe that the government carried out experiments on their detainees in the forts, and that many of the 182,000 'disappeared' during Anfal lost their lives in such places during this period. The forts were two or three storeys high and possessed hundreds of small rooms with barred windows leading off circular corridors. Within was a vast open courtyard area where large numbers of people and vehicles could be assembled as necessary.

The prison in Dohuk is of the same castle-like design as all the forts and obscured from casual view by its location below the main road. Kurdish refugee families now occupy the rooms which were cells for other Kurdish families until the uprising. Our voices and footsteps echo

from the walls as we walk down the long corridors looking into abandoned cells with their shreds of old clothing, odd shoes, notebooks,
schoolbooks, files, and other debris.

An old man emerges from one of these rooms and confirms the worst
stories we have heard about the prison. His former home once looked
out upon this fort and he heard most of the tales at the time they
occurred. Since the *intifada* he has been taking shelter here with surviving
members of his family. Hundreds of Kurdish families were kept prisoner
here, the old man explains indicating the cells off the corridor where we
stand. After the *intifida* many Kurds were found still locked up in here,
their minds destroyed. Women were discovered naked and emaciated,
covered with sores and bruises. After years of interrogation and sexual
abuse some were unable even to remember their own names.

It is like this throughout Iraqi Kurdistan. Sometimes a victim was
spared the fate which befell thousands of his or her countrymen simply
because the area in which they resided was outside the jurisdiction of
the Anfal, or because a family member might have had connections in
the right places.

As twilight settles, Anwar (pseudonym), one of the peshmergas and
nephew of Mohammad our host of the previous night, escorts us to the
former headquarters of the Ba'ath security forces overlooking the commercial centre of Dohuk, its broad concrete walls dominating the school
and shops below. This vast building, like most of the Ba'ath Party's
former institutions in the area has become home to refugees whose towns
have been destroyed in the Anfal, or who come from areas still under
government control, such as Mosul, Sinjar, and Sheikhan.

The walls of the *Amn* building are pockmarked with bullet holes and
deep gashes left by RPG rockets. Kurdish refugee families are lighting
small fires about which they huddle for warmth and on which they cook
their meals. Sacking, canvas and blankets have been erected as boundary
walls between one family and the next. Some have taken occupancy of
the old car park, others the offices of the six-storey administrative complex above, while the latest arrivals have no alternative but to camp for
the night in the basement, cells, and torture rooms with their hooks and
tables reviving the spirits of the dead.

Beneath the firelit walls of the *Amn* building the atmosphere is hushed
save for the echoes of footsteps and the cries of small babies which carry
on the still night air above the open spaces. As darkness nudges in deeper,
the last sound the sleepers hear above that of their own heartbeats is the
steady thud of Iraqi army bombs landing on the hills outside town.

The end of the uprising

The feared Iraqi attack commences suddenly next morning, on 30 March 1991. The first big shells hit Dohuk at about 7.30 a.m., just as we sit down to a sparse breakfast. There is a loud whining overhead followed by a great clattering bang as the first shell falls and explodes in a nearby street. This is immediately followed by another, and then another. Dozens of children, still barefoot and in their nightclothes, stream out through the gates of their houses to find the bombs. Peshmergas promptly arrive in their Toyota Landcruisers, scanning for the tell-tale plumes of rising smoke to determine what has been hit. This is the first time the Iraqi army has attacked Dohuk itself.

After less than half an hour, further shells come screaming in overhead and thud down upon the city. These first bombs seem to be a warning of what is to come, for within 24 hours the resistance will collapse and the entire population of Dohuk – some 80,000 people – will be on the move. As the city's tension grows, the children are hauled indoors and the streets become deserted. For a time I watch this process from the roof. Then women begin to emerge from their doorways. They have bundled up supplies of food and clothing which they load into cars, trucks, tractors – anything with wheels. For a time, the shells stop falling and then an expectant silence builds above the roofs.

At the local headquarters of the Kurdistan Front, peshmergas stream in with reports of strategic Kurdish posts which have been lost to the Iraqis. The jubilant smiles have gone. Trucks and jeeps loaded with armed men accelerate off in the direction of the frontline, blasting their horns as if noise alone will frighten away the enemy.

Fehim Abdullah, who has been our guide ever since we showed up at his 'office' door insists that what we are witnessing is nothing new. But although he struggles to stay cool, ordinary Kurds have already begun leaving the city in a seemingly endless convoy. Fehim interprets this development as a straightforward expedition to areas outside town to wait until the shelling stops. We hope he is right.

We want to see how effective the enemy shelling has been. Fehim lets us visit the hospital. Several women and children lie on stretchers in blood-soaked clothes. Dohuk's modern hospital, renamed the Azadi (Free-dom) Hospital in place of Saddam Hospital, is chaotic. In an upstairs ward where the morning's casualties lie groaning on dirty beds, a dead woman still lies staring into space, massive black stitches across her forehead, unremarked amidst the frenzy as the few remaining doctors and nurses desperately mop and sew up injured children and babies. As many as thirteen people have been killed or wounded in the morning's bombing.

At dusk, the shelling begins again, this time with such intensity no one can be left in any doubt as to the serious intentions of the Iraqi army. The warm spring weather begins an uncanny metamorphosis at the same moment. Storm clouds darken the valleys, lightning flashes across the dry stony mountains. The deep growling of thunder soon becomes indistinguishable from the roar of falling bombs.

Up on the flat roof of Mohammad's house where we have been guests these past three nights, I gaze out upon the gathering storm and trace the flash of rockets as they streak the close-pressed black sky. The camera is mounted nearby, recording the incoming fire. Now, I hear the high garden gate scrape open below me in the dark. Three armed peshmergas rush into the garden. I hear them being greeted by the family downstairs. It is Ramadan and the family has been fasting for several days. Having just finished their prayers, they have now begun the evening meal to end the day's fast.

Anwar, one of the three peshmergas, now climbed the stairs to the roof and as I looked into his eyes I knew he was bringing us bad news. His gentle, spiritual face was anxious, his gaze focused inwardly. He stood in silence for a while just watching the flaring lights of the attack and then quietly told us he had arranged to evacuate the family. He wanted me to leave with Uncle Mohammad, Ayshe and the children although he agreed that Mark, who was responsible for filming on this occasion, could accompany the fighters. Anwar arranged to meet us in the village of Qadish next day. He would remain behind overnight to fight.

I am reluctant to lose sight of the peshmergas and leave with the family; but Anwar is insistent. As I follow him downstairs, I see in the lamplight Ayshe and the other women packing up provisions. The children have already been woken and dressed to go outside. Their eyes are groggy with sleep and surprise. The family is sad and subdued, especially Ayshe and Mohammad who have seen this all before. No one wants to acknowledge that their worst fear has come true: the rebellion is finished.

A steady stream of slow moving traffic crawls through the dark hills leading out of Dohuk to Zawita and eastwards, slow because there are so many people and so many vehicles trying to escape down the narrow road. The rumble of bombs echoes from the mountains encircling the town. It is time to separate. Mark and the three peshmergas bid me a difficult farewell and slip away like shadows into the storm. I wonder if I will ever see them again.

Being shut away indoors with the brooding family makes me nervous, so I retreat back up to the roof and watch the fighting. We are waiting for the truck which Anwar has requested. Hours seem to pass. At last a large vehicle screeches to a stop outside the gate. Kurdish families begin to call out to one another in the road. The streets, the houses, everything is in darkness.

I went outside to join 'Uncle' Mohammad. The driver was urging various families to hurry, trying to stop them from carrying too much with them as there are many other people to be collected from the neighbourhood before leaving Dohuk. With only a few personal belongings and two sacks of flour, Anwar's family heaved themselves up into the gloomy deck. The other travellers crouched there in the dark were almost all women, children and a few non-combatant men. Mohammad's family now compelled me to climb on after them with my lightest baggage. It was final. As I boarded, I envied Mark being able to follow the peshmergas. I felt more at ease with the fighters than among these terrified families. But the segregation of men and women was a fact of life in war as in peace.

We set off into the darkness without headlights. I clung to the steep sides of the truck as it motored through the close back streets beneath the shells being fired upon Dohuk. They were far too near for peace of mind. Desperate people kept trying to clamber into the laden lorry as it slowly withdrew from the neighbourhood. In their determination to escape, those climbing in were trampling underfoot those already within. Fleeing alongside us were hundreds of Dohuk families, carrying their children and bundles, as they laboured along the dark mountain road out of town.

The fall of Dohuk

It was cold now and a sharp rain had begun to fall. Many children were walking barefoot, or wore open plastic sandals; in the panic to get away they remained clad only in their thin night clothes.

My eyes burned with tears of pure rage and frustration. I felt a terrible wrenching as I realised what I was witnessing: the Kurds had been forsaken again, just as in 1988 when Saddam had unleashed his chemical bombs upon them. They were driven to flight once more.

The cold rain hardened into hail as the lorry crawled high up into the hills. There was no shelter. Tired people had stopped in wretched clumps all along the roadside, lighting fires to try to warm themselves. Some were old, some injured, some had already collapsed from the cold or tiredness. As we kept on through the night, the mountains were full of weary people dragging themselves through the storm.

By daybreak, the helicopters that President Bush had failed to halt circled above the fleeing Kurds, and bore down upon the cities. Only those few unable to escape because of the need to protect the lame, blind and infirm, or who had nothing to fear from Saddam, remained to witness what happened next. The rest of Kurdistan was now on the move, fleeing for Turkey or Iran. The roads were choked. The last ones out of town carried horror stories of what the Iraqi army was doing to those who had fallen behind. A few peshmergas and last minute recruits sped in all directions, some away from battle, others into it. Things were chaotic. And the last petrol supplies had also finally run out.

I watched a bleak blue dawn break over the miserable village of Qadish, built by Saddam, just before we were caught in a renewed cloudburst of sharp hailstones and sleet driven into our faces by the wind. Here, after five hours on the road, the lorry lurched to a halt. The villagers of Qadish were still asleep when the first trucks arrived bringing the refugees from Dohuk, wet and afraid, and urging them to wake up. They greeted us as if we carried the plague. I suppose we did – it was a mere hour or so behind us.

Mohammad's family took me with them to a simple one-storey mud and breeze-block house where they roused some sleeping relatives and explained in hushed voices what had happened during the night. The sleepers still did not want to be disturbed and made little space for us. I tried to catch some rest lying in a huddle on the floor, people kicking me as they tried to stretch out. I felt depression surge through me.

Mohammad and his family were now talking about fleeing to Turkey but I was sure that the Turks would not welcome any Kurds. For my part, I decided to take the back route to Zakho on my own, and then try and get across the Khabur river into Syria. No news had reached us that Zakho too had fallen.

I waited until late morning before taking action, wandering around Qadish taking photographs of people preparing to flee, scanning the convoys of trucks that passed for a glimpse of Mohammad's nephew, Anwar, or Mark, our cameraman. A steady stream of cars, trucks and people on foot was heading east. After I had been watching the road for nearly an hour a big lorry crowded with men slowed down alongside me and there, amazingly, was Mark, dishevelled but safe.

There was no sign of Anwar; no one had seen him since he went back to fight on the heights above Dohuk. I was afraid he had been captured or killed. On each occasion after the filming had been arranged by Fehim, it had been Anwar who had accompanied us, kept us informed of developments, arranged interviews with Ba'ath Party prisoners, with the Kurdish guards of the forts and prisons, with the Kurdish commanders, the staff of the hospital. It had been Anwar who had shown us around the former headquarters of Saddam's *Amn*, *Istikhbarat* and *Mukhabarat*[8] and translated the tales of their victims. Now, reluctantly, Mark and I left Qadish without him. His uncle's family, too, was ready to leave for Turkey and had found a car to take them as far as the road went. We wished them well and embraced them warmly before setting off by Land Rover with a small band of peshmergas bound for the headquarters of the Kurdistan Front at Amadiya.

Flight to the mountains

At the Amadiya headquarters of the resistance, situated at the crest of the magnificent stony mountain on which the ancient town is perched, we negotiated the possibility of finding transport back up to Zakho. It was already late afternoon before there was any progress. Darkness struck again all too soon. The back mountain road which loops north west to Zakho via Begova was barely intact. The whole of the Bahdinan region seemed to have become one great camping ground, dense with people on the move. But 'camping' here in the cold hills while the army got closer was simply part of a nightmare from which we all hoped soon to awaken.

Our ride took us as far as Batoufa and there we were left in an isolated barracks at four in the morning to wait for daylight. No one wanted to travel to Zakho. As we stopped, I heard our driver whisper to one of the barracks' guards that Zakho was under attack and that he didn't know what to do with us. He was afraid to tell us this bad news directly in case he became responsible for us. We had lost our friends and were among strangers afraid for their own lives.

At 5.30 a.m. on 1 April and another cold grey daybreak, a peshmerga sleeping on the concrete floor nearby signalled to us to get up, murmuring that a driver had been found to take us to Zakho. True to his word, he was soon greeting the driver of a ruinous looking orange and white taxi which coughed to a halt outside the barracks, its fuel gauge on zero. We agreed a price for petrol with extra for the driver and after the peshmerga had procured a jerry can of the precious fuel we left Batoufa. A few kilometres outside Zakho, it became clear that there were almost no other vehicles still travelling in that direction. On the contrary, the last of Zakho's townspeople were heading the other way. There was a rumble of shelling close at hand.

Our driver delivered us to the KDP headquarters in the middle of town, the old school-house we had visited on arrival in 'Free Kurdistan'. The broadcasting of patriotic poems and music had long since ceased and the place was almost abandoned. A few senior peshmergas remained behind, busy with spies and army deserters who were still being captured and brought to them. A judge was presiding at quick trials.

The peshmergas reported that helicopter gunships were hovering down near Ibrahim Khalil, and the route across the river back to Syria was therefore cut. The head KDP man who spoke a patient, refined sort of English suggested we try to find a vehicle heading back up the Begova road to where it forks off to Shiranish and the Turkish border beyond.

The party's vehicles had already left or were out of fuel. We waited, waving at passing cars without success for an hour or more as Zakho was steadily abandoned. Then, at last someone stopped. We clambered gratefully into the back of a car with a family who were happy to take us with them to Shiranish. The driver carried a Turkish passport, although he was a local Kurd. He was hopeful of being let into Turkey as he had been working there and had kept his papers valid so he was quite cheerful and optimistic.

The main obstacle which faced us now was that the road to Turkey from the Shiranish turn-off ended abruptly at the plain of Deshte Tak and a swollen river. Nor was there any easy way to cross. When we reached the end of the road we found several thousand Kurds already facing the same dilemma.

The sun shone hospitably on the plain below and for a time the Kurds almost forgot that this was a journey of necessity. It looked more like a Newroz picnic as the families spread out on the green grass to eat or rest in little colourful clusters in the sunshine. It was only the sound of gunfire and shelling getting closer that lent any disquiet to an otherwise pastoral scene.

On the far side of the river on the steep hillsides above, columns of Turkish soldiers had begun to patrol the border. The gendarme post stationed atop the highest crags opposite us buzzed with helicopters.

About three hours after our arrival here at Deshte Tak, a lone helicopter finally ventured out above the river towards us. For the Kurds this seemed to mean salvation. A number of males leapt jubilantly to their feet, eyes upon the sky as thousands of leaflets began to flutter down over our heads. They fought to catch them, but on the leaflets was written: 'Warning! If you try to cross into Turkey you are liable to be shot. Do not try to cross!' The message was written in Arabic, Turkish, Persian and 'local dialect'. Turkish officials could still not bring themselves to write the word 'Kurdish' even on a death threat.

At once, the picnic atmosphere evaporated. Children stopped playing. Families began to haul their things up on their backs and move off. Everyone there had to abandon his car, truck or tractor to set off on foot, or else turn back by the road he'd come.

The plain of Deshte Tak was heavily mined, lying close to the Turkish–Iraqi border within the *cordon sanitaire* created by Saddam Hussein. I detected little round landmines scattered everywhere like anemones in the new grass. Once or twice we heard explosions. Someone had strayed from the main path and activated a mine. There were screams, unthinkable injuries. Risking their lives, some Kurdish men began gathering the small mines, deactivating those that were simple, collecting others by the sackful. These they would then detonate away from the crowd to save others from injury.

Such was the painful end of the Kurdish uprising, which had promised so much. Together with the long-suffering people of the region we understood that the time had come to try to cross the border if we were to get away. Saddam's Republican Guards, free to exact their revenge on the Kurds for their defiance, were already occupying the towns behind us.

Midnight. A full moon bloomed above the narrow sheep track, a pale thread winding through the mountains away from the Turkish military post and the churning river. Since sundown we had waited in one of Saddam's border turrets with a few peshmergas and their families discussing the options. A guide had been found to lead us on the path to Turkey, relying on the moonlight to find the way. Many Kurdish families had started off before sunset; others, afraid of being spotted from above and bombed by Iraqi helicopters, had waited for darkness and moonrise like ourselves.

Mark and I gathered our few things together. Most of our equipment had been left behind in Dohuk in the urgency of escape.

The moon gave little light. The night sky was almost constantly clouded over, but the rain held off. The Kurds were trudging in a slow column along a single narrow path. We were constantly warned not to stray from it for fear of landmines. Children and old people slowed this grim procession down still further. They would lean aside, or rest as close to the path as possible to allow the swifter ones to overtake them. Flocks of sheep and goats stumbled along among us.

It was strangely quiet on this mountain march even though we numbered thousands of people. It was like passing through some apocalyptic valley of death, the murmur of voices and the bleating of the animals only audible when we entered deep rock-walled valleys. These valleys were penetrated by a small constant stream which we forded back and forth as it meandered with us through the gloom of the mountains. The atmosphere was hushed not only because of our fallen spirits but also because the Kurds were afraid their voices would alert the Iraqi army as to their whereabouts, terrified that silent clouds of chemicals would once again blossom through the ravines and kill every last soul. No one seemed to know how far it was to the border. Seeing two Westerners, the Kurds would ask us, 'How far is it to Turkey? Will they let us in? When will Europe, America help us? Where is Bush, *Haji* Bush?' It was impossible to answer. Although we were all in the same predicament, the mere fact of our being foreign seemed to offer the people some hope. For our part, we felt far from hopeful.

Shuffling along the narrow sheep track in the dark, I caught up with a young Kurd bearing a crippled man on his back. The man's useless legs dragged behind him through the dust and stones. Other people along the way had fashioned crude stretchers of twisted branches to carry the old and sick. Those who were injured or disabled but could still walk were using branches as crutches. This long trek was a great torment for them.

Around 2 a.m., and still little more than a kilometre or so beyond the guard post at Deshte Tak, we came upon a dead body. On the downward side of the hill lay a long form. The body was absolutely still. He or she had been covered by a blanket and abandoned, unburied. Someone behind me threw a stone at it to see if it would move. It was as if no one wanted to acknowledge death directly by going down to open the blanket. At the time, this quiet unlamented body in the darkness seemed both pathetic and ominous.

As day began to break, a foggy blue light illuminated the stark and craggy features of the valley. The path ahead snaked up and up around the mountains, a steady trail of men, women and children plodding forward, heads down, abject at the collapse of the revolt, too tired even to be afraid any more.

In the blue hours just before dawn, we had stopped and stretched out on the side of the mountain. I pulled the few clothes I still had with me from the bag and draped them over my chilled limbs against the damp night air. I had hardly slept at all in over forty-eight hours and felt flat and dispirited. Mark lay sleeping some yards away in the grass. I extracted the leaves and twigs from my hair and removed the damp covers of my 'bed', then sat up to watch some families lighting fires to make tea and taking dry rounds of bread from their sacks, further down the slope on a little piece of flat ground near the stream. The dwarf oak trees on the hills all around were bare and blighted. Three years before, this wretched valley had been bombed with chemicals. This was one of the same routes by which the Kurds from Bahdinan had fled at the time. The land still looked crabbed and stunted. Perhaps even spring could not heal it.

Time passed and we rejoined the slow procession of people filing up the mountain track. Some had clearly been walking all night and weariness greyed their faces. Children in pyjamas without coats or other warm covering, many barefoot or wearing open shoes, walked in their sleep, fell, and were hauled onto adult shoulders or carried in arms. For those with several children, only babies could be carried while tiny children had to keep up unaided. These whimpered tiredly as they dragged themselves along.

We had not been able to bring any food with us. The Kurds would offer us flat rounds of dry bread or cooked rice but we didn't want to deprive them. We would decline, saying we had already eaten something. Some wanted to expose their injuries to us, or the napalm blisters on the bodies of their wounded children, hoping we were doctors or carried medicine. One of the worst aspects of this journey was being unable to relieve suffering. However, Mark offered to shoulder a huge sack of flour for a family who couldn't manage it. It must have weighed between 30 and 40 kilos. This he lugged over rocks, down slippery declines, and up over the rough mountainsides, pausing every twenty minutes or so to rest before hauling it up on his back once more, aware that the family would ultimately depend on it.

And then suddenly we lost sight of them. They had fallen behind and others had moved into file behind us once the column entered a difficult pass. Here we had to get across a small ravine but were slowed to a standstill by old people and children who required individual help to jump across the gap. This was the worst part of the route thus far and there were several hundreds waiting to get across the small slippery gap, or scaling the cliffs to avoid making the leap altogether.

After several hours more, we reached a barren wood where the track opened into a clearing. Many Kurds had stopped to rest. Here we also stopped and waited, hoping the family whose sack of flour we carried would catch up. An hour went by before a member of their group arrived and we surrendered the flour to him. The women in this group held out a little bread to me, but I was past eating. I just swallowed down a few handfuls of water from the stream which still kept us company, hoping it wasn't contaminated. Others did the same. Then we carried on again.

We trudged steadily upwards all day as the sun rode higher in the sky above and at last reached some ruined villages. These had invariably been blasted to bits by Saddam's helicopters during the long campaign of destruction against the Kurdish countryside and its people. A solitary Kurd identified the village we had come upon just now as Sinaht. The ruined stones of lovely Sinaht lay tumbled across a plateau overlooking the blossoming valley we had just passed through. But now only a few fruit trees and the stony ridges of vineyards remained to testify that this had once been home to a hundred or more Kurdish families. The ruins were blind and dumb. The voices silenced. Not a threshold remained intact. As the late afternoon sun shed its tranquil lemon light over the crests of the mountains above, and pools of blue shadow deepened around our feet, the path suddenly forked. Some took one way, some took the other. Some said one of the two paths led back to Iraq. We didn't know who to follow. The steep rocky ridges of high mountains loomed in front of us. Were these 'Turkey'?

We climbed on upwards for another two or three hours until darkness began to fill the spaces in the naked forest. Reaching the crest of the hill we walked right into a line of Turkish commandos. They wore the blue berets which marked them out as special combat forces. Their guns were already trained upon us.

The Turkish border: Işikveren Camp

The commandos had us under surveillance long before we caught sight of them. The soldiers physically separated us from the Kurds. The leader shouted at us, asking if we'd been with the PKK. It seemed a ridiculous thing to preoccupy their thoughts under the circumstances. I considered it safest to pretend ignorance of the Turkish language lest I be considered a spy. These soldiers were rude fellows and they roughly disarmed every Kurd who stumbled upon the crest of the mountain with the same surprise as we had.

A large assembly of Kurdish men stripped thus of their weapons squatted like prisoners of war behind a growing mound of guns to our left, prevented from crossing the ridge by the soldiers who occasionally fired off belligerently into the ever darkening thickets of the trees. Gunfire erupted from other points along the shadowy ridge. We were left in no doubt as to who was firing at who. Turkish soldiers never seem bothered about shooting anyone inadvertently.

A commando with the unpleasant features of a lizard now swore, 'Hayvan hayvan (animals). How many more of them are coming?'

'Thousands,' I answered pleasantly. 'There are thousands more people behind us – all the way back through the valley.' Seeing his dismay I felt some satisfaction.

'We'll send them all back. We'll send you back too! What are you doing with these people? What were you doing in Iraq? Wait over there!' The iguana grunted a few syllables into his radio and received some crackled response back.

As night wrapped itself bleakly around us, the Kurds had gathered in their hundreds behind. Now the Turkish commandos were joined by a small contingent of their fellows from across the ridge. They ordered Mark and me to follow them.

We emerged from the forest. Below us, a rough camp of several thousand people was spread across the Turkish side of the mountain among the bare wintry trees. Campfires had been lit and small clusters stood or sat around them, fanning the miserable embers alight. These were the first arrivals who'd been allowed across the Turkish border as many as three days before. The Turkish authorities evidently hadn't yet decided what to do with the rest, as the numbers were obviously causing them concern. Although hundreds of weary families kept on arriving at the crest, the majority were being detained on the line of the hill which seemed to represent the border here.

It was a wretched encampment. A muddy slope studded with poor bare trees, already being hacked to pieces for firewood, sloped down sharply to a level grassy plain some half mile below. I could just make out the distinctively shaped huts of a Turkish military post, the base for the soldiers who now had us surrounded. A wind had blown up and a dark bank of cloud rolled in from across the high mountains behind. It began to rain, a cold brittle rain. There was no shelter.

We had been in Işikveren some hours and had asked the most senior of the commandos leave to depart for the nearest town. He refused. Instead, the commander detained us, motioning us to sit down nearby in the rain. He had his own campfire, which he shared with a handful of his men. We reluctantly crouched down beside them, more prisoner than companion, not permitted to return to the Kurds.

As the rain grew fiercer, the fires began to smoke and falter. Smoke and ashes blew into my eyes. My face burned from flying grit and rain. The wind gathered in power and soon the rain had turned into hail. Large hailstones pelted the refugees and the wind whistled through the camp. The night was very dark and close. The poor Kurds stood hunched up around their pathetic campfires, the thinly clad children soaked through.

A few of these families had thought to bring strips of plastic sheeting with them. These they had erected between the branches of the trees, but the powerful wind snatched at it, tearing it free, so that there could be no shelter this night. Caught by a sudden gust of wind, an elderly woman tumbled down the muddy slope and fell into a fire. Her clothes ablaze, she came leaping towards us, shrieking as the flames engulfed her. Someone threw a blanket over the terrified woman and guided her to where the commandos sat, surly and brooding, doing nothing. A soldier tore open the back of her burning dress and ripped away the melting fabric. The woman was not badly hurt. She was sent away again.

As the night wore on, it seemed to get wetter and filthier as the wind pitched the rain ceaselessly against us. We felt more and more dejected. No human being could sleep in this weather. We stood hunched over in the rain, our heads tucked into our necks like birds in a storm, trying to keep the flying sparks and soot from our eyes. But the wind kept blowing the ashes and embers into our faces. To get any warmth one had to stand inches from the fire, which barely stayed alight. Each time that I moved any distance to escape the smoke, the rain chilled my body through. Water streamed from my hair into my eyes and down the back of my neck. My shoes were buried in mud. And Mark was getting sick. He lay shaking on the soldiers' sodden ground sheet, his eyes closed. The soldiers still refused to let us off the mountain. I argued. I coaxed. I cajoled them in ever more articulate Turkish as we became more desperate. I even tried reason. It was in vain.

Not until late in the morning, 3 April, did the iguana finally march us down through the mud for further interrogation in the military hut at the foot of the mountain.

An anxious swarm of local Kurds from nearby villages on the Turkish side of this unreasonable border were by now trying to deliver food to the camp. The villagers had brought in supplies of fresh bread, cheese, milk and other vital foods, but the soldiers would not let them take it up the hillside. It was a disturbing situation and I became quite angry. We knew that many of the Kurds were ill and hadn't eaten, especially the children. But the soldiers seemed to be enjoying the power they had over them.

The villagers confirmed that we were in Işikveren, a short distance from the town of Uludere. A Spanish news crew had also crossed the border the night before some three kilometres further down the ridge. The journalists had been airlifted off the mountain by helicopter before the storm, and were flown straight to Şirnak.

'Can't we be sent out by helicopter?'

'No, it is too windy', the soldiers answered. They had confined us to their hut and we were still not permitted to leave or wander about outside.

We were just envying the Spanish crew their good fortune when we heard that their film had been confiscated in Şirnak by the MİT (Turkish intelligence).

Did we have any film? I hoped they wouldn't look. Film shot in Iraq was of no apparent use to them, but anything about Kurds was considered useful for the counterinsurgency teams.

By three that afternoon, the soldiers set us free from the hut. We were seemingly rescued by some local Kurdish journalists who agreed to drive us to Şirnak, but once on the road we were immediately intercepted by MİT. A black car with tinted windows and blank number plates cruised up behind, clearly tipped off to watch out for us. The car drew up alongside and motioned us to pull over. Those within instructed our driver to proceed directly to Security Headquarters. Here we were led to the Chief's office. Chairs were pulled out for us. Files were opened. These were no doubt the same policemen who had dealt with the Spaniards.

'What were you doing in Northern Iraq? Why did you cross into Turkey illegally?' The questions were beginning, quite amicably at first, then becoming more insistent.

The international press had received word of what was happening out here by this time. While we were trying to get ourselves and our footage out of Turkey, others were trying just as hard to get in to cover the burgeoning tragedy.

We informed Şirnak that we wished to depart for Britain straight away. In fact, we needed immediate access to satellite facilities in Ankara. They responded promptly by dismissing our local Kurdish colleagues, replacing them with one of their own drivers, a bothersome fellow who tried to draw us into conversation about the PKK all the way to Diyarbakir.

MİT clearly wanted us out of the Kurdish area. They radioed ahead for their cronies in Diyarbakir to pick us up the moment we should enter the town's outskirts. Sure enough, the moment we reached Diyarbakir, there they were, stationed in a blue minibus at the turn-off. Several plainclothes police appeared at our heels the moment we freed ourselves from the MİT's driver. Other policemen presented themselves at the hotel check-in as soon as we came through the door. Others loomed beside us when we left our seedy rooms to find a passable restaurant. And there they were again, lurking in reception the next morning, copying details from our passports when we came down to use the hotel telephones.

The oppressive surveillance bothered me and I decided to take my minders on a little harmless walkabout while I went looking for a shoeshine. Pretending to be invisible, they flattened their backs against walls and inspected fruit at every vendor's cart the entire way until I found a shoeshine boy and plonked myself down barefoot on a small stool at his side. The boy laboured and buffed the last mud of Işikveren camp from

my shoes while the men from MİT stood around yawning with disappointment.

'Operation Provide Comfort'

For the next few days that we remained in Turkey, the Turkish government and the Turkish military continued to staunch the flood of Kurds
arriving at the border. They tried jointly to suppress the news by keeping
foreigners out of the area, but still the unfortunate Kurds kept on
arriving by the thousands. On 10 April 1991 there were approximately
eight hundred thousand Kurds suffering in the wretched camps along
the Turkish border and one million more out on the Iranian border. The
international community had now caught wind of what was going on.
The suffering of the Kurds in the mud and snow in the mountains was
to be witnessed almost daily by millions of TV viewers in every part of
the world.

Iran responded to the situation more humanely than Turkey, although it
received less foreign aid due its poor relations with Western donor
countries and the US in particular. America naturally favoured its ally,
Turkey, with the greater contribution.

Figures given by the UN Disaster Relief Operation (UNDRO), 17
May 1991 reveal that: 'Iran received $128.9 million in international
assistance compared to $248 million spent on the Turkish/Iraqi border.
The $248 million figure for the money spent in Turkey combines the
UNDRO accounting of $57 million with the $140.1 million in US
Department of Defense contributions and $31.6 million in Food for
Peace assistance, both of which were distributed as part of Operation
Provide Comfort.' But the hitherto unprecedented public response to
the Kurdish disaster was due primarily to the prominence it had been
accorded by the media. People who had previously known nothing of the
Kurds were now donating money, medical supplies, clothes, blankets and
kerosene heaters.

Eventually, those same Western leaders on whom the Kurds had
counted for help during the uprising were compelled to respond to the
plight of millions of refugees, not simply with humanitarian aid but by
taking decisive political action. On 8 April 1991, Britain's prime minister,
John Major, presented a proposal to the EC for the creation of 'safe
havens' in northern Iraq to enable the Kurds to be brought down from
the mountains. Although reluctant at first to give its backing, the Bush
administration suddenly changed its course and expressed support for
the idea. In fact, thereafter, the US claimed the initiative as its own. On

16 April 1991, Bush ordered 3,500 US troops into the area to carry out humanitarian assistance to the Kurds.

As late as the response was given the Kurds' plight, the fact that it came at all was probably due to public outrage at the sight of human beings left to perish in the mountains. Certainly, many hundreds more lives could have been saved had the Turkish government allowed the refugees to come down from the mountains. Instead they deliberately kept them up on the heights where access was difficult and temperatures hostile.

Mindful of the influx in 1988 of the 100,000 Kurds who had escaped chemical attacks and fled to Turkey, the Turkish administration sought to avoid an even greater Kurdish refugee intake with long-term implications for Turkey by confining the operation to the border region. Any would-be Kurdish influx the government understood in terms of both costly economic relief and the political threat posed to them and their policies towards their own disaffected Kurdish population. Consequently the Turks played for time.

The Kurdish disaster reached its height in May. Ironically, most of the cultural concessions which had been announced by Özal's government to Turkey's Kurds at the time of the Gulf war were largely withdrawn at exactly this juncture.

Özal had introduced 'reforms' which in theory allowed the Kurds to speak, print and even sing songs in the Kurdish language for the first time in 70 years. The hated articles 141, 142 and 163 of the Turkish Penal Code were abolished at the same time. But the Anti-Terror Law which replaced them was to prove even more repressive. Although the use of Kurdish appeared to demonstrate a relaxation in Turkey's attitudes to Kurdish culture and identity, the Anti-Terror Law was exploited in such a way that almost any use of the Kurdish language could still be considered as a 'separatist' offence, under article 8 subject to the most rigorous forms of punishment under the law, including lengthy imprisonment. Consequently, Özal's efforts to open up the Kurdish question proved ineffectual in practice and Turkey commenced a new era of political repression and military aggression towards all sections of Kurdish society. At the same time, it began to play a new game with the Kurds of Iraq. By pretending to help them, it sought to demonstrate concern for the welfare of Kurdish people to the West and silence criticism for the dirty war raging in Turkey.

The Iraqi Kurds were desperate for whatever help they could get. Heartened that the international community had finally responded to their crisis, they accepted the assistance that was given and slowly returned to the little that remained of their homes.

The experience in the mountains when escaping the advancing Iraqi forces had been more horrific than any person could have imagined. Almost every family lost parents, elderly grandparents, uncles or aunts, children, and new babies in the course of the grisly aftermath of the exodus in the mud and snow.

Few would forget scenes like those when Allied helicopters bringing boxes of food buzzed above the camps and simply dumped their heavy crates out the door. Boxes of supplies dropped without parachutes, nor with adequate care for the precise locations of the drop, caused the deaths of a number of civilians not swift enough to dodge the charity which fell upon them from heaven.

Nor too, would we forget the sight of people so desperate for food that they fought one another over loaves of bread like dogs over scraps of meat; children who died from exposure and malnutrition in front of our cameras; people barefoot in the snow trudging through an unbelievable hell on earth.

In the long and trying course of Operation Provide Comfort over the next five years, there would be a number of tragic mistakes from which to draw further lessons about humanitarian intervention.

Notes

1. The name 'Anfal' derives from a verse *(sura)* of the Quran referring to the right to plunder an enemy of wealth and property. The 'plunder' includes taking the lives of the enemy people, their goods and their women. For the Ba'ath Party, anfal was a military code-name for the operation of genocide launched against the Kurds in Northern Iraq between 1997 and 1989. Saddam exploited the *sura* to justify the campaign. For the phases of the Anfal itself, see Kanan Makiya, *Cruelty and Silence: War, Tyranny and Uprising and the Arab World* (Jonathan Cape, London 1993), and Middle East Watch, *Genocide in Iraq: The Anfal Campaign against the Kurds* (New York, 1993). See also Sirwa's Narrative of the Halabja Massacre in chapter 10 and the discussion of the Kurdish question in chapter 11 of this book.

2. The *muezzin* sings the *ezan* (call) which summons the faithful to prayer five times a day.

3. See: Kanan Makiya, *(Samir al-Khalil) Cruelty and Silence: War, Tyranny, Uprising and the Arab World*, Jonathan Cape, London, 1993, pp. 59–60.

4. Faysal Dağli, *Birakuji*, (Fratricide) Belge Yayinlari, Istanbul, 1994, p. 55 (in Turkish).

5. *Jash* literally means 'baby donkey'. It is a derogatory title given to Kurds who serve the regime to the detriment of their own people, doing what the regime commands in the same way that a baby donkey follows its mother.

6. Dağli, *Birakuji*, p. 55.

7. See my previous book *Into Kurdistan: Frontiers Under Fire*, Zed Books, London, 1991 for details of the life of the Iraqi Kurds in the refugee camps in Turkey in the course of the Anfal between 1988 and 1991.

8. *Amn, istikhbarat and Mukhabarat.* The *Amn* are the security police which oversee the population in general; the *istikhbarat* are the intelligence operatives which monitor and screen all state organisations; the *mukhabarat* are the most powerful of the three and have decisive authority over both public and state matters, working within and outside Iraq. Saddam's son, Qusay, is head of the *mukhabarat.*

2

Kurdish *realpolitik* and the failed uprising

> I had a small blue sky
> the occupiers brought it down over me
> I had a trickle of dark blood
> a bouquet of honey dreams
> and a collection of books
> they plundered them all
> But when they came
> to change my skin
> deform my face
> I dressed myself in snow and thunder
> carried my homeland on my shoulders
> and took to the road of the gun
>
> (*The Road of the Gun*, Rafiq Sabir)

Internal and external factors conspired against the Kurds to bring about the collapse of the uprising.

The last year of the Iraq–Iran war had seen the beginning of Saddam's aggressive use of chemical warfare. Thereafter, the Ba'ath systematically used chemicals against the Kurdish civilian population, as part of phase three of the Anfal, in conjunction with the deportation of villagers from their homes for relocation south, or to compound towns in Kurdistan which were easy for the military to control. The subsequent destruction of most of Kurdistan's remaining villages was then carried out.

The Ba'ath regime's campaign effectively restricted the movement of the peshmergas as well as that of ordinary civilians. The guerrilla bases had been dependent on the villages for food, resources and support. The destruction of the villages forced the majority of the Kurdish resistance forces to quit Kurdistan temporarily, leaving only a few small active bases behind. This meant that at the time of the popular uprising in the Kurdish towns in March 1991, the experienced peshmerga fighters of the Kurdistan Front arrived back after the uprising had begun in many areas. The peshmergas did however arrive in time to take part in the liberation of the city of Kirkuk and of some of the most powerful government security strongholds in the other main urban centres.

For the first few days, in the absence of the peshmergas, the people had formed themselves into committees (*shura*) throughout the quarters of the cities and these selected the most prominent and respected personalities from among themselves to organise administration of daily affairs. The committees in the various towns maintained effective communications with one another in order to keep control throughout the uprising. But they did not remain active for long. The return to the scene of the parties of the Kurdish national movement embodied in the Kurdistan Front, created two conflicting centres of power and the forces with the Kurdistan Front subsequently closed down the committees. The Iraqi Kurdistan Front, which represented all the Kurdish political parties, had little difficulty in imposing itself as the main authority for the region. It was strengthened in number and in capacity by the many *jash* and influential leaders of large Kurdish tribes with their supporters who had turned away from Saddam.

But the issue of authority occupied the attention of both the ordinary Kurdish people and the parties, diverting them at a critical moment from focusing on how best to defend their recently liberated country from Saddam at such time as his army would return. As a consequence, when the government's forces did regroup ready to attack Kurdistan, deploying fixed-wing aircraft and helicopter gunships from as early as 25 March 1991, there were no identifiable Kurdish political centres of command. No one really knew what was going on. People ran from place to place seeking a single central authority but found that each of the headquarters gave out its own individual information and instructions, instead of joining to devise a coherent and co-ordinated policy.

Government offices had been looted, vandalised and torched, not only by local Kurds, but also by the retreating government forces early on in the uprising when they withdrew from Kurdistan. Vital equipment, technological resources and vehicles had largely been disabled or spirited away in the chaos of the first days and this made it more difficult for the Kurdistan Front, as the new municipal authority, to adequately administer life in the towns or carry out the business of government. As a result, information about the ongoing situation in liberated Kurdistan passed from mouth to mouth and took shape according to foreign radio broadcasts, generally incomplete and often inaccurate.

The Allies had encouraged the people of Iraq to throw off Saddam, giving the impression that they themselves would provide protection, or at least backing, for such efforts. However, in the moment of greatest

need, Allied help never came. This was primarily due to Western
as to who, or what, would replace Saddam. It has been said that
General Schwarzkopf met with the Iraqi generals to dictate the terms of
the ceasefire, he deliberately communicated that they were permitted to
fly their helicopters, even for military purposes, thereby signalling US
approval for the crushing of the internal rebellions in the north and
south.[1] For the rebels themselves, the sudden conspicuous absence of the
support they had anticipated deeply unsettled the ordinary people and
dealt a death blow to public morale. Kurdish confidence in their ability
to defeat the regime was undermined at a most critical juncture, and
thereafter.

More than twenty-five years of government under Saddam amounted
to a term spanning an entire generation. During this period the regime,
which was economically very powerful, spent billions in buying people
off and in indoctrinating them and their children into executing the
party's orders. People were largely controlled by fear and self-interest.
The population of Kurdistan was also deeply affected by this indoctrina-
tion programme. The Ba'ath government had many loyal servants within
the populace, often unidentified by their fellows and operating under
cover to cause disruption to Kurdish patriotic activities. The Ba'athi
agents worked systematically against the Kurdish movement both before
and during the uprising.

Because liberated Kurdistan is surrounded by powerful neighbours,
all opposed to any kind of Kurdish authority in the region and afraid of
an upsurge in Kurdish separatist activities within the Kurdish areas under
their present control, these neighbours each attempted individually as
well as jointly to block the development of the Kurdish people's passage
towards either independence or regional autonomy. This had been the
case throughout Kurdish history. At any time that the Kurds had sought
to overthrow central government authority their enemies had always
united against them. This was particularly so at the time of the uprising.
The creation of a *de facto* Kurdish state in Iraqi Kurdistan alarmed the
neighbours into holding tripartite talks: quelling Kurdish aspirations has
always provided a basis for a certain level of co-operation between
Turkey, Iraq and Iran.

Finally, the fact that the Kurdish leadership was seen by both Kurdish
and foreign observers to be prepared to negotiate a settlement in Baghdad
with Saddam, so soon after the collapse of the uprising and the resultant
disaster in the mountains, considerably damaged the Kurdish cause which
had just gained significant world-wide attention and support.

Negotiations between the Kurdistan Front and the Iraqi government had become public by 20 April 1991, although talks began between the two sides after the fall of Kirkuk when the government felt it opportune to suggest 'open' negotiations. Saddam promised a great deal in the beginning, but gradually minimised his offers. At the moment when the two sides seemed on the verge of concluding an agreement in principle, PUK leader Jalal Talabani, KDPI leader Sami Abdurrahman and the rest of the delegation exchanged kisses in greeting with the Iraqi president on Iraqi television. These kisses were repeated by KDP leader Massoud Barzani and Saddam, and again broadcast from Baghdad in July 1991. Thousands of Kurdish people both in Kurdistan and abroad felt spiritually as well as politically violated by this deed. Remembering the Anfal, the chemical attacks, the execution of relatives and the flight to the mountains, they asked themselves how such behaviour could be acceptable. Others felt however, as did the leaders themselves, that in the absence of any viable international commitment, the best course for the future might well be to avail themselves of this opportunity when Saddam was weak. They viewed the negotiations, even such as they were, as a breakthrough, seeing in them evidence of Saddam's ultimate collapse. But more cautious voices warned that Saddam was merely buying time until Western pressure on Baghdad and Western support for the Kurds should subside.

Jalal Talabani, PUK leader and spokesman for the Kurdistan Front, announced at press conferences on 21 April that he was confident that Baghdad would formally acknowledge Kurdish autonomy; there would be seats allocated for Kurdish representatives in central government, there would be free elections, freedom of the press, the release of political prisoners, democracy within a pluralist system and a general amnesty for Kurds camped out on the borders or in exile to go back to their towns and villages.

The new agreement under discussion was based on the autonomy pact of 11 March 1970, which had never been ratified. As with the earlier agreement, it was the extent of Kurdish territory to be included in the autonomous region, together with who would control the oil-rich city of Kirkuk, which ultimately proved to be the stumbling block.

The 1970 agreement had sought to determine exactly what area of the former Ottoman Vilayet of Mosul was Kurdish on a per capita population basis. But given the effectiveness of the government's Arabization programme, of the mass deportations, expulsions and massacres carried out by the regime in Kurdistan during the past thirty hostile years, a census-based ethnic distribution agreement was hardly fair to the Kurds. The Kurds also wanted international guarantees for any agreement that they might reach, but Saddam rejected this outright.`

US State Department spokeswoman, Margaret Tutwiler, commented that the agreement itself was purely a matter for the Kurds and Baghdad. Other UN members expressed reservations about becoming involved, sticking to the old line that this was 'an internal affair'.

The British Foreign Office commented, 'We have consistently made clear our support for autonomy for the Kurdish people within Iraq and respect for their political and human rights.'[2] Unfortunately for the Kurds, this was as far as the sought-after 'international guarantees' ever went.

Saddam was not mistaken in his assessment of the West's *interest* in the Kurds, nor of Western concern for other suffering peoples in Iraq. He had long since won the support of a number of mainly anti-Western nations including Yemen, Libya, Somalia and the Palestinians. These accorded him the status of strong man of Arab nationalism for his stand against the Western imperialists and the launching of his scuds against Tel Aviv. But other powerful Arab states, most importantly, Saudi, Egypt and the Gulf states, had turned away and supported Kuwait and the Allies against him; Jordan maintained useful relations with both Saddam and the West.

Although apparently defeated in the war, it was not long before Saddam proved that he was far from finished. Attacks on the Shi'as in the south and Kurdish targets in the north began again, provoking the Allies to establish a second no-fly zone in southern Iraq. This was insufficient to protect the population from attacks on the ground. While bombing the Kurds in the north Saddam was simultaneously poisoning the southern marshes of Iraq, draining the reed beds and driving out their centuries-old inhabitants, the Arab successors of ancient Sumer.

Kurdish representatives need to be considered an equal party to international negotiations affecting their lives and future – if there is to be an end to the Kurdish conflict. In illustration of this argument, I quote the following from a speech by Ali Hassan al-Majid, 'Chemical Ali', on 15 April 1988. The speech was given at a meeting between Majid, fellow Ba'ath Party officials and governors of the 'Autonomous Region' in Iraqi Kurdistan – one month after the chemical bombardment of the Kurdish town of Halabja. Tapes, including the one on which this speech was recorded, were captured from Ba'ath Party offices in Kirkuk during the uprising:

> From now on I won't give the villagers flour, sugar, kerosene, water or electricity as long as they continue living there. Let them come closer to me to hear me, so that I can tell them the things I believe and want in ideology, education and common sense. Why should I let them live there like donkeys who don't know anything? For the wheat? I don't want their

wheat. We have been importing wheat for the last twenty years. Let's increase it for another five years.

I will prohibit large areas; I will prohibit any presence in them. What if we prohibit the whole basin from Qara Dagh to Kifri to Diyala to Darben-dikhan to Sulaimaniya? What good is this basin? What did we ever get from them? Imagine how much we paid out and lost on those areas. How many good citizens are there among those people, and how many bad ones?

What went wrong? What happened? Thirty, twenty, twenty-five years of saboteur activity? Imagine how many martyrs we have! ... Now you can't go from Kirkuk to Arbil any more without an armoured vehicle. All of this basin, from Koysancak to here (Kirkuk) ... I'm going to evacuate it. I will evacuate it as far as Gweir and Mosul. No human beings except on the main roads. For five years I won't allow any human existence there. I don't want their agriculture. I don't want tomatoes; I don't want okra and cucumbers. If we don't act in this way the saboteurs' activities will never end, not for a million years.[3]

'Not for a million years,' Ali Hassan al Majid recognised. The solution: genocide.

Notes

1. Washington analyst Laurie Millroie, of the Washington Institute for Near East Policy, claimed to have seen transcripts of the ceasefire meeting. ITV, *Saddam's Killing Fields*, Viewpoint 93, October 1993, written and directed by Michael Wood.

2. *Independent*, London, 25 April 1991.

3. *Genocide in Iraq: the Anfal Campaign against the Kurds*; Appendix A, the Ali Hassan al-Majid Tapes, Middle East Watch, New York, 1993, pp. 347–53.

3

Summer of the 'safe haven'

It was a hot summer. By mid-June 1991, the countryside around the depleted 'safe haven' at Zakho had become a bleached white-gold in colour. The wheat was in ear, but many harvesters were still inoperative. The rusting hulks of the Iraqi tanks had all but disappeared from the Zakho–Dohuk road. Daily life seemed to have been restored to normality – there was electricity and running water, there were goods in the markets and there were Kurdish citizens without weapons thronging the streets. Most unusual was the lack of Iraqi uniforms and the sizeable coalition presence. The US, Dutch, Italian, Spanish and British coalition forces were patrolling Kurdish roads and manning checkpoints in partnership with the peshmergas. But even as early as this, many soldiers were asking themselves, 'How will it be when we are gone?'.

I was back on a new assignment to film the American withdrawal from the 'haven' and if possible visit the PKK's bases along the Turkish–Iraqi border. We were a two-person crew, the same as during the Kurdish uprising in March three months before. This time Mark and I crossed into 'Free Kurdistan' via the patched up Khabur Bridge, our passports peremptorily stamped with exits from Turkey on 14 June 1991.

At four o'clock in the morning of 15 June 1991, we filmed the remnants of the American military presence in Kurdistan as they finally abandoned their Dohuk headquarters, located in one of the Ba'ath regime's recently built, but unopened, hotels overlooking lush vineyards, the property of a wealthy *jash*, in the heart of Dohuk city. Only a sleepy-eyed Kurdish family and a solitary shepherd prodding a dozen long-haired sheep stood about to witness as the United States army jeeps and trucks slowly purred in convoy out of town, bound for the Turkish border and their military base in Silopi beyond. This would leave only US aerial surveillance in place, with the UN and UN Guards Contingents in Iraq (UNGCI) patrolling on the ground. The departure of the Americans was an anti-climax.

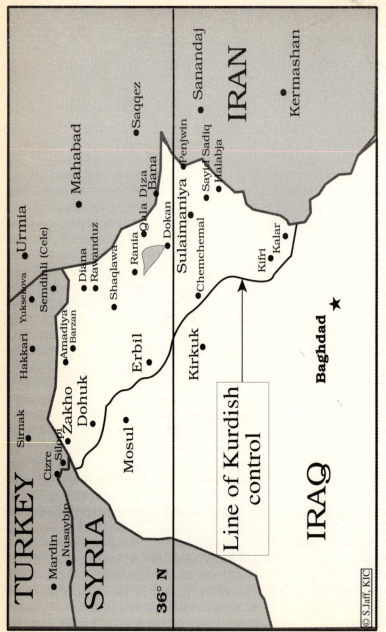

Map 2 Kurdish liberated zone after 1991

Setting off in a Landcruiser with a handful of KDP peshmergas we followed the American soldiers as far as Zakho to see if, as rumoured, there would be protests or demonstrations once the people were aware that they were finally leaving.

A wind storm sprang up gathering the dust. From behind the hills near Batoufa came a rumbling of dry thunder. The vast expanse of UN tents on the Zakho plain blurred like a yellow mirage in the flying dust. Figures bent over against the wind moved between the rows of tents, distorted into ghostly jaundiced silhouettes – the last of the refugees still living in the Zakho 'haven' camp.

The entire area along the Bahdinan stretch of the Turkish border was still heavily mobilised, the roads clogged with Allied military vehicles. The mandate for the British and Dutch soldiers to remain in Kurdistan for a further term had just been renewed. Blond, sunburned European boys kept watch over the main roads side by side with peshmergas of the same age. It was a compelling image. 30,000 foreign troops had been involved in 'Operation Provide Comfort' at its peak. Now only a few thousand were left.

Even as the US forces were pulling out, the Turkish military commenced another crackdown operation against their own Kurds. Bombs exploded around the homes and offices of members of the Human Rights Association. Other attacks were directed at the 'safe haven' itself, killing and wounding Iraqi Kurds, and obliterating newly rebuilt villages, but the US did not condemn its Turkish ally. Rather, their acquiescence in Turkey's brutality was soon to be expressed by a new US outlook. This differentiated Iraqi Kurds ('good Kurds') from Turkish Kurds ('bad Kurds') and ostensibly justified the repression going on in Turkey.

Indeed, the aspirations of the Iraqi Kurds for some form of permanent regional security and control over their part of Kurdistan were now actively manipulated by both Turkey and the West, who agreed to allow humanitarian aid and supplies to pass through Turkey into northern Iraq, and for the Allies to fly the 'Operation Poised Hammer' patrol over Iraqi Kurdistan from Turkish air bases in Incirlik and Silopi – in exchange for intelligence and co-operation against the PKK.

Around four thousand PKK guerrillas had established mobile bases along the Turkish–Iraqi border, an area under the nominal control of the Kurdistan Front, and within the 'protected' zone designated as the 'safe haven'. From here they set forth to launch attacks on Turkish garrisons and police posts, and carried out the training of new recruits who had completed their term in the Syrian-controlled Bekaa valley in Lebanon. The Kurdistan Front was opposed to these practices, especially as they had got themselves into a complicated situation of dependency on Ankara, having to play ball with the Turks in order for 'Operation Provide Comfort' to carry on. The West also supported Turkey, its NATO ally, against the PKK which they likened to the 'Shining Path' in Peru: a threat to the status quo in the region as being beyond Western control. At this stage of their history, the PKK was still avowedly anti-Western, anti-imperialist and somewhat disdainful of the conventions of international diplomacy. Until their fifth congress, the hammer and sickle remained prominent in the PKK's insignia and on its flags. This evidently kept possible friends, including other Kurdish parties, at a distance. However, as an army organised under responsible command, all combatants and victims of the war with Turkey were entitled to protection under the Geneva Convention and Protocols. But Turkey suspended human rights conventions in the Kurdish areas outright, arguing that it was necessary to contain 'terrorism and banditry' and that the armed conflict with the PKK was not subject to the Geneva Convention and Protocols. Alarmed by the burgeoning of Kurdish freedom in Northern Iraq, Turkey also deliberately provoked tensions between the Kurdish parties and relations became increasingly fragile (see Chapter 6 for a discussion of the PKK's role).

It was clear to the PKK from as early as May 1991 that they would soon be subject to Turkish aerial attack. They believed that their positions were being monitored by the Allied overflights ostensibly protecting Iraqi Kurds from Saddam, and suspected the Iraqi Kurdish leadership of providing specific co-ordinates to the Ankara government. This the Kurdistan Front denied.

The establishment of KDP and PUK offices in the Turkish capital and the frequent visits of the representatives of these two parties to meetings with President Turgut Özal and the Turkish government intensified the PKK's suspicions. Conversely, the Kurdistan Front stated that the PKK was supported by the Iraqi government and that their bases and offices in Iraqi Kurdistan were there with Saddam's official consent. This was extremely unlikely given that the PKK's interests were opposite to those of Saddam.

Around the time of the Kurdish uprising in March in which the PKK played a minor role, it established a sister party in Iraqi Kurdistan, the Freedom Party of Kurdistan or PAK (Parti Azadi Kurdistan). PAK was set up with the intention of wooing Iraqi Kurds disillusioned with the Front and disgruntled by the leaders' talks with Saddam.

Both the PAK and the PKK guerrillas moved through the mountains bordering Turkey and focused their military offensives on Turkish military targets. As their goal at the time was for a greater, united

Kurdistan, they did not agree with the Iraqi Kurds' policy of autonomy or federation within Iraq. In their written propaganda they accused the KDP and PUK of betraying the Kurdish people to two of their worst enemies, Turkey and Iraq, stating neither could be trusted to keep their promises. The KDP similarly denounced the PKK as 'terrorist', and a threat to Kurdistan, portraying itself as a reliable, co-operative well-meaning neighbour to Turkey. The KDP claimed that the PKK was occupying its territory and that should the PKK do anything undesirable it would call a halt to its activities. But even then, the KDP's authority was cast under a shadow by the PKK's growing strength in the region. This galled many senior politicians within the KDP who were averse to the PKK's unwillingness to listen to anybody outside its own organisation. They felt that the PKK's war with Turkey jeopardised their own security.

The mood became tense and bitter. It was difficult to discuss the PKK's position or Turkey's repression of the Kurds openly with the Kurdistan Front, which was extremely reluctant to be drawn into the matter at any length. Only those who had done time in the refugee camps in Diyarbakir, Mardin or Muş, or who had experienced the Turkish 'reality' while in the mountain camps in Işikveren, Çukurca (Çele), Silopi or elsewhere seemed to understand that there was justification for Kurds from Turkey to feel as they did. The opposition had already begun to threaten PKK members and supporters in Bahdinan, closing their offices and raiding their safe houses. PKK sympathisers were taken prisoner and roughed up by KDP loyalists. They were forced to go underground in the urban areas during this time.

After many fruitless efforts, we finally made contact with the PKK in a safe house at Zakho, the home of some Iraqi Kurdish PKK sympathisers. I spoke with them for several hours in Turkish as we were vetted and finally told to return the same time the next day for a decision. The following day, the same procedure was repeated but with different PKK representatives asking the questions. On the third day, as we began to wonder whether we would ever be taken 'upstairs' (to the mountains), permission was given.

It was about 4.30 p.m. and the light was fading fast. Mark and I were driven up the Shiranish road by which we had escaped during the uprising. I was not too keen to be climbing the mountains after dark, but there was no alternative. Now that our guides were ready, we had to be also.

The PKK camps

The dirt road came to an abrupt end high up on a mountain track beyond Shiranish. The driver unloaded sacks of flour and sugar for the guerrillas and then turned around and rapidly disappeared in a blur of yellow dust.

Our guide, a university-educated Kurd from Syria, mimicked a series of short bird calls. An answering bird cry rose from the trees below. Almost at once, from out of nowhere, the first of the PKK's ARGK (the Kurdistan Liberation Army) guerrillas materialised from the shadows. They greeted our 'doctor' familiarly and swung the supply sacks up onto their shoulders, before turning and moving off in single file down the slope between the trees. We followed. About five minutes down the mountain we encountered a team of around twenty guerrillas, equal numbers of men and women, heading in the opposite direction. This was the night watch relieving the earlier shift. Each guerrilla shook our hands solemnly and murmured welcome then disappeared, fleet of foot over the dry leaves into the fast gathering gloom.

Half an hour later, a large round moon had risen and the treacherous stony path which wound down the side of the mountain gleamed faintly, a luminous line threading around trees, rocks and tall thistles which caught at my clothes as I swayed and slid, sometimes jumping sheer blind drops. I fell once and got up, dusty but unharmed, hating having to walk blind yet needing to move fast enough to keep up with the guerrillas.

Three hours later we had descended into a valley and were feeling our way over the large smooth stones of a dry stream bed. Another hour passed. Our guide suddenly emitted a low whistle. This was answered in kind from a few hundred yards away. Leaves rustled and we climbed up through a black thicket of trees into a small clearing, a camp dimly lit by a fire over which a smoke-blackened kettle was boiling. Through the clearing I could make out the shapes of about fifteen guerrillas, some sitting around talking in hushed voices, others stretched out asleep on the ground.

The camp leader, Cemil Bayik (Cuma), commander of the ARGK forces and one of the PKK's founders, welcomed us fraternally and we took up places around the fire while tea was brought to us. Cuma chatted with us about what we hoped to do for the next two hours before lying down on the leafy ground. The four of us who had travelled from Zakho stretched out side by side in a row, with a single sleeping bag opened over us to keep out the night air. I could feel little twigs and stones under my back all night long. Just before daybreak, the temperature fell and the air grew cold and damp. There was a constant droning and buzzing of mosquitoes around my ears.

The guerrillas were up by 4 a.m. They assembled in a wide grassy area below to perform the first drill of the day – an oath of allegiance which reaffirmed their reason for being there, *Kurdistan ya naman* ('Kurdistan or death'). The drill lasted no more than seven or eight minutes, then the guerrillas broke ranks and went off in various directions, some to wash and fetch water from the stream nearby, others to boil the tea and fix breakfast. Fires were re-lit to boil water and the big black kettles balanced above the flames.

The sun began to rise revealing the contours of the deep valley we were in, ringed by steep mountains. The camp itself was pitched on the ruins of an ancient Kurdish village, long since abandoned judging by the growth of moss and lichens on the stones. Low, mouldering stone walls and the remains of gardens and fruit trees intimated how beautiful it must once have been. Isolated beyond imagination, the valley was exceptionally peaceful.

As the guerrillas came to life around us, I realised that the camp was more extensive than it had seemed in the night, and that it consisted of a number of levels extending over a wide area. The women had their own patch and occupied a little thicket adjacent to the men's camp where they slept, made their own tea and prepared their own food. They were dressed exactly like the men. Some also wore headscarves. The baggy trousers and jackets (*shal û shapik*) of these guerrillas were subtly different from those of the peshmergas. One would not mistake one group for another. But at this time the PKK and PAK guerrillas were the only Kurds up here in the mountains as the peshmergas had recently become transformed by their unusual circumstances into an urban force with administrative duties in the towns. The PKK guerrillas had a worn and rugged look about them. Their commander, Cuma, had lived for almost sixteen years in the Kurdish mountains. He manifested an almost sage-like presence, his manner commanding silence from all who gathered to hear him. Cuma had been a schoolteacher in an earlier incarnation. A founder member of the PKK, he was both leader and instructor of this camp, training new arrivals in the arts of guerrilla lore.

The guerrilla girls of the women's army took me with them to a stream which bubbled on its course on the other side of the valley. We walked in single file, knee-deep through blonde-coloured grass bright with tall blue flowering thistles and white *hero* flowers (hollyhocks). A little ahead of us the stream ran murmuring over rocks beneath the tall trees, forming deep green pools below. The water was icy cold and perfectly clear.

Berivan crouched down to draw water for the camp. As she filled the water jar she told me how she had decided to join the PKK as the only alternative to being abused by the Turkish army. The Turkish security forces had recently overrun her village and captured one of her brothers in the skirmish which ensued. She was just fourteen years old when she joined the guerrillas.

There were no fewer than nineteen other young women in this small camp. Azimi and her two nieces were from Dersim (Tunceli), but their family had moved to Istanbul because of the 'white massacre', as Azimi called the propaganda and terror tactics of government agents in the schools. She had dropped out of university to join the PKK, sending her family a letter about her decision and enclosing some party information. As she explained, 'from now on it will be me, not the Turkish government, who will give my family the propaganda.'

They all spoke like this. None showed any doubt about her decision despite the harshness of the lifestyle. The girls told us the PKK had several other camps in the area, units of around a hundred members per camp. Some were veteran teams, well seasoned in guerrilla life, others were new arrivals undergoing training like this one. Here they learnt the techniques of guerrilla warfare at the same time as they studied the works of Marx and Lenin, political theory and history. When the sun was at the mid-heaven and the heat greatest, they would shelter from its intense rays under rough canopies of thatch, studying political treatises and answering questions in open-air classes. As the air cooled they went through manoeuvres and mock attacks but used live ammunition to get a real taste of things.

Crossing the grassy valley to the thatched clearing which camouflaged the camp, I heard the drone of aeroplanes nearby. The sound possessed a sinister undertone. The noise of aircraft could mean routine Allied aerial surveillance or it could just as easily signal a Turkish attack.

Cuma reclined in the shade of a tree against a large rock, his gun wedged between his knees. He explained how the PKK had not originally sought an armed solution to their conflict with Turkey, but that finally they felt this had been the only option left to them.

> Countless times we called upon the Turkish government to agree to a ceasefire, saying, 'Let democracy be established, let a free and independent milieu develop, let political activity be conducted freely, let there be the possibility of forming free associations, let there be a referendum in Kurdistan. This could lead to either autonomy or independence. We are ready for anything,' we said. But they completely rejected all our terms.

A strong sense of equality and unity existed between the members of

Cuma's camp. The guerrillas worked together, built their shelters, studied, trained, kept watch, cooked, cleaned, drilled and lived as equals. The atmosphere was relaxed and happy, despite the danger. By night, the guerrillas covered many miles, accustomed to moving in the dark as they crossed the stony slopes, leaving behind the woods of south Kurdistan for the defoliated barren heights of the Turkish side of the border where the regime had burned down the trees and forced the local people to leave their villages, slaughtering the livestock and demolishing their houses in an attempt to wipe out the guerrilla movement by destroying its popular support base.

The guerrillas around us were alert and serious, even the youngest among them; thirteen, fourteen and fifteen years old, they had a surprising degree of personal maturity. The PKK's people seemed to have a clear vision of their role and pursued their training with discipline and commitment. Some had come straight from the villages, some from towns, some from the political prisons, but all were equal here and shared the same outlook.

There was perhaps also an aura of death about them, something disturbing and final. These young people had no life expectancy. Rather, they expected to give their lives and join the hundreds of PKK martyrs, remembered in photographs and ceremonies. It could be a matter of hours, days or months – years, for the lucky few who emerged intact from operations waged against a superior number of Turkish soldiers. (The ratio at this time stood at about one guerrilla for every ten soldiers.)

The guerrillas served us a lunch of oily chicken and lentil soup, which we mopped up with scraps of dry flat bread. This was followed by a dessert of mulberries, which they called *dut*. The berries grew in two varieties on tall trees all around these valleys – a purple species and a white one. One or two friends would climb a tree and shake the branches while their comrades below collected the tumbling berries. After lunch, we hiked across the side of another hill to a second camp. Cuma led the way, extending the butt of his rifle behind for me to grasp hold of for balance as we ascended the stony slope. The pebbles slipped away beneath my feet and rattled down over the rocks into the valley below.

When we reached the camp we found it to be largely populated by young women. Dilan, one of the most distinguished of the PKK's cadres, had arrived from Lebanon a day or so before. Dilan believed that those Western nations which had built Saddam up as their pawn in the region against Iran were also playing a ruthless and deadly game with Kurdistan. After the Gulf war, when the Allies could have toppled Saddam, they chose instead to let him remain, she said; rather than helping the Kurds out of their political dilemma, they chose to follow a devious political course which left Kurdistan high and dry, stranded in political confusion. That was also the view of the party.[1]

Late that afternoon as temperatures grew cooler, we followed one of the guerrilla patrols to an area bordering an icy green stream flowing beside another destroyed village. The devastation here appeared more recent than in the village where Cuma camped. Some Iraqi Kurds driving a flock of sheep, smuggled from the Turkish side of the border, to sell in Zakho appeared in the distance. Our companions stopped them, sat down with them in a circle and began to talk politics. The smugglers looked frightened. An hour went by. Then they rounded up their sheep and proceeded on their way with evident relief, plunging across the stream in the direction of Cuma's camp. One of our companions was immediately despatched to warn the camp to keep quiet. He would try to divert the Iraqi Kurds to another path lest they ascertain and thereafter divulge the whereabouts of the base to any interested parties back in Zakho. For security reasons the guerrillas moved camp every few weeks, or days, as necessary. They rightly mistrusted all but their own people. Rumours had been heard of PKK sympathisers being attacked by the KDP, some fatally. The KDP deeply resented the PKK's presence in what they viewed as their territory, and traditionally Bahdinan had always been under the KDP's control.

Turkish attacks on the 'safe haven'

The first Turkish aerial attack on the 'safe haven' came on 4 August 1991 and continued until 15 August. Turkish F-14 and F-104 fighter jets completed 132 sorties over Northern Iraq. On the way they dropped a number of bombs on Kurdish villages on the Turkish side of the border in the vicinity of the Cudi, Gabarve and Herakol mountains. In Iraqi Kurdistan, figures for civilian casualties indicated that by the fourth day at least eleven people had been killed, and as many as a further twelve lost their lives thereafter.[2]

The second Turkish operation was staged at the beginning of October 1991. Turkish warplanes crossed the border penetrating 35 km into Iraqi Kurdistan, again in the Zakho region. Fields, orchards and houses were burned. At least two people were killed and another eight injured.

The third operation commenced on 25 October 1991. Turkish forces again attacked Kurdish areas across the border, hitting Banik, Kani, Silan, Siyar, Surya, Dereluk, Begova, Berze and Barzan. I saw evidence of some of these attacks when I was back in the area shortly after. The injured were mostly women and children whose men had been 'disappeared' during the Anfal.

The Turkish attacks were also witnessed by a number of foreign organisations working in Kurdistan, including the International Rescue Committee (Zakho) and the UN (Diana). A number of victims of the bombing were hospitalised in Dohuk, where I met them at the end of November and recorded accounts of the families involved. Although after the second operation Turkey had promised the Kurdistan Front that it would not repeat its action, it did so again after only three weeks. It was not the PKK who suffered. The guerrillas reported very few casualties and the bases were missed altogether. The Kurds widely believed that the attacks were intended as a warning to the Iraqi Kurds not to become over ambitious in their regional aspirations. By 1992, Turkish strikes on both sides of the border would become a regular occurrence.[3]

Intimidation and murder within Turkey

Even prior to the August bombing attacks, daily life had become a nightmare for the Kurdish inhabitants of south-east Turkey. On 5 July 1991, Vedat Aydin, chairman of the Diyarbakir branch of HEP (the People's Labour Party) and schoolteacher, whom I had met several times in 1990, was abducted from his home late at night by unidentified persons. He never returned. On 8 July, Vedat's dead body was discovered near Maden, about forty miles outside town, on Diyarbakir's provincial border with Elazig. He had been brutally tortured before his corpse was casually dumped at the side of the road.

Vedat had been a well-known and popular figure in town, and his funeral on 10 July 1991 attracted tens of thousands of angry Kurds who marched in protest through the streets of Diyarbakir to the cemetery. The procession included several MPs from HEP, Human Rights Association members, patriotic Kurdish citizens as well as PKK sympathisers. It marked a turning point in Kurdish relations with the Turkish government. Vedat's murder also provoked a new mass sympathy among ordinary Kurds for the PKK.

As the crowd drew near the cemetery, police marshalled along the black city walls above the graveyard opened fire. As the first dead and injured fell, others ran for their lives and scattered in all directions, some leaping over the old walls down a sheer drop twenty to thirty feet to the orchards below. Turkish Security Forces joined the marksmen. Witnesses later told of having seen armed men, their faces masked in balaclavas, up on the walls before the attack. It had evidently been pre-planned.

Although nobody was brought to trial for Vedat's murder, Turkish contra-guerrillas were identified as having been responsible. The contra-guerrillas were behind many similar murders, including those of journalists and Kurdish activists. Again, there were no trials.[4] The PKK grew stronger as state terror in Kurdistan became less discerning in its choice of victims.

Iraqi government collaboration with the Kurds

Meanwhile, back in the 'safe haven', although the coalition forces had driven most of Saddam's secret police and security agents from the area (after the police station in Zakho was bombed by Kurds on 26 April 1991), a few Iraqi policemen remained behind to follow new instructions. These now worked alongside the Kurdistan Front to maintain order in the towns. They helped to guard the banks and supervised the dispensing of pensions and other state payments to the poor. For a time, Iraqi soldiers also assisted the peshmergas with clearing and detonating land-mines in Zakho and around Ibrahim Khalil. This desirable arrangement only lasted for the duration of the autonomy negotiations with Saddam.

Thereafter, Ba'ath security agents started to infiltrate the Kurdish towns once more, threatening to punish any locals who assisted the Allies. This unnerved the ordinary people, especially as the Allied Forces were fast disappearing from their midst.

When the Kurdistan Front's negotiations with the Iraqi government finally floundered in October 1991, Saddam recalled his men, imposed an embargo on Kurdistan in addition to the UN sanctions, and tried to starve out civil servants and teachers by cutting the payment of wages to the region. At the same time, he reduced petrol supplies to one-quarter of the usual amount. The Kurdish economy suffered an enormous blow, bringing misery upon ordinary Kurds, a misery which could only deepen as winter set in.

Notes

1. Planet Television for Channel Four News, June/July 1991.
2. *Guardian*, 8 August 1991.
3. See chapters 5 and 6.
4. Further accounts are detailed in chapter 6.

4

Waiting in the cold

By late November 1991, the winter rain and snow had arrived. The problem of providing shelter for thousands of refugees, some one in ten people, who had been unable to return home, or who had no homes left to return to, had not been resolved and so the Kurds remained under canvas and plastic. The shelters which the UN were to have had ready before winter were still not in place. I arrived back to this appalling scene at the beginning of December. Having crossed the Turkish border, I found Zakho looking so much sadder and shabbier drenched by a thick rain, the roads awash with mud. This Zakho reminded me of Kurdistan during the exodus, with people hard-pressed and having to take shelter where they found it.

The blockade imposed by Saddam had bitten deeply into the life of the enclave. The effect was one of paralysis. Only one-quarter of the usual amount of petrol was being sold; there was little fuel for heating and almost everyone was cold. Supplies of food and medicine were lower than ever. Saddam's embargo, in place since October, compounded the deprivation already caused by UN sanctions. Ordinary Kurds were barely able to carry on feeding their families. Virtually no government supplies reached Kurdistan at all.

Returning to Dohuk, I located a few friends from the days of the uprising, busy with administrative duties, their role as peshmergas having been overtaken by the unfamiliar task of running a city. Anwar laboured behind an empty desk in a former Ba'ath Party office converted into the KDP's administrative headquarters for Dohuk. Dealing with insurmountable problems, Anwar had evidently not seen a barber for weeks and in his general state of fatigue looked to have shed ten kilos from an already slight frame. Spiritless groups of bedraggled Kurds would call at his office, passing from one desk to the next, from one party building to another, living only on party chits and hope.

The offices of the new Kurdish administration were barely warmed, if at all, by the single kerosene heaters placed in the centre of each room. Outside, muddy water spewed through the streets from broken drains. Pipes and sewers were still broken and storm-water gushed along the main roads. Large sections of residential areas had been dynamited in April when the vengeful Iraqi army recaptured Dohuk. Now, the afflicted families pitched their tents on top of the rubble and struggled to carry on with daily life. But everything was wet and nearly everyone was ill.

Petrol queues at gas stations stretched all the way around the corner and out of sight. Drivers would park their cars and simply leave them overnight or until the next delivery came, moving up the queue one by one, hoping to get to the head of the line before the supply ran out again.

The economic embargo imposed on Kurdistan by Baghdad simply represented a further attempt by the Iraqi president to break the resolve of the Kurdish people and usurp ongoing negotiations with the Kurdish leadership to regain control of the region. Although this internal embargo clearly constituted a breach of Security Council Resolution 688, again no punitory action was taken against Saddam by the international community or the UN. Despite the considerable hardships at this stage, few Kurds would have wished to see things return to the way they were before the uprising.

The rebuilding programme was progressing satisfactorily. Reconstruction was being carried out by NGOs including the KRO (the Kurdistan Reconstruction Organisation), KURDS, the KSRO (Kurdistan Shelter Reconstruction Organisation) and the KRA (Kurdish Relief Association) in conjunction with NGOs from Switzerland, France (such as Madame Mitterrand's France Libertés); with Germany (Caritas), Australia (CARE) and with Britain (Save the Children, Oxfam and Christian Aid). Christian Aid was also supporting the Mines Advisory Group's project for land-mine clearance, site marking and a mine awareness programme. British charities also contributed finance for the reintroduction of livestock to the villages and seed for spring planting, together with fertiliser and pesticides to protect new crops. The intention was to assist the newly reconstructed villages to become self-sufficient as soon as possible. Some four hundred villages had been rebuilt, complete with plumbing, drainage and irrigation. Former inhabitants of villages undergoing reconstruction tended to camp nearby to take part in the completion of the new homes.

By this time, some fifty or so families had also returned to the village of Barzan which was rising like a phoenix from the rubble. The families consisted almost entirely of women and children. Most of the Barzani males had been rounded up and taken away by Iraqi soldiers in 1983. It is widely believed that they were executed immediately afterwards. To date neither the missing Barzani men nor any trace of them has been found. But numbers of mass graves of Kurdish victims of the Anfal are constantly being discovered within the liberated area.

In the summer of 1991 the first of a number of bombs from Turkish jet fighters had struck Barzan village and injured several civilians. The victims of the attacks on the region were taken to Dohuk Hospital.[1] The Kurdistan Front's negotiations with the Baghdad government over the same period had also failed to prevent the Iraqi regime from attacking frontline areas where Iraqi and peshmerga forces maintained an uneasy stand-off. There had been shelling by the Iraqi army, especially around Sulaimaniya and Kirkuk. Hundreds of families had again been made homeless by Iraqi attacks on the outskirts of Chemchemal – the last town held by the Kurds on the Kirkuk road – and on Kalar and Kifri, swelling the number of displaced people still in need of international assistance to tens of thousands.

Chemchemal reported nightly fire. Sizeable units of Iraqi tank troops were dug in just outside town and remain so at the time of writing. Hospitals were busy with casualties. Mine injuries also exacerbated the problem as Kurds were forced, by economic hardship, to forage for wood among the ruins of their villages for heating and building materials.

The ruined town of Sayid Sadiq, south of Sulaimaniya, had failed to cope with a state of emergency as the first 70,000 refugees returned to the rubble of their former homes. Sayid Sadiq, like most towns in the area, had been dynamited to bits by Saddam's army during the Anfal. Now its people lacked adequate means of winter shelter. The few light-weight tents they shared between them were no match for the severe Kurdish winter weather. By the time we arrived there in early December, the population of homeless families had swollen to around 90,000 people. These families were now literally 'camping' in the mud and frozen snow.

There had been another storm during the night. Muddy water surged through the plain and flooded the few tents which had withstood the fierce winds and the lash of rain. Most of Sayid Sadiq's children went barefoot and wore the same thin clothes as during the Kurdish exodus seven months before. A few families were still trying to move their tents to higher ground, or took shelter under the concrete rubble of dynamited houses and shops – all that remained of their town. In shivering clusters, the rest simply stood waiting for the rain to stop and for the water which lapped through their tents to abate. It never did. Not that day, nor the next, nor the day after that.

At Halabja (best known to the international community for Iraq's chemical attacks on the town in 1988) there were 60,000 homeless people seeking shelter and, at Penjwin, another 50,000. Most had only recently returned from Iran where they had sheltered since the failed uprising. New arrivals had joined them from Kirkuk, Chemchemal, Kalar and Kifri within the past two weeks, due to attacks by the government. Although the majority of these displaced people were of Kurdish origin, there were also numbers of Turkoman and Assyrian families among them.

The mountain town of Penjwin had been cut off by snow a few days before our arrival. Virtually no supplies had been able to get through since. But now the snow had melted sufficiently in the heavy rain that fell overnight to allow us into the miserable place.

Huddled at the entrance to the UNHCR supply tents in Penjwin was a family from Kirkuk. I learned that for the past three days they had received no food on account of the weather, which had forced the local food distribution points to close. One of the Kirkuki women trailed listlessly behind me into the UNHCR's yard, where her problem received no attention from aid workers. The woman finally gave up asking for food and left with two blankets. A token gesture. The family would have to wait for the distribution points to reopen the next day, the day after that or possibly even the day after, before they could get any food. What could be said?

The UN, UNHCR and UN guards

Part of the problem faced by the Kurds lay in the inadequacy of the UN's winter 1991–92 plan. This had failed to allow for either the cessation of Iraqi government supplies, or for the increased numbers of Kurdish families displaced through government attacks on the region. Bands of desperate people mobbed our vehicle as we drove through Penjwin. Some of these were black-shrouded Kurdish widows whose men had been 'lost' in the Anfal. They had neither homes, property, livelihood, nor anyone to care for them; the Kurdish political parties could do nothing to help them. Nor was foreign aid reaching them. Therefore they besieged newcomers such as ourselves in the hope of getting a little food or money. These women were proud and angry; they clearly resented having to beg. They waved the photographs of their martyrs before our eyes and shouted. Our crew filled as many open palms as they could before taking to the road once more. Enormous hailstones battered the roof and windows of our car, thunder struck the mountainsides and sheet lightning flashed across the thick black sky. The road before us swirled with water. Vast rivers of mud churned through the heart of Sayid Sadiq camp, even more widespread than in the morning. The inhabitants stood still as scarecrows in the storm, their tents beyond use. They would doubtless remain that way the entire night. Only a dozen or so families now bothered to dig trenches to channel away the rushing brown water.

The UN's winterisation plan

The UN and UNHCR were unable to cope. Part of the 'winterisation' project included the construction of pre-fabricated huts at Shanaderi, a kilometre or so up the road from the tents at Sayid Sadiq. However, only fifty buildings were ready for 140,000 displaced people in the area. Because the UN changed its money at Baghdad's official rate, most of its funds were lost to the government. Other NGOs working in Kurdistan had thirty times the buying power of the UN – simply by changing their currency through the Kurds at the going black-market rate.

The UN was severely handicapped in a number of other significant ways by having to operate through Baghdad. UN personnel entered the country through Baghdad, took Iraqi visas and were thereafter subjected to government harassment, interference and all manner of bureaucratic delays. Impeded by their own bureaucracy and paperwork, the UN lost much valuable time when time was their most precious asset. The UN had had eight months during which to prepare for winter and launch the winterisation programme for the Kurdish refugees. Why were they so late in getting started?

First, there had been internal setbacks. UN offices and phones were bugged, their operation centres infiltrated by Ba'ath party undercover agents, and their documents were being stolen.[2]

Second, Baghdad did everything in its power to obstruct the UN in all aspects of its work throughout the country. When the 'safe haven' was first set up, 20,000 allied troops had been put in place to protect the relief efforts in Kurdistan. But when, in June 1991, the UNHCR took over these responsibilities, no international body guaranteed the security of the Kurds with the Iraqi government nor with the Kurdish parties of the Kurdistan Front. Although a Memorandum of Understanding (MOU) was signed between the UN and the Iraqi regime, as customary, Baghdad failed to honour its content.[3]

UN and UNHCR delays and massive inefficiency provoked the Kurds into reacting. Hunger strikes and marches were organised in every part of 'Free Kurdistan', thousands demonstrating outside the UN's offices in Arbil and Sulaimaniya. Mass demonstrations were organised both in protest and to demand that the area of UN protection be extended to the 34th parallel to include Kirkuk, Kalar and Kifri which were still under attack from Saddam's military. Schoolchildren, women's groups, students, refugees and workers all joined these demonstrations.

The Kurds' protests and hunger strikes endured throughout December, as people became increasingly angry and disillusioned, aware that the resolve of the international community was weakening. Women, young and old, chanted slogans outside the UN's headquarters day after day. They waved banners at the blue uniforms in front of them, urging a breakthrough which never came.

The UN guards were not actually in a position to do anything. They were mainly ex-army personnel, security men and policemen brought in to do a difficult job for which they had little heart. Many secretly hoped for a better posting elsewhere and were eager to finish their time and move on. For the ambitious among them, there was little status attached to being posted to Kurdistan.

Although the Kurds were led to believe that UN guards were there to protect them from the Iraqi government, it became clear that the guards were equally in need of protection, incapable by virtue of their mandate and small numbers to offer protection to anyone. By the end of 1991, the peshmergas were being called upon to protect foreign NGOs in Kurdistan, including the UN and UN guards. All foreign personnel, vehicles, and headquarters became the main target of the government's sabotage.

While the Kurds' protests fell on deaf ears, the bureaucratic inadequacies of the UN itself had become increasingly apparent. A scandal over UN mismanagement of funds was already breaking. Although entrusted with the duty of behaving as the world's policeman, like a 'global 999', the UN was unable to police itself. Its confidential audit in 1993 revealed 'incompetence and thievery'. The UN had a workforce of 80,000 people and a budget of $10 billion. The public information office was grossly overstaffed and in 48 years had never fired anyone. Staff were retiring, taking their pensions, and then returning as consultants on long-term contracts. Reports were often published as many as nine years late.

Charles Lichenstein, the US ambassador to the UN between 1981 and 1984, asserted:

> It's a train that runs almost completely out of control ... there's a culture at the UN – you enrich yourself and you loot your country, forget about other impoverished countries and the public, you are on a lifetime gravy train.

At the expense of other projects, UN officials financed massive conference centres such as in Addis Ababa ($100 million). One powerful member can launch a building boom by himself, as for example with Kurt Waldheim when he was head of the UN in Austria ... .There had been no prosecution of UN officials for corruption etc. After the audit, Boutros Boutros Ghali promised to take action. He declined to be interviewed as to what he would do.[4]

Landmines and security of life

Two metres of snow blocked the Haj Omran pass to Iran. Many hundreds of Kurdish refugees remained in the area to avail themselves of an escape route should the Iraqi government return. For others, winter in Iran seemed preferable.

Our four-wheel drive had conveyed us thus far successfully up the snowy road to within three miles of the Iranian border. Here we came to a sad halt, banked up behind a number of similar vehicles and two large trucks stuck in the snowdrift which had finally impeded movement in either direction. Several Kurdish families carried on to the Iranian border on foot, hauling large bundles behind them through the snow. They walked with their heads down, keeping to the icy slush of the road rather than risk walking in the frozen snow which hid thousands of mines planted during the Iraq–Iran war the length of the road between Choman and Haj Omran.

Pondering our dilemma, the crew wandered away to investigate the sole surviving building in the area. Kurds were shovelling snow from the roof. Two refugee families had taken occupancy of this former local schoolhouse, although it was virtually in ruins. These families had recently fled from Kirkuk and had chosen to spend the winter here, unable to return home. Two smoke-darkened rooms had been sealed off as sleeping quarters. These looked reasonably watertight, but within other parts of the building, the rotten ceiling leaked badly and a small steady trickle of water snaked across the floor.

A boy now hip-hopped towards us, leaving a small dark room where a wood fire was burning. His mother went to him swiftly and hoisted him up on her hip. Only three months before, one of the child's feet had been blown off by a concealed mine when he was taking the goats up to graze on the hill opposite the school. The boy smiled shyly at us, evidently the focus of the family's attention since his accident. German doctors from the Cap Anamur tent hospital in Choman had treated him. Two survivors of another mine explosion lay in the German tents awaiting amputation. Several other adults and children from the Choman settlement had been blown to pieces when a bonfire was lit on top of a buried mine.

The German doctors, nurses and volunteers from the project had established this canvas 'hospital' because mine injuries in the region were so high. The doctors said they were treating more than twenty local mine casualties each week, but the cold, the snow and the lack of adequate operating facilities were now seriously hampering their work. One of their operating tents had collapsed in a recent snowstorm and they were waiting for the UN to vacate its supply hall across the road so that they could adapt it for the surgical amputations that needed to be performed.

We drank tea at the Cap Anamur hospital before returning to the KDP's eyrie, hovering in the mists of the Massif (Salahaddin) where Massoud Barzani maintained his headquarters. The hotels we stayed in were part of the former tourist resort at Salahaddin, which had been enjoyed by Saddam and by Arab tourists from the plains before the uprising.

It was bitterly cold on the mountain top; the kind of damp cold that penetrates to the marrow and leaves you aching, wet through inside your clothes. The 'Green Hotel' was poorly heated, boasting but a single kerosene heater set in the middle of a huge deserted lounge adjoining the dining area. Still wearing our thickest winter jackets, we huddled in a small group around the kerosene heater, exchanging observations with fellow guests Kurt Schork from Reuters and Siegfried March from the German Green Party, before sharing a meagre dinner. Siegfried and Kurds from the various political parties who joined us in the dining room were deeply concerned about the West's lack of political commit- ment to the enclave, and firmly believed that Western governments were responsible for the predicament the Kurdish people found themselves in that winter. The same anxieties were expressed to us next day by the KDP's leader, Massoud Barzani, who warned:

> If there is no political decision, this so-called 'safe haven' is short-lived, whether it be six months or a year. And what then? That is the question. We want a lasting solution – a political one. Our question is not simply a humanitarian issue. This humanitarian disaster is the consequence of our problem not being solved politically.[5]

In view of the imminent collapse of their negotiations with the regime, the fears of the Kurdish leadership were amply justified. They under- stood that foreign interest was declining and saw that there was no initiative to bring about the urgent political solution they sought.

The winter of 1991 proved to be the most severe in several years. Kurdistan's gloom deepened as the months dragged by. Poor villagers and refugees continued to die of cold and hunger in the tents and ruins of their former homes while Saddam remained snugly in power.

By February 1992, shortly before the end of winter, talks between the Kurdistan Front and Baghdad finally collapsed. Although the Kurds had met every condition the regime laid down, Saddam constantly moved the goalposts. Ultimately, the talks failed as the two sides could not concur over the administration of Kirkuk and whether or not Kirkuk was to be included in the autonomous region. Definitive details concerning the proposed autonomy for the Kurdish region also remained elusive, as did the question of internal security and who should provide it.

The discord caused the first serious cracks to form in the fabric of unity hitherto maintained between the Kurdish parties. The Kurdish leadership realised they must pursue alternatives other than negotiations with Saddam if they were to win support for their fragile freedom.

Playing off the Kurds of Iraq against the Kurds of Turkey

Continuing Turkish attacks on the enclave proved of additional concern to the Kurdistan Front. In response, the Front sought to reassure the Turks that Kurdish democracy in northern Iraq posed no threat to any of its neighbours. Visits by the Kurdish leaders to Turkey and negotiations with the Turkish government continued in earnest. The Turks had allowed the PUK and KDP to open offices in Ankara. The Kurds in Turkey interpreted this as the sell-out of their own revolution.

The Turks urged the Kurdistan Front to position its peshmergas along the Turkish–Iraqi border to obstruct the PKK's attacks against Turkey from that quarter. One KDP loyalist commented that at least three hundred peshmerga fighters had been dispatched to the border areas, saying 'They will help prevent people going across to Turkey to throw bombs'.[6] Tensions between the PKK and the Iraqi Kurds rose dramatically thereafter. The Allies supported the Kurdistan Front and Turkey's position and omitted to condemn Turkish strikes against the PKK in Northern Iraq. Instead, Western leaders continued to back Turkey's militarism on the basis that the PKK was a 'terrorist' organisation, despite its popular basis in Turkish Kurdistan.

In nationwide elections held in Turkey that October, 22 Kurdish MPs in the Kurdish region were elected to office on the SHP–HEP ticket. HEP (the People's Labour Party), as a newly established political party, had not qualified to put candidates up for election as it had not been in existence for the prerequisite period. Its candidates were only allowed to stand because HEP linked itself with the SHP (People's Socialist Party) led by Erdal Inönü. The elections resulted in a coalition between Süleyman Demirel's right of centre DYP (True Path Party) and Inönü's centre-left SHP. Demirel took office as prime minister.

It did not take the new government long to denounce the Kurdish HEP MPs as 'PKK sympathisers' and for the SHP coalition partner to disassociate itself entirely from the pro-Kurdish lobby. Following the official denouncement of the HEP MPs, political representatives and prominent members became targets of the state's death squads (Special Forces and contra-guerrillas); political murders in the Kurdish region became increasingly rife.

The mutual hostility between the Turkish Kurds and the Iraqi Kurds continued to mount as the winter of 1991 gave way to the spring of 1992. The Turkish security forces also intensified their offensives, and carried out daylight massacres coinciding with Kurdish New Year celebrations, in patriotic Kurdish towns such as Cizre and Şirnak.

Like the Kurds of Iraq, the oppressed Kurds of Turkey waited for the international community to condemn the repression they suffered at the hands of the Turkish government. In its first few months, the new coalition led by Demirel was proving even more aggressive than its predecessor in its policies towards the Kurds. But in view of the West's close relations with Turkey, no foreign nation emerged as a friend to the Turkish Kurds, willing or able to generate any useful progress towards a democratic solution of the Kurdish question. As the Kurds of Iraq rose in the West's favour, the Kurds of Turkey were allowed to slip further from sight.

Like the doomed Kurdish Republic of Mahabad of 1946, the Kurds found themselves beleagured by regional *realpolitik*. The mood was very like that expressed by Shaikh Mahmoud in the 1940s to Qazi Mohammad in Mahabad (Iranian Kurdistan), exhorting him to succeed in his struggle to free Kurdistan in Iran when he himself had failed in Iraq.

Poem to Qazi Mohammad

My years were plundered in neglected places
I swam in a bottomless sea
the ignorance of the people
was a weight upon my shoulders
but I was a falcon on the enemy's battlefield.
Look at the scars of my hands
they are testimony to my deeds
but hestitation became my chains
and I cannot bear another snare.

No, I am not afraid to die
to overthrow the foreigners

nor can I drink any deeper bitterness.
I am an old wolf whose fangs have broken
I no longer possess the strength to hunt
but even now I am ready
to keep my feet on the path towards nationhood.
You who are chief of the Kurds
it is a great pity to lag behind the people

Join hands and don't abandon your hopes.
When you are firm in your path
You may grasp the opportunities you want.
The enemies and the foreigners
cannot determine a nation's rights.
The love you bear for your country
is like the Sufi's love of God.

(Shaikh Mahmoud)[7]

Notes

1. Before leaving Dohuk on 3 December, I interviewed families and filmed several children who had been badly burned or maimed by the explosions. Witnesses described how they had been surprised when Turkish planes dropped bombs on the village. They had become accustomed to the sound of the American overflights and had not taken cover.

2. A UN supervisor confided to me that UN files had been copied by a clandestine computer expert, a Ba'ath agent, working undercover in their office as a UN employee. Although the infiltrator had been discovered and sacked, the damage had already been done.

3. See David Keen's report for Save the Children Fund, *The Kurds in Iraq – How Safe is their Haven now?*, May 1993.

4. *60 minutes*, ITV, 27 September 1993. The programme concerned an ongoing investigation into highly detailed charges of corruption levelled against the UN and UNHCR.

5. Massoud Barzani, interviewed for S4C (Wales) and BBC *Breakfast News*, Insight Television, December 1991.

6. *Guardian*, 26 October 1991, quoting S. Banaa.

7. Original Kurdish poem in text of M. R. Hawar (see bibliography).

5

The fratricidal war

Background to internal divisions

Since the Gulf war, as throughout Kurdish history, internal divisions between Kurdish groups and political parties have remained a major block to cohesion of purpose or activity among the four severed parts of Kurdistan.

Attempts to realise political unity in 'Free Kurdistan' had practical benefits for the population, coming as they did at a time of great economic weakness and political uncertainty. But factional violence between the KDP, PUK and PKK threatened to shatter the formal unity of the status quo achieved by the elections of May 1992. The political objectives of the leaders of each of these three parties, their style of politics, past alliances, enmities and differences in their ways and means of attaining goals continued to pose significant obstacles for peace and Kurdish unity.

On 19 May 1992 elections were held in Iraqi Kurdistan to elect representatives for a Kurdish parliament. The parliament was thereafter established with two main parties – the KDP and the PUK – holding the balance of power between them, with 50 seats apiece out of the total of 105 seats (even though, ironically, the leaders did not hold seats themselves). The remaining five seats were allocated to the Christian Assyrian minority and representatives of the Islamic movement. But it did not need a sage to see that the 50/50 power share between the KDP and the PUK would lead to serious problems in the future.

The parliament met regularly at first and functioned along the lines of other democratic assemblies. In comparison with the House of Commons, the Kurdish MPs behaved with considerably more decorum. But while parliamentary debates put forward practical democratic solutions to many of Kurdistan's problems, it was frequently the means of putting them into effect which proved to be the most difficult task of the new administration.

Most of the region's problems derived from the political dilemma in which the *de facto* state found itself. The situation of Iraqi Kurdistan was quite unparalleled in history, for here was a UN-protected enclave within a recognised foreign state, at the same time economically severed from that state and to all outward purposes functioning as an independent territory. Iraqi President Saddam Hussein also behaved towards the Kurdish enclave as if it were a separate territory, as did the neighbouring governments in their negotiations with the Kurdish leadership. This situation aggravated internal Kurdish relations and led to increasing rifts between the main parties.

Any reader of Kurdish history will be aware of the inter-party rivalries which have so often erupted into armed conflict in the past; struggles and warfare between the KDP and the PUK, between the PUK and the Iraqi Communist Party, between the KDP of Iraq and the KDP of Iran (KDPI), between the KDPI and Komala, between Kurdish and non-Kurdish opposition parties in Iran, Iraq, Turkey and, to a lesser degree, Syria. All these divisions have been further complicated by the instability created by Kurdish *jash* groups in each of these countries and moreover, by the rising tide of Islamic fundamentalism. This last factor will be dealt with more fully in later chapters.

Such tensions between the left and the right, between secular government and Islamic *shari'a* rule, and between the numerous factions are rarely manifest to such a bewildering degree as they are in Kurdistan. It has always been the lack of a legitimate Kurdish state that has made this situation particularly fraught. Where there is diversity, however, there is also a chance for democracy. Although many would wish to see a single democratic party emerge in Kurdistan able to speak for a substantial section of the population, differences between the Kurds in the countries in which they find themselves have made unity of view and purpose extremely difficult. At the same time, the Kurds have also realised that their greatest hope and strength lies in just such a unity.

Birakuji – fratricidal war

Although predicted more than a year before by the PKK in 1991, the outbreak of war on 2 October 1992 (between themselves, the KDP, PUK and Turkish Armed Forces) signified a perilous new period in Kurdish affairs. The old regional policy of divide-and-rule had proved successful once again. Kurds were killing Kurds because the neighbouring countries manipulated the Kurdish leaders so effectively. The Turkish government took advantage of the economic weakness of south Kurdistan and its dependence on foreign aid to force Iraqi Kurds into a position where they had little alternative but to fight against the Kurds from Turkey.

The Turks may have employed new arguments to trigger the conflict but they resorted to the same old tricks as in the past.

These tactics included making promises to the KDP to support their efforts to realise political supremacy in 'Free Kurdistan' over both the PKK and the PUK; co-operating with the KDP, to the detriment of the PUK, in collecting border levies at Khabur customs post; courting Iraqi Kurdish leaders in Ankara to placate the West, while at the same time condemning the Turkish Kurds as 'terrorists', whom they likened to the IRA; provoking the already considerable tensions between the PKK and the Kurdish Administration by reiterating the threat that if the Iraqi Kurds continued to 'permit' the PKK to operate from bases in Northern Iraq, aid would be cut off and the border closed. At the same time, the Turks maintained the image of all the Kurdish leaders, via the Turkish media, as untrustworthy bandits and dangerous neighbours whom Turkey had to keep under control. This kept the Turkish majority happy. The Turkish government also emphasised to the folks at home that their presence in Northern Iraq was necessary for Turkey's national security and that Operation Provide Comfort had a solely humanitarian objective; any attempt by the Iraqi Kurds to establish a separate Kurdish state in Northern Iraq would be crushed.

The more the Iraqi Kurds sought to reassure Turkey that their objective was not to create an independent state at all, the more the PKK despised them for failing to make the most of a historic opportunity to wrest back what had been taken from them: their traditional land, Kurdistan. Looking at world events taking place at the time, such as the conflict in Bosnia, pro-independence Kurds agreed with the PKK.

Europe and America were also opposed to Kurdish independence. They could see no advantage in any redrawing of international borders and viewed the Kurdish leaders as highly unstable. They also deeply distrusted the PKK and were averse to the PKK's increasing prominence in Kurdish regional politics, a threat far more dangerous to Western interests in the Middle East than any other Kurdish political party had been thus far. Although Western countries continued to insist on respect for human rights, one right was never mentioned: the right of the Kurds to self-determination. No help was ever forthcoming from the West to assist the Kurds in realising such a right.

The bloody inter-Kurdish war had been under way for nearly ten days by the time I set off for Kurdistan, arriving at Batman's military airport in south-east Turkey (north Kurdistan) on 12 October 1992. The touchdown was not a pleasant experience. The airport was buzzing with Turkish army personnel: contra-guerrillas, special forces, uniformed men in dark glasses with tight faces. Judging by the mood around the base, a major military advance was imminent.

To reach the Iraqi border it was necessary to pass through scores of roadblocks and checkpoints. These were sometimes reinforced by tanks, their long-range guns trained on the road and low hills beyond. This level of militarisation was rarely seen in the region, except during Kurdish New Year (Newroz) rebellions. It signified that the Turkish authorities were preparing a new onslaught against the PKK. Land forces were being moved towards the border with Iraq at Şemdinli, Işikveren and Hakkari ready to back the aerial assault from the ground.

The Turkish army and Özel Tim (special forces) had attacked two sizeable Kurdish towns, Kulp and Cizre, early in September, firebombing and shelling shops, factories and houses. The government had authorised the attack on civilian property in Kulp in retaliation for a minor PKK assault on a military checkpoint in which two soldiers were killed. The authorities blamed the wanton destruction of the town on the PKK, but local witnesses confirmed that government forces had been responsible. Turkish tanks continued to patrol the burnt-out commercial centre of Kulp while the victims stood in clusters outside their charred shops, their faces closed. Any murmurs of outrage petered out as soon as they came within the sights of the tank again.

A similar air of disquiet and foreboding hung above the border post at Khabur. The Turkish officials were tense and surly. A PKK embargo on all traffic and trade with south Kurdistan was in force and few petrol or goods vehicles moved along the roads. Three lorries had been burned to a shell as a warning to drivers not to cross the border. They heeded the message. Now the Turkish side of the border was deserted and the last Turkish trucks carrying fuel were just crossing back from Iraq, slopping a slick of crude oil across the road from their illegal tanks. Two weeks later, the trucks too had disappeared and the roads were deserted. The Front condemned the PKK and inflamed public and international opinion against them. Ordinary Kurds were feeling the effects of the embargo as prices of commodities soared in the markets and stocks grew low. While the first PKK embargo had been of short duration, its second embargo was more serious. Most of the supplies first reached the upper echelons of the KDP, the merchants and middlemen who sold off the aid which had been marked for distribution to the people.

The PKK imposed the embargo in reaction to the KDP's blockade on their own supply routes through Derkar to the bases along the border in Bahdinan as well as in objection to Turkish traders who were making significant sums of money out of the depression in South Kurdistan. They were also demonstrating their authority in the area to the KDP which had long considered Bahdinan solely their possession. At this period, the PKK also operated a visa system, providing passes to any visitor to Kurdish areas under their jurisdiction.

Both the KDP and the PUK had been obliged to court the Turks in order to keep humanitarian aid and commodities rolling in. But the price the Turks had set to keep the border open was the expulsion of the PKK. War became inevitable as early as July 1992 when the KDP and PUK delivered ultimatums to the PKK to leave south Kurdistan altogether. The intensity of contacts between Ankara and the Kurdistan Front increased over the next few months until finally war became inevitable.

My destination on arrival in south Kurdistan was to be whichever part of the war front might prove the most accessible. I quit Zakho at once as no help was forthcoming, having been informed that Fazil Mutni (Mirani), the KDP's politburo member in charge of Dohuk, was away directing the KDP's operations in Haftanin. Without his personal permission no one was allowed access to the area.

Accordingly, we drove a further eight hours on the long road through Aqra, crossing the Zab river heading for Salahaddin and Shaqlawa to obtain briefings there. It was important to speak with everyone, both those parties involved in the war and those who were not. Even in the towns, the PKK was being witch-hunted by Iraqi Kurds party to the conflict and Turkish secret police and special forces who had infiltrated the area disguised as Kurds. It was not only extremely difficult to try to make contact with the PKK, it was potentially 'fatal'. PKK and PAK sympathisers were being arrested and imprisoned in Zakho, Dohuk, Arbil and Sulaimaniya. There was substantiated evidence of ill-treatment.

The fighting was focused on two main fronts – the area around Bahdinan known as Haftanin, and the Xakurk/Biradost region close to the Iranian border where the PKK guerrillas were being 'sandwiched' – a word coined by the Turkish press from a statement made by Jalal Talabani – between Turkish warplanes on bombing missions and peshmerga forces, mainly from the KDP, PUK and Biradost tribe's own militia on the ground. The three-pronged advance came to be codenamed the 'Sandwich Operation'.

Passing through several villages, I asked the locals' opinion of the fratricidal infighting. They shook their heads wearily and clicked their tongues. Ordinary Kurds were against it, but what could they do? They were not the ones in power. They had seen it all before. This war was to become a tragic new example of Kurdish *realpolitik*, the betrayal of Kurd by Kurd.

The southern (Iraqi) Kurds were generally reluctant to express any opinion about this war but were clearly embarrassed by it. The KDP and other party officials initially denied all collaboration with the Turks while simultaneously justifying their position. Their main argument was that the PKK was a threat to security in the region and had to be expelled; the guerrillas' presence provided an excuse for the frequent Turkish attacks on Iraqi Kurdish villages. Tensions between the PKK and Kurdistan Front had been growing steadily as the PKK's attacks on Turkish targets proved more effective, provoking the Turks into retaliating on a scale hitherto unseen in the region.

Hostilities between the KDP and the PKK dated back to the collapse of a joint agreement signed in July 1983, when the PKK first commenced its armed struggle in Eruh and Şemdinli in August 1984. These operations against Turkish targets had been launched without the KDP's prior knowledge.

For years, the KDP and various tribes living along the Turko-Iraqi border had maintained a working alliance with Turkish military personnel stationed in the *karakol* (bases) along the frontier. These Iraqi Kurdish families lived from the profits of border smuggling. As the Turks also took a cut, they turned a blind eye. The PKK's new border operations threatened to disrupt this trade and to damage the Iraqi Kurds' relations with the Turkish border officials. Additional numbers of Turkish military reinforcements began to pour into the area to the alarm of all those with an interest in preserving the old status quo.

Under the terms of the KDP–PKK agreement, the KDP was to have provided support to the PKK for any armed struggle against an enemy of the Kurds, but in fact, the reverse soon proved to be true. Rather than supporting the PKK, the KDP exhorted them to close down all their border bases and locate their operations entirely within Turkey. Most of the border tribes in Zakho, Amadiya and Biradost supported the KDP's position excepting those tribes which had begun to develop good relations with the guerrillas, including sections of the Sindi tribe.[1] This situation had smouldered for some eight years, during which period the KDP would sometimes hand captured or wounded PKK guerrillas over to the Turks in exchange for money.[2] A number of KDP commanders kept up their relations with the Turkish border posts for mutual benefit.

The PKK had also entered an agreement with the PUK for mutual co-operation in the armed struggle against the common enemy. The agreement was signed on 1 May 1988 during the Anfal but was never put into effect. On a visit to the United States soon after, speaking at a press conference, Jalal Talabani advocated an end to the armed struggle, saying it could not succeed. In July 1992, Jalal Talabani was flown to Turkey to meet with senior representatives of the Turkish military and military intelligence joined by the PUK's Ankara representative Sarchil Qazzaz. At this meeting, Talabani allegedly proposed co-operating with the Turks by deploying PUK forces in the south, with the Turks attacking from the north in a joint endeavour to 'wipe out the PKK'.[3] General Eshref Bitlis took up the plan with enthusiasm. A delegation of Turkish officers was thereafter dispatched to south Kurdistan to gather intelligence and prepare the groundwork for the plan.

After the first few days of clashes between the PKK and Kurdistan Front, as reported in *Özgür Gündem* newspaper (4 October 1992), Jalal Talabani's most senior representative, Noshirwan Mustafa, announced:

> The Kurdish government is responsible for all the borders. The presence of PKK camps on our soil is provoking all the world against us. As far as the PKK's own tactics and strategies go, they are free to do as they choose in Turkish Kurdistan, but not here. We do not want the PKK to use Iraqi Kurdistan for its own objectives. We wish to resolve this problem with trust and peace. Our concern is for the interests of the Kurdish people. I have no way of knowing if the PKK will vacate the area or not. We have sent in a delegation to hold talks.[4]

The sandwich operation

The Iraqi Communist Party (ICP) had not been drawn into the war and I therefore knocked discreetly upon their door. ICP committee members in Shaqlawa obliged us by arranging a car and driver and I set off accompanied by producer Ron McCullagh, doubling in this instance as cameraman.

Before leaving Shaqlawa we were obliged to obtain written authorisation to visit the front at Xakurk from Kamal Mufti, the minister of peshmergas. Mufti's authorisation was to be delivered in person to Mustafa Chawresh, the PUK's commander at the front. Journalistic access had been severely restricted and journalists from Turkey had been kept under close surveillance by both the KDP and the PUK throughout their travels in southern Kurdistan. Having obtained our permission, and the written authorisation dry in my hand, the ICP's car sped forth at daybreak, a tawny autumn sun rising over Mount Sefin, leaving the leafy little town of Shaqlawa nestled at its foot behind us.

The Communist Party's saloon slowly ascended the unpaved mountain roads closer and closer towards Iran until at last Turkish warplanes came into view, circling like birds of death in twos and threes above the mountain peaks before swooping into the hidden valleys below to discharge their load of bombs. The roar of their engines filled the sky.

For two hours more the car struggled up into the mountains, and then refused to budge, overpowered by the steep gradient. But after much patient coaxing on the part of our obstinate driver we finally chugged into Siddiqan. Heavily armed peshmergas halted us at a road-block.

Unusually delicate negotiations about journalistic access to the war-front ensued. The peshmergas said they would have to contact Kerim Xan Biradost, the leader of the Biradost tribe for further authorisation (Kerim Xan had switched sides from Saddam to the 'patriots' during the uprising, distributing his arms to the rebels). Like Jalal Talabani, Kerim Xan had also presented a similar proposal to Ankara to undertake a sandwich operation against the PKK as early as June 1992.[5]

A loyal clutch of Kerim Xan's men tried to establish radio contact with the war front about our request. It seemed doubtful whether the car would be able to cope with the steeper climb ahead, so we were dependent upon the peshmergas to take us to the top of the mountain ranges where their forces were positioned. There was still some kind of problem about letting journalists proceed to the front, despite Kamal Mufti's authoritative letter. In time, we came to suspect this may have been due to the presence of Turkish, and allegedly also American, military advisers in the area – a classified secret.

We sat fidgeting with impatience in the old khan (roadhouse) beside the roadblock, participating in a tense tea ceremony, lulled into a false security by the fragrant scent of late summer roses, while the pesh-mergas' radios crackled and spat out inaudible internal understandings. Finally, accompanied by additional peshmergas from Siddiqan, the ubi-quitous Landcruiser materialised and the driver accelerated away from the roadblock in a hail of stones.

Several hundred peshmergas were camped along the narrow mountain road. Tents had been pitched and guns positioned to face the mountain-sides opposite. Some of the fighters were catching up on their sleep at the side of the road after the previous night of combat. They were on a war footing and fighting in shifts.

The dirt road extended to the uppermost ridges parallel with the peak ranges of the Iranian frontier. The PKK's forces had occupied these same heights two days previously, but the peshmergas and Turkish warplanes had combined their strength to drive the Turkish Kurds in an easterly direction towards Iran. PKK guerrillas were returning the peshmergas' fire from the next valley over. The Turkish warplanes were momentarily lost from sight but smoke rose from freshly blackened patches on the mountainside where their bombs had just fallen. We wondered if the delay imposed upon us at the old khan in Siddiqan had been with the intention of preventing us from filming the latest Turkish bombardment.

The Landcruiser braked and pulled up below a short ridge. Enquiries for Mustafa Chawresh proved productive. We scaled a small knoll to where peshmergas swarmed between the black rocks, to find Mustafa Chawresh scrutinising the heights through a pair of binoculars. At his side was Kerim Xan. Chawresh indicated the PKK's positions and spoke into his radio. From deep in the valley below one of his commanders responded. The two commanders chatted like city men on a telephone.

Apart from the aerial bombardments by the Turks, most of the action in this war was concentrated after dark, peshmerga against guerrilla. It was not possible to get any closer to the battle, concealed as it was within the deep valleys of these mountains. One could see only the smoke of shells, the trace of small arms fire, the semi-camouflaged forms of the fighters merging with the scrub and dark rocks, and the sharp outlines of the Turkish bombers diving out of the sky between the shoulders of the mountains. The atmosphere of war was unmistakable – the nervous excitement, the tensions and suspicions, the sudden movements of large numbers of armed fighters on the mountain roads and through the passes as they sped off to man sensitive positions along the front.

We pressed the PUK's commander as to whether the Iraqi Kurdish forces were collaborating with the Turks: were they giving the Turks co-ordinates for the locations for bombing, and were the Americans involved? Although he denied that this was so and reiterated that the Turks were not operating from the Iraqi side at all, this information belied the evidence of many eyes other than ours. Their contacts were also captured on film.

Why war?

Although the KDP and PUK knew that they were serving Turkey in its nationalist conflict with the PKK better than they served themselves and Kurdish interests, it was largely the fear that their practical relations with the Turks would collapse, giving the Turks the excuse they sought to close the border, which forced their hand. At the same time, the Iraqi Kurds distrusted Turkey and suspected that the Turkish military might choose to launch a comprehensive assault against the enclave itself; the Iraqi Kurdish leaders were in no position to call the shots.

A week later, their concerns proved to have been well founded. A column of Turkish tanks crossed the border at Khabur and rumbled into Zakho. Turkish ground forces simultaneously pushed 25 kilometres over the border into Kurdistan, claiming legitimacy for their actions on the basis of a previous 'hot pursuit' agreement with Saddam signed in 1983 for 'border security and co-operation'. This permitted both governments to pursue and attack Kurdish rebels across each other's borders.

The KDP and PUK sent urgent appeals to Western leaders to demand Turkey's withdrawal. Turkish army sources retorted that in the absence of regional security along its border they would create a 'cordon sanitaire' five kilometres deep into Iraq. The Allies did not agree and the Turks were obliged to withdraw.

It had long been necessary for the Kurdistan Front, or the Kurdish parliament on which the Kurdish administration of northern Iraq had become centred, to conclude a workable agreement with the PKK over its activities in the 'liberated' area. Unfortunately no agreement proved sufficiently equitable or lasting to prevent the war. Five months previously when the Kurdish parliament had been inaugurated, the PKK failed to recognise it as a legitimate authority for the region since the PKK itself had chosen not to stand for election. However, PAK, its sister party, had been allowed to campaign, although its name did not appear on the ballot cards.

The PKK based its actions in northern Iraq on the concept of the historical and geographical integrity of Kurdistan as a single nation. The PKK's struggle was focused on the realisation of the goal of a single, united independent Kurdistan. While most Kurdish parties throughout divided Kurdistan have shared this dream – the vision of a single country – past relations with the great powers during the Cold War and with neighbouring states always forced them to compromise their political demands. The eight Kurdish parties constituting the Kurdistan Front argued that political experience had taught them to put realism before idealism; almost seventy years of armed conflict against successive Iraqi governments had failed to bring their goal any closer; the Kurds of Iraq had been unable to achieve either autonomy or federation within Iraq. Worn down by the killing, they sought a return to political dialogue with their historical enemies to bring about a peaceful solution to the Kurdish question.

But even such negotiations proved ineffectual. The neighbouring states did not want to negotiate anything with the Kurds. They do not want, or intend, to concede a single inch of any part of Kurdish-populated territory to the Kurds, or relinquish control. And therein lies the real problem. Throughout the history of their struggle, the Kurds have always got far less than what they asked for. For this very reason, the PKK demanded no less than what they wanted – their ultimate rights. As in October 1992, this led to Kurds from one side of the border fighting with Kurds from the other, and on Kurdish soil, causing deep satisfaction to their enemies.

The real losses in the October 1992 war may never be known. The Turkish government's figure for casualties inflicted on the PKK – more than one thousand eight hundred guerrillas – is certainly exaggerated.

Perhaps it ran to between three and five hundred. *Serxwebun* newspaper accounted for 193 guerrilla fatalities. The peshmergas also suffered losses. Again there are no reliable figures, but a safe estimate might set it at around one thousand.

The Turkish army lost four helicopters, five warplanes, 270 soldiers as a result of landmines, at least twelve high ranking personnel, political morale and a great deal of money. No accurate figure for casualties emerged, although it was almost certainly several hundreds. Villagers living along the border were ordered and paid by the Turkish army to retrieve the bodies of dead soldiers and convey them on the backs of their mules from the deep mountain valleys to areas accessible to transport by the army.[6]

Ultimately, the October conflict was a costly, futile war with neither resolution nor victor. Its main victims were the ordinary Kurdish people.

With the cessation of fighting, the Kurdistan Front signed an agreement with the PKK which saw the latter temporarily pull back from its bases along the Iraqi border. The Kurdistan Front also agreed that the PKK might use alternative bases further south, such as Zelê, and maintain headquarters in the cities for their political activities. The ceasefire was signed on 30 October 1992 and the following protocol came into effect.

Agreement between the Kurdistan Regional Government and the PKK[7]

On 29 October 1992, PKK representative Osman Öcalan (Ferhat) visited the seat of the Kurdistan Regional Government where it was announced that all those on the soil of south Kurdistan were obliged to respect the decision passed on 5 October by the Kurdistan Regional Government and the National Parliament.

Namely:

A. All PKK fighters and its members to be found on the soil of Iraqi Kurdistan and whenever on this territory are constrained to respect the laws of the Kurdistan region.

In this respect:

1. To undertake no activities whatsover of a military nature on the soil of Iraqi Kurdistan.
2. PKK members wishing to remain on Iraqi Kurdistan soil would move away from the border with Turkey to locations designated by the regional Government.
3. They are able to travel in freedom through the region with papers issued by the Interior Ministry (of the Kurdistan Government).
4. They will not be involved in political activities opposed to the Kurdistan Government and its front.

B.

1. The Kurdistan Government will protect Turkish Kurdistan citizens wishing to remain in this region.

2. PKK members can retain possession of all goods belonging to them.

3. The right of the PKK to undertake political activities within the region will be upheld.

4. The regional administration will provide health services to the sick and injured.

30 October 1992

Signatories to the agreement

Iraqi Kurdistan Regional Government

Fuad Mahsoum (President)
Roj Nur Shaweis (Vice President)

For the PKK Central Committee

Osman Öcalan
Numan Simo (PKK Delegation Member)

Turkey was required to withdraw its tanks and ground forces from south Kurdistan as a result of international pressure. On 12 and 13 November, 200 armoured cars, tanks, transporters and ambulances returned to Turkey; at the same time more than two thousand Turkish troops also went back to their bases on Turkish soil.[8]

The Turkish government's attitude to the war was best revealed in the state-controlled press. It implied that this had not been a real fight; that the Kurds had not seriously fought one another. The *Turkish Daily News* quoted one Turkish commander saying, 'Dogs don't bite dogs', of the warring Kurdish factions.

Surveys were published to reveal that, first, the majority of the Turkish population was against the establishment of a Kurdish state in northern Iraq; second, that the Turkish people no longer wished to host the Allied rapid reaction forces (known in Turkish as the *Çekiç Güç*, Operation Poised Hammer) on Turkish soil; and third, that 'Mr Barzani' and 'Mr Talabani' were 'bandits', as was 'Apo' (the PKK leader), and not one of them could be 'trusted'. The same survey also reported that the Kurdish population of the south-east did not share this view. Kurdish civilians were certain the recent fighting would have no significant impact on the Kurdish struggle in Turkey, nor would it weaken popular support for the PKK.

After-effects of fratricidal war on the Kurdish people

Kurdish families living close to border areas have been physically divided by the artificial frontier which cuts through their midst. Brother and sister are separated by these borders and have to obtain visas to visit each other in their own homeland. Any problem affecting Kurds on one side of the border affects those on the other. In the past this meant that Turkish Kurds had always rallied to help the Iraqi Kurds whenever they were in difficulty, embracing the problem as their own. During Iraq's chemical attacks on the Kurds in 1988, and again after the uprising of 1991, the Kurds from Turkey and Iran sped to give all the help they could to their fleeing brothers. Iranian Kurdish families would look after Iraqi Kurds in their homes, often taking on the burden of two extra families into already large households.

For Kurdish families in Turkey, it was difficult to do the same because of the Turkish military presence in the area. Instead, the Turkish Kurds would take food, clothes, blankets and, if possible, medicines to the camps under cover of darkness and would quickly pass them to the many open hands beneath the barbed wire. Some managed to help the relatives of Iraqi Kurds escape from the camps and spirited them away to nearby villages. The Kurds from the Turkish side of the border identified with the suffering of the Iraqi Kurds. To them, it was the Kurdish nation which had suffered the blow.

The deep feelings of ordinary Kurds were injured in the war of 1992 by the short-term policies of the Kurdish leadership.

Whenever internal conflict develops between parties active in the same territory, it is manifested as a contest for power and ultimate political superiority. While at a personal level the leaders may remain detached, relations between ordinary people deteriorate. Such injuries are difficult to heal. While political leaders can repair their relations fairly readily, ordinary people cannot. When a political party gives priority to its strategic and tactical relations with neighbouring governments over the preservation of social and political relations between ordinary Kurdish people, fraternal bonds break down at grassroots level.

This is precisely what occurred after the war of October 1992. Grass-roots relations, the bonds of sympathy which previously existed between ordinary Kurds in Iraq and those in Turkey, were severely damaged; Kurdish people felt that they had become alienated from one other. Kurds on the Turkish side of the border remembered how they had helped Iraqi Kurds in the past, and felt betrayed. Consequently, their enthusiasm for the freedom the Kurds across the border currently enjoyed was spoiled, for they understood it was only maintained at the cost of their own freedom. Despite this, the leadership of the Kurdistan Front continued to press for diplomatic relations with Ankara; Ankara responded by increasing the size of its military deployment in Turkish Kurdistan while playing the Iraqi Kurds for time.

Kurdish interests do not coincide with the interests of any one neighbouring country, nor evidently with those of the West. Western governments had avoided the full implications of the Kurdish issue, speaking of 'human rights', rather than advocating negotiations geared towards a political solution – the only kind of solution that can guarantee the Kurds their rights.

The Kurds of Iraq asked, 'As the West is against the creation of an independent Kurdistan, what can we do alone? If the West should cease to support the enclave it would almost certainly collapse allowing Saddam to return.'

The Kurds of Turkey argued, 'From now on we must depend on our own people; depend on yourselves, don't lean on the West, and don't rely on your historical enemy, every one of them wants to see you lose.' But even they have derived a certain level of assistance from external powers, such as Syria and Iran.

Without military might and technology in a world which relies on sophisticated weapons, economic persuasion and violence to determine the status quo, could the Kurds place their reliance solely on their own poorly armed people and their power to negotiate in order to achieve a lasting peace?

The limited freedom of south Kurdistan was entirely dependent on external support and goodwill. Such freedom carried with it the stupefying fear that everything might be lost in five minutes if that international support were removed. This was a perilous basis for national self-confidence.

Notes

1. For any reader able to read Turkish I strongly recommend Faysal Dağli's *Birakuji*, Belge Yayinlari, Istanbul, 1994. This book is the main source of written information on the inter-Kurdish war of October 1992, and rich in document and detail. I gratefully acknowledge my debt to Faysal Dağli's authoritative book for much of the supporting material supplied in this chapter. This reference, pp. 37–9.

2. Ibid., pp. 78–9.

3. *Aydinlik* magazine, 9 June 1993, quoted in Dağli, p. 75.

4. Dağli, pp. 92–3.

5. Ibid., p. 75, quoting *Aydinlik* magazine; *A. Cem Ersever Anlatiyor*, 9 June 1993.

6. Ibid., pp. 207–9.

7. Ibid., p. 183, source: *Medya Güneşi*, 16–31 November 1992.

8. Ibid., p. 208.

6

The dirty war in Turkey

It is 7 o'clock in the morning, 21 March 1993 – Newroz (Kurdish New Year) in the frontier town of Cizre, Kurdistan in Turkey. I wake sharply to the metallic drumming of tanks arriving to take up positions in the main square. I look out of the window. It is still dark, raining, the streets empty of anyone save members of the Turkish Special Forces, the army, contra-guerrillas and police. Heavily armed, helmeted, waiting, they have lined up in the shadows along the walls of shuttered shops and offices. The bleak rain comes down. They stand about, idle, watchful and menacing.

This is what Kurdish New Year means here – an intensification of military and police presence; there are twenty new tanks parked up at the base on the top of the hill. A military tent camp of special re-inforcements has also set up there in the past few days.

Two nights before, on 19 March, bullets rained down on the town for 40 minutes in an attack staged by village guards and Turkish Security Forces, to make the Kurds and others believe that Abdullah Öcalan, the PKK leader, had broken the ceasefire announced three days before at his Lebanon press conference.

Added to the constant crackle of gunfire directly overhead were the deeper noises of exploding rockets being fired from German-made armoured personnel carriers (locally known as 'panzers') used by the police. Rockets destroyed three Kurdish homes. Furnishings and family possessions were all burnt to a gluey mess. It was sheer good fortune that on this occasion the Kurdish family within escaped alive. Such attacks were frequent and indiscriminate.

Outside in the wet street, the tanks were now joined by two black and white police panzers, army personnel carriers and several jeeps packed with soldiers. I wondered how the Kurdish people would celebrate their New Year in such an atmosphere of hatred and aggression. The Newroz fires lit the previous night smoked and smouldered in the rain, and nothing and nobody moved in the streets.

An hour later, small groups of Kurdish women and children began to form circles in the muddy back streets of Cudi Quarter to chant and dance. Young men appeared, their faces masked to the eyes with *jemadane* (traditional Kurdish scarves). The sun came out, but just as celebrations began, Turkish panzers sped into the quarter. Flinging open their hatches, gunmen in black balaclavas trained their machine guns on the celebrants and, steering towards them, scattered them.

'These streets belong to the government, not to you,' the contra-guerrillas warned.

Yet as soon as the panzers disappeared off elsewhere, the circles of dancers reassembled.

The dance begins again. But the dancers are mostly children, perhaps too young to be arrested, dressed in red, yellow and green clothes, the Kurdish national colours. The dancers chant patriotic slogans, 'Long Live Kurdistan, long live Newroz, long live the PKK', and wave their fingers in the air making the sign of victory. Teenage girls have tied red, yellow and green scarves, plaited ribbons and ornaments over their hair or in bands around their foreheads. Others have masked their identity, wrapping the lower part of their faces as the guerrillas do.

By noon a crowd of several hundred throngs a large open square between the houses to sing, dance and listen to speeches.

Journalists and human rights monitors catch word of the assembly and join the thousands celebrating in the spring sunshine. I have film rolling. Colin Thomas, our producer for *Blood and Belonging*, is recording sound. We are swallowed up among the crowd of Kurdish celebrants, unarmed and colourful in their Newroz clothes, when suddenly an old man cries out, 'Panzers!'

I look up from the viewfinder to spot two black-and-white armoured cars descending the hill above us, undoubtedly on their way to what is in their eyes nothing other than an unlawful assembly. All festive gatherings have been forbidden by the Turkish authorities except for a few indoor events in some western cities for which permission had been obtained beforehand.

The ugly mood of the morning returned. We knew we were in for trouble. The panzers arrived faster than one would have thought possible. Suddenly they jolted into the square and began to charge towards the Kurds, guns mounted ready to fire, the eyes of the gunmen steady, their faces concealed by the hideous balaclavas which revealed only the eyes and the mouth. The atmosphere turned nasty. The bolder Kurds around the square stood their ground. Hundreds of others scattered into nearby alleys as scores of women ululated a scream. I carried on filming.

One of the armoured cars made a sudden lunge at a group of Kurds and deliberately drove into the wall of a house on the edge of the arena. Kurdish children responded by taunting them, shouting Kurdish national slogans and making the victory sign.

Several armed figures leapt from the hatches of the panzers. Loping forwards with their rifles, they attempted to catch whoever was closest. These unlucky victims were then dragged, struggling, their heels scraping along the ground, towards the panzers. Here, armed security police began to beat and kick them. One gripped a youth by the hair and banged the boy's head against the side of the armoured car before bundling him inside through its door. Women ululated again: a sound as chilling as the scene we witnessed.

Even as the camera rolled I prayed that someone below might somehow be able to stop the police from abducting defenceless spectators. Torture was guaranteed. Suddenly, the security forces raised their guns and took aim at the rooftop where I was standing. Bullets hissed overhead. The rooftop was flat and exposed. I pulled the camera back behind a washing line. Bullets hit the roof nearby, stirring up little whirls of dust beyond me. A few more rounds of gunfire came. I hunched down clutching the camera, still awkwardly on its tripod.

The panzer drivers had begun revving their engines, preparing to leave the square. They now entered the lane directly below and carried on past. It was later said that seven innocent people had been abducted. I feared what would be done to them once they were out of sight.

The PKK ceasefire

Similar incidents took place simultaneously in most Kurdish towns in the south-east. Many Kurds suffered arbitrary arrest, others were shot at, or beaten in public. Police in Istanbul used tear-gas against Kurds dancing in the streets.

The actual death toll for Newroz 1993 was well down on that of 1992. This was solely due to the unilateral ceasefire announced by the PKK two days before. The Turkish government had already made full preparations to use military force to impede the celebrations and crush any demonstrations One side effect, however, was the realisation among ordinary Kurds in the south-east of the vulnerable position they were in without the protection of the guerrillas while the ceasefire held. Village guards paid by the state took advantage of the ceasefire to intimidate patriotic Kurdish families, fire-bombing homes and attacking unarmed Kurds in the back streets.

At the same time, Kurdish people welcomed the PKK's peace initiative.

Turkish and Kurdish democrats alike hailed the move as a breakthrough, a serious chance for peace. Unfortunately, the response of the Turkish government and the military was negative and uncompromising. Kemal Atatürk's dictum of 'Turkey is for the Turks' held fast. The Turkish authorities stuck to the old line that they would not do business with 'bandits'. They refused to enter any dialogue with the PKK. An opportunity to stop the bloodshed was dismissed out of hand.

In Diyarbakir some time afterwards, we raised the matter of Kurdish freedom and Newroz with Ünal Erkan, Super Governor of the State of Emergency Region since late 1991. Erkan was a well-known supporter of the Grey Wolf (Bozkurt) fascist party, the MHP (Nationalist Movement Party), trained in the United States in intelligence and countersubversion.

'Were people free to celebrate at all? Could the Turkish government cede control to Kurdish areas of the country in some form of autonomy agreement?' Michael Ignatieff asked as I translated.

The governor intoned the official answers:

'Constitutionally, the Turkish government is a unitary state. There is a single authority in this country and all citizens living within the borders of the state are equal. This is a constitutional system. Within the legal framework of the constitution it is not only impossible to consider anything outside this, it is also unnecessary,' he smiled.[1] The Kurds wanted to celebrate Newroz and practice their own traditions, we suggested.

> There is no legal impediment to those who want to celebrate Newroz. But at Newroz, it is wrong to stage operations which erupt into violence and aim to divide one piece of the country from the rest ... If organisations celebrate Newroz by staging unlawful operations of course the security forces will enforce the law ... In the region where I am in charge, five million people inhabit thirteen provinces. They are Turkish citizens; people of Turkish origin, citizens of Arab origin, citizens of Assyrian origin and other citizens. It is not possible to register all their various beliefs on the same parallel, but every one of them is treated with equal rights, in accordance with our constitution.[2]

My thoughts returned to the recent Newroz assembly where we had been shot at while watching the Governor's security forces harassing the civilian population. Any person there was liable to arrest for attending an illegal demonstration.

In the Kurdish region, following Newroz and the PKK's offer of a ceasefire, violence intensified. The death squads targeted Kurdish journalists and HEP members. Accordingly, it was only a matter of 84 days – 8 June – before the ceasefire of 20 March 1993 finally collapsed. Military attacks on Kurdish villages accelerated. The bodies of slain guerrillas and other Kurdish patriots were left mutilated and disfigured by their killers. Funerals for guerrillas were prohibited. The army dumped the unwashed bodies in instant graves and covered them over. The PKK's attempt to initiate peace had not been given a chance.

Gagging Kurdish MPs and the Kurdish press

The dirty war had entered its ninth bloody year. The death toll stood at 18,000 people. The Turkish government's vow to 'finish the PKK in 1994' left no one in doubt as to what to expect in Kurdistan thereafter.

On 12 July 1993, the term in office for the military chief of staff, General Doğan Güreş, was exceptionally extended. A decision was passed to mount an all-out offensive in the state of emergency region. This decision was duly approved by the National Security Council.[3]

Since her election in June 1993 (by her own party) to become the first woman prime minister of Turkey, Tansu Çiller, while presenting an outwardly democratic face to the rest of the world, gave consent to the escalation of the military conflict in Kurdistan and increased the powers of the army. Çiller authorised an additional 10,000 special forces to be posted to Kurdistan by the end of 1993.

The coalition government under Süleyman Demirel, which had come to power eighteen months before on its liberal ticket of promising Kurdish reforms, had almost immediately revealed itself as more ruthless than its predecessor. The late President Turgut Özal's attempts at reform were trampled underfoot. Özal's death proved to be an untimely blow to hopes for a democratic resolution of the Kurdish problem in Turkey.

Before his sudden death on 17 April 1993, Turgut Özal had at last lifted the ban on the use of Kurdish for speech and print. Accordingly, a proliferation of patriotic Kurdish publications appeared on sale. These were, however, still subjected to rigorous censorship or systematically banned, title by title, under the Anti-Terror Law as constituting separatist propaganda. Newspaper and magazine editors and their staff were regularly arrested. The printing presses ground to a halt just as before. The state described the systematic persecution of writers, journalists and publishers as 'Freedom of Expression' and 'Freedom of the Press'.

Journalists expressing support for Kurdish independence, or even for recognition of basic human rights, were almost all subject to death threats or assassination attempts by 'persons unknown' (faili meçhul).

The vice-president of the Diyarbakir branch of the Human Rights Association, Sedat Aslantaş, explained how local people had more reason to fear being murdered than being arrested. Even the grand old man of

Kurdish literature, an esteemed writer and journalist, Musa Anter, 70, was lured to his death and murdered in Diyarbakir on the night of 20 September 1992 by a state-sponsored death squad.

The *Özgür Gündem* (Free Agenda) newspaper, which had gone to press on 30 May 1992,[4] had also become a highly conspicuous target for the death squads. More than nine of its journalists were murdered by unidentified agents; their killings are widely believed to have been ordered by the authorities. Over eighty issues of *Özgür Gündem* were either banned or confiscated. Death threats to *Özgür Gündem* journalists and their families became an everyday reality. Both the paper's offices and workers' homes were regularly ransacked. Shots were fired, sometimes fatally, at various *Özgür Gündem* personnel as they left their offices for the day, or when distributing the newspaper by car, or even while walking in the street. On 14 April 1994 *Özgür Gündem* was ordered closed by a writ of the state. It was succeeded by *Özgür Ülke* (Free Country) on 27 April. The case brought by *Özgür Gündem* against Turkey was declared admissible by the European Community on 27 October 1995.

Over the period, working in Kurdistan, I came in contact with a number of *Özgür Gündem*, and *Özgür Ülke*'s dedicated correspondents – people who placed their professional responsibilities above personal safety. A journalist was frequently obliged to go into hiding as a consequence of reporting events, particularly in the Kurdish region. MİT carried out dawn raids on their homes *in absentia*, and more often than not a brother, sister, spouse or parent would be taken into custody and interrogated on their account. Torture was almost always used to extract confessions.

In one such instance, police arrested Hassan (pseudonym), the younger brother of Ali (pseudonym), an *Özgür Gündem* journalist in Diyarbakir. They also arrested his girlfriend. The police acted with almost complete impunity. They did not need to provide anybody with a formal reason for arrest. Evin (pseudonym), Ali's innocent girlfriend, was simply hauled from her university classroom and taken away by the police without any explanation. She was detained in police custody for more than a month. Both Hassan and Evin were arrested simply to flush Ali out of hiding. Hassan was tortured; Evin was threatened and intimidated.

Prior to the arrests, Ali and every member of his family received regular death threats by telephone. Ali had left home to protect his family and seek sanctuary elsewhere. But the police continued to raid Ali's home, often late at night or just before dawn. Cassette-tapes, books, even the cassette-player were confiscated. Furniture and other household possessions were damaged and the home was ransacked by the police. The raids left a deep impression on the younger children. They were terrified that their missing brother would soon be killed. But the more this harassment went on, the more the resentment felt by Kurdish families in Diyarbakir and elsewhere grew.

The official response to the killing of journalists was summed up by President Süleyman Demirel in the following terms. Demirel argued in the state-controlled press that: 'Those killed were not real journalists at all'. Government spokesman Yildirim Aktuna claimed: 'Some terrorists could have gone into journalism. This needs investigating.'[5]

Despite numerous calls by Amnesty International, Helsinki Watch, Article 19 and other international human rights and press organisations for investigation into the murders of writers and journalists, not only have there been no trials, there have not even been any suspects. There was not the slightest response or change in the conduct of the state. Extra-judicial killings and political murders of the democratic opposition continued. Trials were rare.

In September 1993, Mehmet Sincar, a Kurdish MP from the recently established (Kurdish) Democracy Party (DEP) was gunned down in the streets of Batman. Paying her respects at the Sincar's family home in Kiziltepe, Mardin, fellow DEP MP Leyla Zana narrowly escaped a bomb attack on the house which left six people injured. It is widely believed that Leyla Zana herself was the target. Since her election as an MP the frequency of death threats against her had intensified. Written proof of death threats to Leyla Zana were published by Amnesty International.

The Kurdish MPs formerly with HEP (closed by the government and reconstituted under the DEP banner) were also threatened with the lifting of their parliamentary immunity. The state finally carried out this threat and passed its decision in the National Assembly. As a result, five of the DEP MPs were arrested and detained. The trial would not take place until eight months later. The MPs were to be tried under Article 125 of the Turkish Penal Code (which carried the death penalty), for seeking to undermine the territorial integrity of the Turkish state. In this way, Çiller's government sought to silence Kurdish political demands and aspirations by constitutional means.

Most significant here is that it was *not* just the PKK and its supporters which were the target of the government's intimidation. Any pro-Kurdish person in Turkey, or abroad, was liable to be labelled as a 'separatist' or 'terrorist'. This was true not only of Kurdish MPs, human rights activists and journalists, but also of teachers, lawyers, singers, actors, engineers, trade-union members and students as well as their families and close friends, shepherds, villagers and farmers.

There was no freedom of the press, no freedom of speech, nor even freedom of thought in Turkey at this time. Turkey cannot be called a democracy. Western governments supporting the Turkish government have been guilty of masking the truth about their Nato ally. Although Turkey was criticised for its appalling human rights record, trade continued, as did the flow of Western arms to the Turkish government. US representatives declared quite unashamedly that their 'interests in the region far outweighed their concern for the abuse of human rights'. (See *Air Force Times*, December 1994).

Germany, Britain, France and the USA continued to supply Turkey with military equipment despite conclusive evidence that this was being used against the Kurds, contravening NATO agreements. The European Parliament has unanimously condemned Turkey's violations of their agreements and called for a ban on the supply of arms to the Turks, but individual governments have taken no notice. It is too profitable.

The village guard system: the *jash* of Turkish Kurdistan

The Turkish government could not be so effective in its repression of the Kurdish population without the collaboration of the *korucular*, village guards. Kurdish villagers who refused to become village guards and take a salary from the state to fight against their compatriots in the PKK suffered harsh reprisals from the military. Such reprisals were manifested in the destruction of livestock, homes and property or, failing such methods of persuasion, execution of family members. If they accepted to become village guards, they often suffered a similar fate at the hands of the PKK for 'having betrayed the Kurdish cause'.

The PKK could decide to 'pass the death sentence' on a village guard to prevent him from carrying out further crimes of treason against the guerrillas; or, just as likely, the village guards might be offered an amnesty in exchange for renouncing to bear arms for the enemy. But for most of the village guards, the big payments they received from the Turkish government were a powerful inducement. The salary of a village guard was the same as that of a Turkish civil servant. The money superseded any amount that an unqualified worker might have expected to earn in the Kurdish provinces. In May 1993, the monthly salary of a village guard was TL 2,195,000, the equivalent of about £107 at the time. By mid-1993, there were an estimated two hundred or more Kurdish villages in south-east Turkey under the control of village guards, who were reinforced by 50,000 soldiers and 5,000 special forces.

It became extremely dangerous for any local Kurd to be caught talking with foreigners, especially journalists or human rights monitors visiting the area. Secret police, contra-guerrillas and the mysterious Hizb-i Kontras (see p. 87) infested most Kurdish towns, keeping the local Kurds under surveillance. Informers (*itirafçilar*) too were everywhere. The bodies of murdered Kurds began to turn up in the rubbish dumps, in the coal cellars, down wells – eyes missing, ears and genitals cut off and even severed heads sometimes sent as a warning to their relatives.[6]

The Hizb-i Kontras were trained by the government and were allegedly organised by Ünal Erkan, the 'Super Governor'. After Erkan became Governor over the Kurdish provinces under a state of emergency, it was reported that:

> the level of murders carried out by the contra-guerrillas rose in the Kurdish provinces. Ünal lodged contra-guerrilla teams in the State of Emergency Region's (*Olağanüstü Hal*) special buildings. Organised inside the prisons, the special teams were then set loose to carry out their activities These teams, dependent on Erkan, were allegedly responsible for the murders of DEP MP Mehmet Sincar, 16 journalists, Human Rights monitors, lawyers, unionists, doctors, Kurdish intellectuals and others. The contra-guerrillas became an official wing of the security department along with the special army organised from the ranks of the fascist MHP militants, death squads, and Hizbullah.'[7]

– and, of course, the village guards. In any Kurdish area, one half of the occupants may have taken up the state's offer to become village guards while the other half would remain adamantly opposed to doing so. The security forces and the army would constantly provoke conflicts between the two sides with the aim of setting Kurd against Kurd.

A large wall-map hangs behind the desk of the military commander in his expensive new headquarters in Diyarbakir. The map has red markers for every village controlled by village guards in the Kurdish provinces. Non-village-guard villages are also marked. These will be systematically targeted until such time as they too carry red markers or are wiped from the map altogether, the inhabitants driven out, arrested or executed.

State terror and death

Should a suspect happen to die in police custody before a case is brought to trial, it requires a superhuman effort on the part of local lawyers, Human Rights Association (HRA) personnel, MPs and relatives of the deceased to expose the actual cause of death. To attempt to bring the guilty to trial and obtain satisfaction for the victim's family is all the more fraught with obstructions and danger.

In 1992, cases of death as a result of torture and of political murder were brought against the Turkish government in the European Court of Human Rights for the first time. One such case was that of Yakup Aktaş, a 24–year-old Kurdish youth brutally murdered in police custody. Yakup lost his life while in custody at the Mardin Gendarmerie Regimental Command's interrogation centre. He died as a result of torture. An initial investigation into his death was undertaken on 28 November 1990 by a special delegation consisting of the HRA assistant chairperson, Zubeyir Aydar, also a practising solicitor; an HRA management committee member and chair of the Diyarbakir branch of the HRA, Hatip Dicle; Diyarbakir president of the law bar, solicitor Fethi Gümüş; Socialist Party assistant secretary-general Azad Kutlay; an HEP (People's Labour Party) provincial management committee member, Esat Bingom; the provincial secretary of the (illegal) Turkish Communist Party, Ahmet Kilil; HRA Nusaybin district representative, Dr Cemal Kahraman; a Chamber of Architects provincial representative, Kemal Acil, together with members of the press.

The high-calibre delegation, formed to investigate the cause of death in the Aktaş case, found that death had indeed occurred as a result of torture. Proving it was another matter. The case typified the way in which death by torture routinely occurred in police custody. Having translated the documents in this case for submission to the European Court of Human Rights in 1993 for the Kurdistan Human Rights Project, and having had access to all legal documents, the autopsy report and the court verdicts, I can verify the case as absolutely genuine.

Yakup Aktaş was arrested on Sunday, 18 November 1990, in Derik, Mardin, and taken the next morning to the Mardin Regimental Command's central interrogation bureau. A week later, on Sunday, 25 November, Yakup's uncle, Süleyman Aktaş, was notified that his nephew had just died from 'heart failure'. The body was released by the Mardin State Hospital morgue for burial the next day. The Security Forces made sure that the burial took place immediately.

According to statements given by Yakup Aktaş's uncle, and the person who washed his body for burial, there were bruises and scratches on his left and right wrists, on his arms and on his back; the rear of his head was completely crushed and still bleeding; his forehead and eyebrow area was also bruised and had sustained injuries. These injuries indicate that Yakup Aktaş died as a result of torture, not, as stated on the death certificate, of 'heart failure'.

At the European Conference on Security and Co-operation (ECSC), shortly before Yakup's death, Turkey had pledged to take a stand against torture and inhumane acts.

A new investigation under the contol of the Mardin State Prosecutor, (case No. 1990/2216) led to a verdict of 'non-responsibility' being returned on 29 November 1990, (no. 1990/158).

Such circumstances would seem to indicate that the 'cause of death' certificate, the autopsy report and the report of the forensic department were all falsified by the authorities with the intention of protecting the state and its agents; or less likely, that they were shown a different corpse altogether. It is widely known that Turkish doctors may be compelled by the state to falsify medical records, examination notes, autopsies and other investigations. Such a thing almost certainly occurred in the case of Yakup Aktaş.

Conversely, doctors who do not co-operate with the authorities in assisting torture, concealing evidence of torture, or officially sanctioned murder may themselves be tortured, accused of membership of an illegal organisation (such as the PKK), and their testimonies discredited. A recent book, *Medicine Betrayed: the Participation of Doctors in Human Rights Abuses*, prepared by the British Medical Association, cites several examples of such cases in Turkey.[8]

Yakup Aktaş's relatives and the HRA delegation have since requested that Yakup's grave be reopened, a new autopsy performed and those responsible for Yakup's death under torture be brought to trial. It was hoped that once the case came before the European Court, pressure would be exerted on Turkey to comply with the human rights conventions to which it is signatory.

The Aktaş case is one of thousands. Reports by Amnesty International and Helsinki Watch on torture and human rights abuses since 1993 confirm that there has been a worsening in Turkey's human rights record. Yet Turkey's President Süleyman Demirel recently stated: 'There is no such thing as torture in Turkey'. In the same interview he chose to present the Kurdish struggle as a problem of 'terrorism', explaining: 'We do not want to give any part of Turkey to anyone else. For the time being, Turkey is subject to a struggle against terrorism. A Kurdish state in northern Iraq would create lots of problems for the Middle East, worse than any problem existing now.'[9]

Arms and allies

Turkey was deeply afraid of the new Kurdish freedom in Iraq, seeing in it a premonition of Turkey's own future. The United States, Britain and Germany continued to assist Turkey militarily and, in so doing, assisted in the mass murder of Turkish Kurds. These same nations have invariably supported Turkey, their ally, at a political level by accepting denunciations of the PKK as a 'terrorist' organisation despite its popular support in the Kurdish region.

In 1993, America agreed to export 95 Black Hawk military helicopters

to Turkey. Turkish Aerospace Industries are involved in a joint manufacturing venture with American firms, General Electric and General
Dynamic, in co-producing F-16 C/D warplanes for export and defence.
From Russia, Turkey bought Mi-17 'Hip M' helicopters, armoured
personnel carriers and night vision equipment for the gendarmerie and
for the General Directorate of Security. Sikorsky also supplied helicopters
to the gendarmerie and police. NATO has additionally provided for
surplus stores of its weapons to be based on Greek and Turkish soil as
part of its 'cascading' policy (see pp. 194–5). As *Jane's Defence Weekly*
observed: 'The equipment will be used against the outlawed PKK in the
south east. US supplied AH1 and UH-60 Black Hawk helicopters are
currently used in the region.'[10] In 1994, Turkey spent more than one
fifth of its entire budget fighting the PKK, around $8.2 billion. It had
spent $7 billion on the war in 1993. In that same year the PKK inflicted
losses of $1 to $1.5 billion on Turkish tourism.

The involvement of Western companies in Turkey's military industries
has been as considerable as their profits were high. But Western governments accepted no outward responsibility for their involvement in the
Kurdish conflict – just as they failed to make public details of the supply
to Iraq of machine tools and chemical components for weapons of mass
destruction. Britain had even doubled its credits to Baghdad following
Saddam's attempted genocide of the Kurds by chemical gas in 1988.
The British government consistently advised the Iraqi Kurdish leadership
to reach an accommodation with Saddam, to renounce independence and
seek a federal solution in Iraq.

A similar problem has arisen in the case of Turkey. Details of the war
against the Kurds in Turkey are concealed from the public. Despite the
heavy casualties in the south east, press coverage is kept to a minimum.
European statesmen do not wish to arouse public interest in the Kurdish
question because of the economic and political advantages they derive
from their friendship with the regime. In this light, it is difficult to see
how the Kurds can trust the West to safeguard their right to life, let
alone champion the cause of democracy.

Kurdish protests in European countries against Turkish atrocities are
frequently met with hostility by the host nations. Kurdish protesters are
seen as criminals and troublemakers. Background information supplying
reasons for protest is regularly omitted from the news reports.

In Britain, France, Belgium and Germany, police have broken up
peaceful Kurdish demonstrations by violent means. Kurdish refugee
organisations and pro-PKK information centres have been forced to close
in both France and Germany. Kurdish bank accounts have been frozen,
Kurdish documents, possessions and campaigning literature confiscated,

especially in connection with the PKK. Kani Yilmaz, the political representative of the ERNK, the PKK's political wing, was arrested in October
1994 and detained in maximum security at Belmarsh prison as a 'threat
to national security', despite the fact that he had been invited to Britain
by British MPs to discuss peace. Other arrests of prominent PKK
members followed (see chapter 11).

The death squads and Hizb-i Kontras

The red sun is slowly setting behind the graveyard on the hill. People
quickly leave the streets. Traffic along the roads ceases. After dark there
is no protection from the death squads in this area. Ancient, weathered
stone houses cling to the slopes of Mazidağ, a small Kurdish town half
an hour's drive from Mardin, afflicted by intrigue and political killings.

Travelling in a van we have hired in Diyarbakir, complete with a
patriotic Kurdish driver, our five-person crew drives watchfully past
Mazidağ, heading down the main road. We reach the town of Derik
shortly before the road joins the southern highway which ascends to the
hilltop town of Mardin. We turn a corner into the town centre. This is
the place where Yakup Aktaş was arrested and possibly also where he
was murdered. The town is couched in shadow. Scrawled in blood-red
paint on the walls of several shops is written: 'Death to the PKK traitors
– the PKK will drown in blood'. Some of these slogans have also been
altered to read: 'TC [the Turkish Republic] will drown in its own blood'.

Disembarking from our vehicle without any equipment, we descend
upon a tea house to stop for a short break. A crowd of Kurdish men,
most wearing cloth caps, presses in close about us. I leave the teahouse
with one of the crew to buy some *börek* (pastries) to have with the tea
outside in the fading sunlight.

In the tiny pastry shop we are approached by a gaunt middle-aged
man. The man has a tired but kindly face. I notice that he wears a
Human Rights Association (HRA) pin in the lapel of his worn jacket. It
is clear that he badly wants to talk to us, but just as he introduces
himself and asks who we are, I see another figure loom behind him in
the doorway, walkie-talkie in hand. For a moment, everything is frozen.
Then the plainclothes policeman glances distastefully at the man's pin
and fixes his eyes coolly on us. The walls of the shop seem to contract.
Although we are merely buying *börek* and *baklava* for our tea, we have
become suspects by virtue of the presence of the two men who have
followed us into the shop. An unpleasant atmosphere develops. The pastry
shop proprietor passes me the parcel of *baklava* without meeting my
eyes. He wants us to pay up and get out before he too is implicated.

As I pass through the door, the policeman catches the HRA man by the sleeve and detains him. A few words of warning are spoken. Both of them cross the street and follow us to the teahouse. I break through the circle of men pressed tightly around Michael Ignatieff and the crew drinking their tea. A youth about Yakup Aktaş's age sits talking with them. His earnest entreaty falters when he sees the plainclothes man with the walkie-talkie behind us. Kurdish men offer us their stools to seat our friends, then stand back and wait, alert now.

It is almost impossible to consume the sticky, dense baklava or drink the tea under such expectant scrutiny. The policeman broods. The kindly-faced Kurd from the HRA calmly draws up a stool and sits down with us, ready to take the risk. He is glad to see foreigners here in his town. He explains that a European delegation visited Derik a month or two before, just after the murders in one of the nearby villages. Had they sent us to follow up?

No, we were not connected with any previous delegation, we told him, but we too had heard about the killings. It would be unwise to speak in any detail, so we cut our conversation short, and reassure the HRA representative that we will do our best to find out what had happened. We drink the tea quickly and leave Derik before attracting further attention.

The police did not bother to pursue us far. Once we turned back on to the Mazidağ road, the white Toros car with no number plates also turned back. The road was empty now. We carried on, stopping only to ask a villager by the roadside if he knew the way to Karataş, the name of the village where village guards had murdered some Kurdish civilians. He supplied us with the necessary directions in Kurdish and so on we went. The sky was growing darker now. This in itself was a worry. It is not a good idea to be caught on the road in this area after dark.

The turn-off to the village we sought looked unpromising; there were no houses in sight and the road was rough and deserted. But after a few minutes we were surprised by an approaching car. Two young Kurds were inside. We signalled to them to pull over, and asked if this was the right way to Karataş. They confirmed that it was and offered to guide us to the next turn-off, explaining that one fork led to the village we sought whereas the other went straight to the gendarme post of the Etibank Phosphorous Factory.

The boys executed a swift U-turn and guided us to the crossroad. Here, the driver indicated the correct way, and warning us again not to be seen by the gendarmes, sped quickly on his way. Behind some low hills, we finally caught sight of a small sombre village lying about half a mile off. Although we had to pass precariously near the Etibank phosphate Gendarme station, no soldiers appeared, so we drove straight on to the village. I guessed that from this distance our minibus looked like a public taxi (*dolmuş*). In this region public transport between the villages mainly consisted of vans like ours. Because of this, we were probably overlooked by the gendarmes.

The light was rapidly fading now and the small stone houses of the martyrs' village lay nestled in deep shadow. There were few people about. We still possessed some apprehensions that the place might turn out to be a village-guard village, in which case our presence would soon be reported to the gendarme post. Big shaggy village dogs roamed freely everywhere. These barked and snapped fiercely at our vehicle as we drove into a dusty square between the stone cottages of the village. Our driver parked behind its low stone walls – out of sight, we hoped, of the gendarmes.

Had there been a clash here recently between the village and the government? Yes, they replied bitterly. Village guards had attacked the village. Men wearing army camouflage clothing and balaclavas had murdered a family of three, shooting them at close range inside their own house. The village was then subjected to a rocket attack as a further warning to its inhabitants. The Kurds explained that this had taken place because they had refused to become village guards.

I asked which of their houses had been attacked. The villagers led us *en masse* some two hundred yards or so deeper into the neighbourhood. As we approached the location of the murders, a young Kurd detached himself from the crowd and declared himself to be the surviving son of the family who had been killed. His mother, father and brother had been executed that night.

Ercan Önen led us to the door of the house. It was locked now and the house abandoned. He probably did not want to live there anymore. The boy explained how his father had gone to answer a knock on the door at around 9 p.m. Those outside said they were soldiers come to carry out a search. 'When my father said, "If you are soldiers, then come with the *muhtar* (village mayor), or I will not open the door," the voice outside said: "The mayor isn't here, he has gone to Istanbul, don't be afraid of us, we are going to do a search and go away."'[11] But when Ercan's father opened the door, masked intruders burst inside. They opened the bedroom door and shot his brother Orhan while he lay in bed. The killers then shot and killed his father because he had witnessed the murder and could identify those responsible. His mother was also shot when struggling with the assailants and died several hours later on the way to hospital, having been denied assistance or an ambulance by the gendarme station nearby – the gendarmes claimed they could not go out after dark for 'security reasons'. Ercan believed the shooting had happened because his brother was sympathetic to the PKK. All the villagers here were sympathetic to the Kurdish liberation movement. They belonged to one of the Kurdish tribes of Mardin.

The killings had taken place on 16 March 1993 and still (two months later) no one had been charged even though the family had identified the two village guards (from Belpinar village, Batman) by name.

It was well known that the Hizb-i Kontras were particularly active in Batman. The Hizb-i Kontras were death squads, organised on a secret basis to carry out the state's contra-guerrilla activities in conjunction with the special forces, commandos and contra-guerrilla teams. Organised under a religious cover, they were not in fact a religious organisation, but a right-wing fascist group and were almost certainly being trained by the security forces. They roved throughout the Kurdish region, where they were responsible for carrying out numerous politically motivated killings. Batman itself had become one of the foremost cities in the country for murders of this type. There were a total of 139 killings by 'unknown persons' in Batman in 1992, and 25 more in the first month of 1993.[12]

The Hizb-i Kontras were allegedly organised by Abdulkadir Aksu, former interior minister under Özal and the Motherland Party (Anavatan Parti), a Diyarbakir Kurd, also former governor of Gaziantep, whose sympathies lay with the extreme right pro-Islamic fascist wing within the party. Aksu was the chief of police (Emniyet Müdürü) of Karahmanmaraş at the time of the massacre of the mainly Alevi populace by right-wing extremists supporting the MHP led by Alparslan Türkeş. Aksu is considered to have been one of the main forces behind the co-ordination of the Hizb-i Kontras. He failed to be re-elected in 1992 in Diyarbakir, superseded by pro-Kurdish politician Hatip Dicle.

The Hizb-i Kontras are not to be confused with Hizbullah (the Party of God), first set up by Ayatollah Mohammad Gafari in Iran in 1973, which has only limited support in Turkey and Turkish (north) Kurdistan.

Ercan's uncle pushed through the crowd and opened his palms to reveal several metal shell fragments collected from the rockets fired upon the house. He had taken the trouble to go home and fetch them for us as proof of what his people were telling us. These Kurds all spoke in that intense quiet way which showed how frightened they were. Even as we talked, we feared the police might arrive and these innocent people be punished for telling us their story. The longer we stayed in this unhappy village, the greater the risk became. The deepening darkness was a threat to everyone's safety. We agreed to stay 15 minutes or so longer and accompanied the villagers as they pointed out first one house and then another, all bearing the pockmarks of gunfire.

The villagers were considering abandoning their homes and heading west, afraid that the village guards and gendarmes would come back to finish them off. Yet they did not want to abandon the homes that had always been a part of their lives. Torn between commitment to the past and anxiety for the future, they had no protection in this isolated place. They complained bitterly about the lack of justice in Turkey: life here was cheap.[13]

Perhaps even more horrific than the story of the villagers of Karataş was that of the Kurdish villagers of Yeşilyürt. These had been rounded up by the army, forced to lie face down in the dirt of the village square and made to eat human excrement.[14]

In incidents in other villages, Kurdish men were separated from the women, some singled out for execution, others subjected to *falaka* (beating on the soles of the feet) and other forms of torture to extract information or 'confessions' from them; women were sexually violated. The villagers' houses and barns were then either bombed or doused with paraffin and torched. So it was in Ormanci, Tepecik, Lice, Kulp, Cizre, Şirnak, Idil and numerous smaller villages.

By the summer of 1993, military attacks on civilian areas had spread north-east to Dersim, Ağri, Doğubeyazit, Kars, Bingöl, Yüksekova and Hakkari. Every Kurdish town faced increasing military aggression after the collapse of the PKK ceasefire.

Challenge to the Turkish constitution and penal code

Because of the unitary character of the Turkish constitution, there can be but one nation, one people, within the boundaries of the Turkish state. The country is therefore constitutionally indivisible. This also means that a citizen is and must be 'Turkish' and that by extension Turkish is the language of the country. This leaves no room for Kurdish or any other national or ethnic identity, culture or non-Turkish political activity. Open expressions of 'Kurdishness' become illegal and as such are effectively reinforced by the Turkish penal code.

Article 3 of the constitution uncompromisingly declares that the Turkish state, its territory and nation, is an indivisible entity, and its language is Turkish. The major obstacle to the resolution of the Kurdish question is the Turkish constitution itself and the laws based upon it.

Article 125 of the penal code states that: 'Any person ... who carries out any action intended to destroy the unity of the Turkish state or to separate any part of the territory from the control of the Turkish state shall be punished by death.'

Then there is the Anti-Terror Law, passed in April 1991 under Turgut Özal. Under this law a person may be suspected of being a 'terrorist' and accused of 'terrorist' activities for any attempt to change the present political system or the characteristics of the Turkish republic.

Article 8 of the Law declares that: 'Written and oral propaganda and assemblies, meetings and demonstrations aimed at damaging the in-divisible unity of the state of the Turkish republic with its territory and nation are forbidden, regardless of the method, intention and ideas behind it.' These provisions make it illegal to discuss separate forms of administration for the Kurdish region, from devolution to independence.

The present-day repression practised by the Turkish authorities against the Kurds has been justified under articles of Turkish law from the time of the collapse of the Ottoman Empire (see appendix for the specific laws by which military rule has been legitimised in Kurdistan). Kurdistan in Turkey has been controlled through martial law for more than seventy years. During the Newroz 'celebrations' in Cizre described at the beginning of this chapter, Turkish security forces beat and arrested an elderly Kurdish woman simply because she was standing close by. Young women and children were shot at. The state justified this be-haviour and backed it through the Anti-Terror Law by branding civilians 'terrorists' for having demonstrated support for the PKK, for carrying PKK flags or portraits of Abdullah Öcalan, the PKK leader. The only possibility for protection from state violence lies in labelling yourself a 'Turk', whether you happen to be one or not, or in aligning yourself with the state, becoming perhaps a village guard, a spy, an informer, a member of the death squads or perhaps even a civil administrator.

There are persons of Kurdish origin in the Turkish government as there are in the government of Saddam and Hafiz Asad. But in none of these parliaments are Kurds able to represent the interests of their own people. Nor is that the reason why they hold office; those who rise to power in the central governments do so as a result of their work against Kurdish and other minority interests. The state uses them to lend authen-ticity to its work, saying, 'Look, Kurds can become prime minister or even president in our democracy, if they choose!' At the same time Kurdistan is plundered of all its natural resources – its petrol, water, minerals, metals and agricultural products – but little is put back into the region, and certainly not into Kurdish hands to be controlled by Kurds themselves.

The PKK's role

It is a weighty task to describe adequately the PKK's contribution to the Kurdish struggle, to analyse its appeal, its successes and its mistakes. But certain facts emerge when it comes to any frank discussion of the party.

In the 1990s, the PKK rose to become the most powerful Kurdish party in Turkey. This was due to the Turkish government's silence over the extra-judicial killings in Kurdistan, the military's attacks on civilian targets and the commencement of the destruction of Kurdish villages. Nineteen ninety was also significant as the year in which popular democratic Kurdish intellectuals like Vedat Aydin were murdered by contra-guerrillas, fuelling public outrage at the same time as increasing grassroots support for the PKK as the only party strong enough to fight back.

In 1990 for the first time massive demonstrations in support of the PKK erupted in Botan province in the large Kurdish towns like Cizre and Şirnak. During Newroz ordinary Kurds hurled stones at the army and security forces, and marched openly in the streets waving PKK flags and holding up portraits of Abdullah Öcalan.

After 1992 and the war in south Kurdistan, the PKK emerged as the only Kurdish party in that particular conflict whose deeds matched its maxims. This brought the PKK even greater support in both north and south Kurdistan.

Although the PKK was founded on principles of Marxist-Leninist philosophy it also advocated democracy and was not opposed to Islam, nor to the teachings of Mohammad. This was one of its internal political contradictions, but as the Kurds are fundamentally Muslim, these principles had to be reconciled within the overall political outlook. In fact, the Islamic philosophy of equality and opposition to unfairness is in harmony with the principles of Marxism. This can be considered one of the PKK's most successful aspects – the rare marriage of Islam and socialism. Although the party was opposed to the 'real socialism' of Moscow, the teachings of Marx and Lenin were passed on to hundreds of guerrillas and party recruits side by side with democratic theories.

The PKK was opposed to amalgamation with other Kurdish parties, all of which it inevitably labelled 'reformist'. It has always taken its political decisions without consultation, being highly critical of the other Kurdish parties and their leaders. The party claims to depend solely on the Kurdish people and on itself, refusing to rely on the dubious support of outside movements or nations where no good reason exists for doing so – history having illustrated that the Kurdish people have been betrayed by foreign powers on every occasion that a Kurdish leader relied on them.

Although the PKK has been fighting for an independent, secular, socialist Kurdistan on an armed basis since 15 August 1984, the party does not champion violence *per se*; the armed struggle waged by its ARGK guerrillas must be understood in the context of defence. From a Kurdish perspective, the guerrillas are Kurdish soldiers, fighting against an occupying military and nationalist colonial presence for their people's national and human rights, and for the preservation and development of their ancient homeland, Kurdistan.

The PKK stood out from other Kurdish political groups in Turkey because it viewed armed struggle as a necessary means to resolving the Kurdish question. However, in 1991, as conditions worsened in Turkey, the leadership changed its tone, saying the party favoured a solution through democratic means and political dialogue. For the first time in the early 1990s, PKK leader Abdullah Öcalan began to speak about the possibility of political negotiation with the Turkish government over autonomy, or federation, provided that full rights would be granted to the Kurdish people. Independence itself, he said, was no longer a prerequisite. He presented the government with a demand to lift its restrictions on Kurdish culture, education, language and identity – in Turkey, even calling oneself a Kurd was still illegal. However, the Turks refused to sit down and negotiate with them. They also refused to negotiate with any other Kurdish party from Turkey, preferring to be seen to court the Iraqi Kurds as allies against their own Kurds. The attitude of the Turkish military was best summed up by its general chief of staff, Doğan Güreş, who warned: 'The PKK will die like dogs in their own blood.'[15]

Tansu Çiller's government continued to reject all the PKK's offers to reach a political settlement through negotiation, vowing instead to end Kurdish resistance militarily. But short of genocide, it certainly seemed that the Turks were and are incapable of defeating the PKK, or of solving the Kurdish problem by force. Indeed, other Kurdish groups were also continuing to resist. *Yekbûn* (Unity) had recently sent its own small guerrilla force, known as *Brûsk* (Thunder), into the mountains to train and defend Kurdish interests.

Although vastly outnumbered, the PKK's (ARGK) guerrillas (10–20,000) have succeeded in holding down more than 350,000 Turkish troops in the tenth year of their war for Kurdish rights and independence. Support for the PKK grew because the PKK guerrillas have been prepared to fight and die for Kurdish freedom.

Although the guerrillas availed themselves of mobile bases in Kurdish

Iraq and Iran, they also continued to operate from bases on the Turkish side of the border, moving about as conditions determined. The Turkish army and air force, which showed equal disrespect for the international borders dissecting Kurdistan, pursued the guerrillas into the heart of Kurdistan, destroying any obstacle in their path. It was of little importance to the Turks whether it was Kurds with the PKK or other Kurds they cut down. Kurds were Kurds, after all.

Following the October 1992 war, the PKK temporarily withdrew from their bases along the Turko-Iraqi border and established a new training site far to the south in Zelê, bordering Iran in the Zagros mountains. Yet even here, far from the Turkish border, in the summer of 1993 and thereafter, Turkish warplanes penetrated Iraqi airspace 130 kilometres deep and bombed the camp indiscriminately. This was despite Zelê's proximity to a number of Iraqi and Iranian Kurd villages occupied by non-combatant families. It was virtually impossible from above to distinguish one from the other, as the villages interlaced the camps. Iran resorted to the same tactics in pursuit of the Kurdish Democratic Party of Iran (KDPI) guerrillas in adjacent locations. (see pp. 118–22).

Aiming at focusing world attention more effectively on the dirty war in Turkey, and the destruction of the Kurdish way of life, the PKK resorted to taking small numbers of Western tourists hostage in areas under their control. But the European public, ignorant of the PKK's motives, and generally frightened by hostage-taking, tended to jump to the wrong conclusions: namely, that the lives of Western tourists and travellers were in jeopardy when travelling through Kurdistan. The British Foreign Office issued an official warning advising all travellers against entering the region. Although the hostages were always well treated and released unharmed, those concerned were caught up in a struggle about which they usually had very little prior knowledge. The press sensationalised their stories, ignoring the fundamental political message and focusing on intimate details of the captives themselves: romance, physical hardships, abduction.

Most reporting in the West on the PKK has demonstrated a distinctly negative bias, stemming frequently from ignorance and the fact that writers' sources have invariably been the Turkish government, parties or individuals opposed to the PKK. Despite the gross disproportion between abuses carried out by the government and those of which the PKK are accused, the government has got considerable mileage out of allegations that the PKK has murdered schoolteachers working in Kurdish areas. It is worth looking at this charge in more detail.

The Turkish government continues to impose its Turkification programme through the education system upon all children. In the Kurdish

provinces, where education in the Kurdish mother tongue is still prohibited, education becomes a highly politicized arena. From the moment
they begin school Kurdish children are denied their identity, forced each
morning to recite the creed: 'Türküm, doğruyum, çalişkanim' (I am a
Turk, I am correct, I am hardworking). Non-compliance or claims to be
a Kurd or an Armenian are punished. The school may report the family
to the authorities or inform the military, who will then take the matter
into their own hands. Teachers sent into Kurdistan are first armed by the
government, and not only with propaganda. Kurds allege that numbers
of teachers are in fact contra-guerrillas masked as teachers and trained to
perform darker functions than simple brainwashing: the identities of
Kurdish patriots and dissidents are established through the children in
the schools, leading to pogroms. The PKK claims to have unmasked this
clandestine activity, locating and attacking contra-guerrillas lodged in the
school buildings – hence the origin of the allegations against the PKK.
It is indeed likely that authentic teachers can also get caught up in the
ugly conflict. The PKK has certainly been responsible for torching post
offices, electrical and other government installations, including telecommunications pylons, government offices, as well as schools.

After 1993 and the ceasefire, the PKK changed its policy towards
collaborators, informers and village guards. Human rights reports documenting PKK violations showed a proportionate decrease in extrajudicial
revenge killings. For all their self-confessed faults, the PKK have never
exhibited the sadistic brutality characteristic of the Turkish security
forces. Kurdish women are raped and sexually humiliated every day; in
the course of routine torture, village men and guerrillas alike are later
found mutilated, eyes gouged, ears, noses and genitals hacked off, their
naked bodies dumped or hastily buried. Souvenir snapshots are taken
showing individual members of the special forces displaying their human
conquests like trophies after a hunt. The casualness and sadism evident
in these pictures is shocking.

Listening to a speech delivered by Mustafa Karasu, a prominent
spokesman for the ERNK (Eniya Rizgaria Netewa Kurdistan, the political
wing of the PKK), to an audience in Europe, I understood how the
PKK's message had come to be so compelling for a people deprived not
only of their rights but also of their identity. Mustafa Karasu had spent
at least a decade in a Diyarbakir prison. There he had lived according to
his political beliefs and still survived. He reminded those who had
gathered to hear him:

> This is not just a bachelors' war. It is everyone's war. Young and old, men
> and women, we must now fight side by side. Our enemies do not believe in
> peace and democracy. Our neighbours are brutal and corrupt, ruling their

countries by force and through terror. Are we seriously to believe that we Kurds can win our rights by sitting down and talking? After all that has happened how can we believe we will gain our rights by sitting down and talking quietly? No one wants to listen. No one wants to concede an inch to the Kurds. We do not want to fight, but our neighbours know nothing else but fighting and killing. Tell me, does democracy exist in any country bordering our homeland?

The PKK expects and demands absolute loyalty and integrity from its members and supporters, a loyalty that places the party and its objectives above all other goals and relationships. In Kurdish society, the good of the family has always been placed above that of the individual members. Individualism is not of value in itself. In the same way, no merit is attached to privacy, solitary contemplation, personal space or personal growth and fulfilment. By extension, it has not been difficult for the political parties to demand this same sacrifice of individualism for the greater good of the whole (although for many Kurds, submission of personality and individual choice to a supreme chairman and his central committee is both alien and abhorrent). This ideal is also cherished by the PKK. Here, individuality is submerged into the composite identity of the party. Within the party the individual slots him or herself into a hierarchical structure and a chain of command which rejects personal self-expression. Participants are not encouraged to dispute the contents of the party's manifesto but are taught to familiarise themselves with it so thoroughly as to be able to reproduce its teachings in thought, word and action. I am reminded of Jung Chang's *Wild Swans – Three Daughters of China*, a vivid account of life under Chairman Mao and the applicability of *The Four Seasons* by Lei Feng which, in 1964, Chang and her fellow students committed to memory:

> Like spring, I treat my comrades warmly.
> Like summer, I am full of ardour for my
> revolutionary work.
> I eliminate my individualism as an autumn gale
> sweeps away fallen leaves,
> And to the class enemy, I am cruel and ruthless
> like harsh winter.
>
> (From Jung Chang, *Wild Swans*, pp. 340–1, Flamingo,
> London 1993.)

For those who want to understand the PKK, publications by the pro-PKK publishing houses are recommended. These include the Kurdistan Reports produced in virtually every European language. *Berxwedan*

(Resistance), *Serxwebûn* (Liberation), *Bawer* (Faith), *Welat* (Homeland) *Welate Me* (Our Country), and *Axina Welat* (Oh, Homeland) are published abroad in Turkish, Kurdish or a combination of both. Then there were the dailies like *Yeni Gündem* (New Agenda), *Özgür Gündem* (Free Agenda), *Yeni Ülke* (New Country), *Özgür Ülke* (Free Country) and *Yeni Politika* (New Politics), all of which have been banned in Turkey on the grounds that each was the successor of the last and prohibited under article 8 as constituting separatist propaganda. *Özgür Politika* (Free Politics) which commenced publication following the closure of *Yeni Politika* was printed only in Europe.

The Kurdistan Socialist Party and the PKK: a new political era?

The Kurdistan Socialist Party (KSP), previously opposed to an armed solution to the Kurdish conflict, adopted a position of support for the PKK on 19 March 1993 when KSP General Secretary Kemal Burkay signed a protocol in Bar Elias, Lebanon with PKK General Secretary Abdullah Öcalan. The protocol was signed in support of joint peace efforts and future co-operation. Ten other Kurdish groups in Turkey also joined the pact to bring about democracy and end Turkish state repression. Amongst their foremost demands were the abolition of the village guard system; an end to state of emergency rule in the Kurdish provinces; freedom of speech, of expression and the freedom to speak, teach, publish and broadcast the Kurdish language; and the commencement of a political dialogue between Kurdish representatives of the people and the Turkish government as a means of resolving the Kurdish problem.

The KSP (formerly the TKSP; it has now dropped the 'T' for 'Turkey') had consistently sought to resolve the Kurdish problem in Turkey by political means, envisioning a national democratic socialist revolution within Turkish Kurdistan. Its programme advocated the abolition of the old Kurdish feudal structure, in which Kurdish aghas and wealthy businessmen exploited the greater part of Kurdish society for their own profits and collaborated both with the colonialist central governments controlling Kurdistan and their 'Western imperialist and capitalist' allies. It took the view that each of the four main parts of divided Kurdistan was subject to different conditions and optimum circumstances affecting individual revolution in each part, and that revolutionary endeavours by one part were to be supported by each of the other parts in the natural course of their own struggle. (This view is not shared by the PKK, which advocated struggle throughout greater Kurdistan simultaneously and regardless of prevailing circumstances or geopolitical trends.)

In 1975–79, and opposing the military coup, the party was responsible for setting up legal organisations promoting Kurdish culture and education in almost every Kurdish town. These were known as the Devrimci Halk Kültür Dernekleri (Revolutionary People's Cultural Associations, DHKD). After the coup many of the DHKD's members were arrested, imprisoned and the centres abolished. During the same interval, in 1977, for the first time two of the party's delegates were elected to office as mayors in the cities of Diyarbakir and Ağri.

While in practice supporting *every* means for achieving Kurdish freedom, the KSP has not been disposed towards the armed struggle in principle. Diyar Budak, a senior London representative of the party, put it to me this way:

We do not believe that it is sensible to align ourselves with any of our neighbouring countries, particularly when it comes to armed struggle in the Middle East, and an armed struggle usually demands alliances. The armed struggle in Turkey, as in Iraq before it, destroyed nature and agricultural production in Kurdistan. In Kurdistan now you cannot find an egg or a chicken … We also condemn the internal fighting which has wrecked people's lives in south Kurdistan, especially as it focuses on something potentially as manageable as control and allocation of the Ibrahim Khalil border post revenues.

The KSP is a peaceful organisation which supports the principles of democracy and diplomacy. But the generals continue to exert control over Turkey and there can be no talking with them. We can hold strikes, boycott the trade of Turkish goods, support the external boycott of tourism and carry out similar pacifist practices. Unfortunately Turkish unionists do not sufficiently support the Kurdish people in their struggle for this to be successful in its own right. If you read it you will see that our programme states that:

'the KSP views the national liberation of the Kurdish people as being implicit in our people's right to determine its own destiny. The Kurdish people must govern itself. We believe that there could be two possibilities for this in northern Kurdistan: the Kurdish people could secede and establish a state of its own, or it could choose democratic unity with the Turkish people. In the second case, the unity would have to consist of a federation of two republics having equal rights. Kurdistan would have to organise itself as an independent republic with its own parliament and its own government, and it would have the same rights as Turkey in every respect. As soon as the appropriate conditions have evolved for the Kurdish people's right to determine its own destiny, the Kurdish people can choose one of these two possibilities. In both cases it would have the status of an independent state.'[16]

Practically speaking however, democratic unity is more feasible than secession even if just for economic reasons.'[17]

The KSP has always published and continues to produce serious literature, political magazines and newspapers, including *Roja Welat* (Sun of the Homeland), the first newspaper to be published in the Kurdish language which had a circulation of 40,000 copies, *Özgürlük Yolu* (The Path of Freedom), *Deng* (Voice), *Dengê Azadî* (Voice of Freedom) and, more recently, *Ronahî* (Enlightenment) to reach Kurdish people and encourage them to support the peaceful resistance movement. The high literary quality of many Kurdish books and papers produced by the respective parties still puts their material beyond the reach of ordinary villagers and especially of Kurdish women. In the towns and villages illiteracy remains high, and women receive little or no education. The power of books, magazines and newspapers to bring about change is necessarily limited. Ordinary Kurds needed a party, or mass movement, which could defend their immediate security interests, and political and cultural rights. Support was manifest for the HEP and DEP before their closure by the state, from quarters in sympathy with both the KSP and PKK respectively. This support has carried over since 1994 into the DDP (Demokrat Değişim Parti, Democratic Change Party) and HADEP (People's Democratic Party).

While many workers, students, educated Kurds, intellectuals and business people support the KSP – evidenced from the sizeable member-ship of its European associations such as Komkar – the armed struggle has focused attention away from the largely non-violent Kurdish parties and left the spotlight firmly centred on the PKK.

The PKK's use of force against force in the defence of the Kurds has provided the Turkish government and its Western allies with the excuse they need to continue military offensives throughout Kurdistan under the cloak of 'fighting terrorism'. Continued Turkish military aggression in the Kurdish provinces (particularly over the past five years) has effectively seen to it that there is no longer even the most minimal security of life for ordinary civilians in Kurdistan, and at the present rate of destruction there will be no villages left standing in Kurdistan twelve months hence.

Sections of the older generation have had difficulty in understanding the 'Marxist revolutionary' PKK. This has been particularly true in the case of practising Muslims, who were incapable of comprehending, or accepting, why young Kurdish women choose to become guerrillas, living as men and in the company of men, up in the mountains. Kurdish society observes basic practices of segregation in everyday life. Challenge to traditional gender roles, whether from within or from outside, is not readily appreciated.

The PKK's political aims include improving the position of women within Kurdish society and creating gender equality within the movement. Women may rise to the same political or military ranks as men within the party. However, their femininity is compromised. As in Mao's China, the PKK family is being sacrificed for the greater good of the party. Political members are encouraged to put the party first, frequently spending months or even years apart from partners and children, sometimes in different countries, while they strive meanwhile to achieve the liberation of Kurdistan. The PKK regards this as a necessary sacrifice for the struggle.

Outline of the Kurdish political movement in Turkey 1960–85

There have been a number of important Kurdish parties and movements active in Turkey in addition to the PKK and the KSP. The earliest of these was the Kurdistan Democratic Party of Turkey (TKDP), founded in 1965, virtually a branch of Massoud Barzani's KDP of Iraq and banned in Turkey. The TKDP formed the basis for several other parties, including the Kurdistan National Liberation Movements (KUK) but excluding the PKK, which developed from the Turkish left wing.

Other Kurdish political movements in Turkey which became influential after 1969 included the Eastern Revolutionary Cultural Centres (DDKO), a legal movement which provided a forum for those whose political alliances and activities were of necessity clandestine, all Kurdish national parties being outlawed. The DDKO was banned after the 1970 military coup which overthrew the repressive Demirel government. Thereafter, military action against the Kurds intensified.

The successes of a number of revolutionary liberation movements at the time, as for example in Vietnam, Cambodia, Laos and Mozambique, influenced left-wing movements in Turkey and Kurdistan.

Although many Kurds had membership in the Turkish Workers Party (TIP) and Dev Genç (Revolutionary Youth), issues centred on Kurdish identity and Kurdish independence led numbers of Kurds to break away and establish a distinctly Kurdish movement of their own as in the Turkish Kurdistan Socialist Party (TKSP) (the forerunner of today's Kurdistan Socialist Party), and the Kurdish Workers Party (PKK), a conceptual forerunner, not the root of today's PKK. The former evolved into the Vanguard Workers Party of Kurdistan (PPKK), now known as the People's Unity Party of Kurdistan (Yekbûn).

These groups were all components of the legal Revolutionary Democratic Cultural Associations (DDKD), as was the Liberation (Rizgarî) Movement and KAWA, the former evolving into the Kurdistan Liberation Party in 1988, and KAWA continuing in much the same fashion into the present. They felt the need to represent themselves and considered that the Kurdish cause was being used by the Turkish left for its own ends. In 1970, the TIP was banned for having formally recognised the Kurds as a distinct and separate people within Turkey.[18]

Armed clashes between the PKK and the Turkish army began on 15 August 1984. David McDowall, in *The Kurds: A Nation Denied*, underlines that this same year the Turkish state: 'correctly recognised the PKK as the single most serious threat to state security, and was stringent with those PKK members it captured. By 1985 it had demanded the death sentence in over six hundred cases in mass trials. It also took strong measures in the field, militarising the whole of eastern and south-eastern Anatolia.'[19]

Summary of the Kurdish movement in Turkey in the 1990s

By the 1990s, there were twelve main political movements in Turkish Kurdistan varying in size and outlook. These comprised the KDP–Bakur, KAWA, KKP (the Kurdistan Communist Party – not linked with the Kurdistan Communist Party in Iraq), KUK and its offshoot, the RNK (Kurdistan Liberation Movement Party), PİK (Islamic Party of Kurdistan), PRK/Rizgarî, KSP (Kurdistan Socialist Party), Tekoşîna Socyalist, TSK (United Socialists of Kurdistan), the PKK and Yekbûn. (Yekbûn comprises three former left-wing parties: Peşheng, KUK-SE and KAK) and reflects a broad spectrum of socialist–communist political views.)[20]

Circumstances have encouraged a proliferation of Kurdish parties and movements in Turkey. For example, the resumption of 'civil' government in 1983 under Prime Minister Özal following the military coup brought about a number of significant changes which affected Kurdish issues and the ways these were approached, not only by the Kurds but by the Turkish mainstream, legal political parties. The collapse of the Soviet Union in 1991 similarly triggered a variety of political splits within left-wing groups. These factors led to radical changes in their political programmes and fundamental reformations of their manifestos.

One major change in the ideology and goals of most groups has been the change towards adopting a stance firmly centred on Kurdistan, rather than deriving an ideological basis from political parties having the same political manifesto based in other countries.

In 1994–95, KAWA, Tekoşîna Sosyalist, TSK, KUK-RNK and Yekbûn formed the Kurdistan Socialist Unity Platform, sharing 'the common goal of an independent, democratic Kurdistan and supporting armed struggle against economic targets adversely affecting the lives of Kurds in the region'. (*Medya Güneşi* newspaper, April 1995). This alliance did not take in the KDP–Bakur, (KDP–North) Rizgari, the PKK or the KSP.

With the exception of the PKK and Yekbûn, whose programmes focused on the resolution of the Kurdish problem within the whole of Kurdistan, the political programmes of the aforementioned groups had, by and large, been concerned with the Kurdish struggle solely as it existed *within* Turkey or on a regional and conditional basis.

Identifying self-determination for the Kurdish people as a prerequisite, each party thereafter differed mainly over whether or not secession, federation or independence (and eventual unity with other parts of Kurdistan) should follow. But they shared the view that it was immaterial which parts of Kurdistan should gain independence first and that the model of administration best suited to Kurdistan was socialism.

However, after the end of the Cold War and particularly after the Gulf war, Kurdish political views underwent a change as a consequence of the campaign of state terror and widespread devastation of the Kurdish countryside unleashed by the Turkish government and its war machine. Kurdish leaders increasingly demanded political dialogue and proposed a democratic solution, inviting the participation of observer countries or international monitoring bodies in ending the bloodshed which had claimed more than ten thousand Kurdish and Turkish lives and seen the destruction of over two thousand Kurdish villages within the borders of Turkey alone.

By the time the Kurdish Federated Parliament was established in south Kurdistan (northern Iraq) in 1992, the Kurds of Turkey increasingly pressed for the achievement of short-term goals including *real* democracy in Turkey, recognition of Kurdish identity, democratic representation and possibly even a federal solution, rather than autonomy. Turkey still refused to discuss any of these alternatives.

Summary of economic issues and differing viewpoints in Turkey[21]

Between 1973 and the military coup of 1980, there had been an easing up on left-wing publications and on the expression of left-wing views; restrictions on trade unions were also eased, and workers' rights acknowledged. However, this outward lifting of restrictions was effectively counteracted in practice by the state's support of the extreme right wing, represented by the MHP (Turkish Nationalist Movement Party, or 'Grey Wolves'). The Islamic sector also supported Türkeş and violent clashes erupted between left- and right-wing factions, particularly students, workers, trade unionists and the dissident population of the Kurdish provinces still under military rule. Thousands died in the ensuing violence, especially in Karahmanmaraş and Çorum.

By 1978, the three most prominent right-wing parties had combined to form a National Front coalition government. During this term, attacks on the left continued, finally erupting into the military coup of 1980 and the dissolution of parliament itself.

Under the military, intensive and brutal operations were carried out against the two remaining enemies of the Turkish state: the Kurds and the Communists. Turkish prisons filled up with prisoners of conscience and political activists. Torture was routine and frequently ended in death. The victims of torture included the first independent Kurdish Mayor of Diyarbakir, Mehdi Zana – husband of Leyla Zana, who remained in prison for the next eleven years suffering regular abuse. Executions of political prisoners in detention became commonplace. The victims were mostly trade unionists, activists, writers and intellectuals.

The rule of the generals did not adversely target the religious sector of the population. In fact, during the next three years of military rule numerous new Koranic courses were permitted – attended, among others, by thousands of children. It also became known that Saudi Arabia's *Rabita* was secretly financing the courses as well as paying the Mullahs' salaries. Once public, the news became a scandal.

Religion was exploited as a means of depoliticizing society with the aim of combating Communist tendencies and undermining the growth of national awareness amongst the country's estimated 12–15 million Kurds. The Turkish state's religious policy found cohesion with Western governments' anti-Communist policy which supported Islamic countries neighbouring the Soviet bloc – known as the 'Green Border'. The West therefore did not oppose the resurgence of Islamic practices in Turkey.

Although 'civil' government was restored in 1984 under Turgut Özal and his Motherland Party, policies towards Kurds and Communists hitherto applied by the military continued virtually unchanged. But now for the first time, radical Islamicists were freely admitted at all levels into state administration. Özal and many of his ministers began a new practice of attending the mosque near parliament each Friday. Özal, his wife Semra, and several ministers also went on the Haj to Mecca; the pilgrimage was broadcast on state television. The national education ministry was put under the control of the Islamicists. One of these, Vehbi Dincerler, a confirmed anti-Darwinist, objected to the theory of evolution being taught in Turkish schools, claiming that he was 'descended from Adam, not from monkeys'. The theory of evolution was removed from the state's text books. Religious education in schools became compulsory from elementary school until the end of secondary school. At university level, graduates from the Faculty of Religion were allowed to pursue any additional profession of their choosing – banking, economy, etc. The greatest item of the state's annual expenditure, after military expenditure, was now allocated to religion, via the Religious Affairs Ministry (Diyanet İşleri Başkanliği). Turkish State Television (TRT) commenced live broadcasts of religious ceremonies direct from the mosques.

The Islamic fraternity within the government, and relatives of ministers, including the brother of Prime Minister Özal, gained enormous financial benefits from their political alliances, obtaining credit from the government (deriving from Islamic countries) and making private and corporate investments in oil, undertaking their own businesses in import and export, and ultimately amassing considerable personal fortunes. Arab banks were opened in Turkey for the first time; profit from interest being prohibited in Islam, a share-holding system was practised. Wealthy Arab shaikhs were allowed to buy property in the best parts of the country after a special amendment was made to the law concerning foreign purchase of property in Turkey.

Özal advocated a free market system in Turkey and made a number of significant changes which included the building of modern highways, the modernisation of telecommunications, new housing and the free import of foreign goods such as cars and electronic appliances.

The gap between the rich and the poor widened with the creation of a new upper class. Hand in hand with these social and economic changes came a new way of looking at life. Capitalism greatly influenced the young, whose goal became one of getting rich quick and putting the interests of the individual above of those of the greater society. The *nouveaux riches* knew nothing about financial management, however, nor how to manage their new resources. Swift gains on the stock market were often just as quickly lost again. The new trends had a damaging effect on the poorer Turkish and Kurdish masses, whose standards of living worsened as their buying power decreased. The resultant inflation hit them hard. Economic deprivation also resulted in a sudden increase in prostitution and a collapse of public moral values, introducing enormous changes into traditional Turkish society.

A number of new political parties were founded at this time. The Kurdish issue grew hotter. Previously underestimated by the government, a section of the left Kurdish opposition began their armed struggle for Kurdish rights and independence under the leadership of the PKK. The armed struggle which began with an initial two hundred or so guerrillas rapidly developed into a force of thousands. The state denounced them as 'bandits and brigands seeking to destroy the indivisible unity of the Turkish state'.

Mehmet Ali Eren, a Kurdish MP and a member of the SHP (Social Democrat Popular Party) dared to speak out in parliament, describing himself as a Kurd. This statement met with violent opposition from Turkish MPs, the ruling Motherland Party and the Right. It was unheard of to consider oneself anything but a Turk: the word 'Kurd' was taboo.

The Turkish government henceforth committed a greater percentage of its armed forces, formerly based in the west of the country, to the escalating armed conflict in the Kurdish south east. But its early attempts to destroy the guerrillas were unsuccessful. It was Prime Minister Özal who proclaimed the state of emergency in the Kurdish provinces and pronounced a military curfew upon the region. This was to be administered by a new postholder designated as the 'Super Governor' and accorded special powers to act with virtual independence. Özal also introduced teams of foreign-trained Special Forces (Özel Tim) into the area, counter-insurgency squads fittingly nicknamed 'Rambos'.

Young people who had been studying the Koran in the state-sponsored Koran schools were encouraged to join government-directed Hizbullah, anti-PKK squads. The government secretly armed them to fight against the PKK and other Kurds in Turkey who championed separatist views. Despite such extreme measures, the number of guerrillas supporting the PKK continued to increase. Popular support for the Kurdish armed struggle also increased in direct proportion to military repression in the Kurdish towns and villages.

In response, Turgut Özal introduced new laws and abolished the infamous articles 141, 142 and 163. In their place he set up an even more stringent Anti-Terror Law, article 8 of which covered all aspects previously subsumed under the abolished article 142 but which went still further in identifying anybody helping, feeding, or sheltering a Kurdish guerrilla or 'separatist', as guilty by association. Kurdish dissidents began to be labelled 'terrorists' in the state-controlled media. Conversely, the law covering Islam was softened.

Of the Turkish republic's three traditional enemies, Islam had became a friend – albeit under state control; the traditional Left had been tamed following the collapse of the Soviet Union. For example, the Turkish Communist Party's leaders in exile abroad were induced to return home after secret talks and concessions. After going through the motions of 'punishment', they were invariably set free, and the Communist Party was thereafter legalised as it was no longer seen as constituting any serious threat to the Turkish state. As the Communist Party aroused little interest, before long it closed its offices. Some of the party's former activists went on to become MPs in alternative parties, others advisers of some of the richest holding-companies in the country. (The entire advertising sector in Turkey is mainly comprised of former left-wing activists.) The Kurds, who had become an even more serious opponent of the government, emerged as the sole enemy of the state. In 1989, seven Kurdish MPs from the SHP were expelled from parliament for having attended the International Conference on Kurdish Identity held in Paris. They went on to form the first pro-Kurdish party in Turkey, the HEP (People's Labour Party).

In 1991, Özal's Motherland Party (ANAP) lost its majority and a new coalition government came to power comprising Demirel's True Path Party and the SHP, under Erdal İnönü. The promises which had carried them to power had been twofold; the True Path Party had promised economic progress and the SHP had promised democratic reforms – including the resolution of the Kurdish problem and the safeguarding of minority rights. But contrary to expectations, under the new coalition, military expenditure increased to 40 per cent of the state's total budget. Hopes among the Kurds and the working classes for greater democracy in Turkey soon died as the true face of the coalition government became apparent. Demirel's campaign promise of 'two keys': 'a home and a car for everyone' proved hollow, just as did İnönü's promise that human rights for all would be respected.

Although for the first time a Turkish prime minister officially declared that a 'Kurdish reality would be recognised', no practical steps were taken to do this, nor were any legal reforms carried out which might have improved the state's treatment of the Kurdish population. Instead, even more public money was spent on a military solution. This expenditure brought the Turkish economy to the brink of collapse and revealed the coalition's promises as false. Newspapers quoted people as saying of Demirel: 'Our Father has let us down.'

Whereas the pro-Islamic Welfare Party (Refah) had won only 7 per cent of the vote during ANAP's term of government (1984–91), after mounting popular disillusion with Demirel, support for Refah soared amongst the poor masses who no longer recognised any alternative. Refah obtained 22 per cent of the vote in the local elections of March 1994. People who had tried all the main parties found them all equally guilty of abusing power and failing to bring economic improvement to the country as a whole. As had happened under Özal, a number of those in the coalition government closest to the leadership derived financial benefit from their close proximity to the seat of power. There was widespread talk of bribes, pay-offs, insider-trading and secret deals. Demirel's nephew, for example, was accused of taking $20,000 from the state bank and, having declared himself bankrupt, escaped to Cyprus where he opened his own bank. Although he was sentenced to 15 months' imprisonment he was not extradited.

Popular general disappointment in the government presented Refah, with a real opportunity. It was the only legal party which had not hitherto had a chance to try its hand at power. Accordingly its candidates went from house to house, particularly in the poorer quarters and the sprawling urban shanty towns, speaking with the discontented populace who readily accepted their promises of a new just order. Nor did they overplay their pro-Islamic card at this stage of the campaign.

The Welfare Party had considerable money to spend on the campaign deriving from Islamic sources overseas; in the build-up to the March 1994 elections it spent more than any other party. Its campaign also sought to appeal to the military and, accordingly, the party took on board a number of retired generals. The party particularly needed this support as there had been a well-publicised scare about the imminent possibility of another military coup.

Opinion poll results helped to create panic amongst the rival parties; Refah candidates were targeted by the pro-government press in a libellous smear campaign; Kemalist loyalists from the centre-left and centre-right staged rallies demonstrating their loyalties to Atatürk's (secular) principles and protesting against the Welfare Party. However, Refah took the majority vote in both Istanbul and Ankara and obtained control of the city councils with an astonishing 22 per cent. As a direct consequence, the pro-Islamic sector of the population once again was seen as an enemy of the state.

While military activity against the PKK guerrillas had intensified under the coalition, extrajudicial killings against ordinary Kurdish citizens and Kurdish activists, educated and poor alike, had also become systematic. The Demirel–İnönü coalition government failed to respond. President Özal, touring in Kazakhistan at the time, announced that upon his return to Ankara he would make an important statement on the issue. A day after his return, however, he died of a heart attack. Confusion reigned.

Upon Özal's untimely death in April 1993, Süleyman Demirel became the new president and Tansu Çiller, elected by her party, stepped into Demirel's shoes as Turkey's new prime minister. Öcalan's peace initiative went unanswered and war intensified in Kurdistan.

As Turkey's new prime minister, Tansu Çiller announced that in future the Kurdish language might be broadcast on radio and television. Whilst on a visit to Spain, she discussed favourably the 'Basque model' with Prime Minister Felipe Gonzalez, but upon her return, pressurised by the hard-nosed members of her cabinet and the military, she denied having ever considered it. Indeed, Çiller thereafter made a complete about-face and left the 'Kurdish problem' to the generals. The ultimate power in Turkey was concentrated, as in the past, in the State Security Organisation (Milli Güvenlik Kuruluşu). Further capital was committed to the war effort in the Kurdish provinces, but as the military remained unsuccessful in its efforts to finish off the PKK ordinary Kurds became the government's next target of repression.

Echoing an old saying of Chairman Mao, the military warned: 'We'll drain the seas to catch the fish', referring to the PKK in the sea of the Kurdish people. But the government had plunged the country into economic despair having spent billions of dollars on its war against the Kurds, to the extent that even the privileged upper class was affected. Commodity prices and taxes rose day by day, killing off business and industry and bringing mass unemployment.

By mid-1994, the value of the Turkish lira hit an all-time low at TL46,000 to the US dollar on the international exchange. The Turkish government hastily announced an emergency economic package and called upon the people to make sacrifices for their country. The package doubled prices overnight and then froze them; people's savings were halved, as were their means. The trade unions held a one-day general strike.

Despite these extreme measures, the government still refused to revise its Kurdish policy. Seven Kurdish MPs from the DEP (Democracy Party) were imprisoned, and six others fled the country when their diplomatic immunity was lifted. They had been accused of separatist propaganda. The entire staff of the pro-Kurdish *Özgür Gündem* (Free Agenda) newspaper was arrested, including the tea-makers, for uncensored reporting of the Kurdish issue.

Not only were ordinary people disillusioned with the coalition government and its policies, the intellectuals and business class had also reached the limit of their tolerance. Cem Boyner, an intellectual and prosperous businessman, publicly proposed the formation of a new model Turkish republic, claiming that the old model was bankrupt and rotten beyond repair. Among other changes, he proposed that the existing model be replaced by a state respectful of the Kurds as a people who should have their own local administration. Boyner's democracy movement also advocated freedom of religious belief and religious observance. His circle held numerous meetings and debates and, from the beginning of 1994, Boyner formally spearheaded what was called the New Democratic Movement. He began touring Turkey province by province, town by town and talking with the people. A small spark of hope was kindled amongst the middle classes and intellectuals that here might lie the answer.

Of its three former enemies, the Turkish government continued to treat the Kurds as Enemy Number One. But its old enemy, Islam, was also rising in new guise, its radical disaffected youth avowedly anti-secular and fearing no one.

In 1993, 37 intellectuals and singers meeting for a special Alevi festival in Sivas were burned to death in an arson attack on the hotel where they were staying. The attack was carried out by Islamic extremists supporting Refah and was provoked by the presence of Aziz Nesin, the Turkish leftist writer who had translated Salman Rushdie's *Satanic Verses* into Turkish. Nesin was one of the lucky few to escape Sivas alive.

Criticised on a US trip for her government's Kurdish policy Prime Minister Çiller defended her actions, saying that an Islamic upsurge was threatening Turkey's secular 'democracy' and Turkey needed American support. She implied that it was in America's interest to help Turkey combat Islamic fundamentalism; Turkey's rough-handling of its Kurdish problem should be overlooked.

While Turkey received the West's support, real efforts were made to restrict Iran's influence, particularly upon northern Iraq. The Kurdish enclave was quietly left to rot. Meanwhile the Middle East's secret policemen took up positions in the area, the better to further their own interests.

The international community should have registered greater alarm over the kind of negotiations that began to take place between the governments of Turkey, Iran, Syria and, on a clandestine basis, Iraq from 1993 onwards. These negotiations had as their goal the defeat and extinction of the Kurdish enclave in Iraq, and of Kurdish resistance in each of the four states so represented. This final goal was to be achieved through combined military means involving political and military co-operation and intelligence-sharing across their respective borders.

The international community, however, remained silent. The dirty war became dirtier.

Notes

1. Excerpts from an interview with Ünal Erkan filmed in May 1993 for *Blood and Belonging – Dreaming Kurdistan*, BBC2, 18 November 1993, written and presented by Michael Ignatieff.

2. Ibid.

3. See Eric Avebury, *Kurdistan Report*, London, October 1993, p. 3.

4. Stated by Gurbutelli Ersöz, editorial board member for *Özgür Gündem*, Istanbul, reprinted in *Kurdistan Report*, London, October 1993, pp. 6–7.

5. Jonathan Rugman, 'Atrocity Times', *Guardian*, 23 August 1993.

6. Serdar Çelik, *Türk Kontra-Gerillasi – ölüm makinasi* (The Turkish Contra-Guerrilla – Death Machine) Ülkem Presse, Germany, 1995, pp. 117–21, 152.

7. Ibid., pp. 412–13.

8. British Medical Association, *Medicine Betrayed: The participation of Doctors in Human Rights Abuses*, Zed Books, London 1992; see pp. 46–7, 51, 58, 161, 162 and 173.

9. Interview recorded, October 1992, Insight Television News, Kurds – Turkey and Northern Iraq.

10. See *Kurdistan Report*, London, issue 14, April/May 1993, p. 27.

11. The case brought by Şemse Önen, Ercan Önen's sister, was declared admissable by the European Commission of Human Rights (ECHR) (Application No. 22876/93) and registered on 4 November 1993. Source: ECHR Decision. 15 May 1995.

12. Aydin Engin, 'The State is Turning a Blind Eye to the Hizbullah', *Kurdistan Report*, April / May 1993, London, pp 24–6.

13. Önen, op. cit.; European Commission of Human Rights, 15 May 1995.

14. This case was also taken to the European Commission of Human Rights, which found against Turkey.

15. Faysal Dağli, *Birakuji*, Belge Yayinlari, Istanbul, 1994.

16. *Socialist Party of Kurdistan Programme*, KSP Publications, October 1993, pp. 8–10.

17. Interviewed in London, 20 August 1995.

18. *Seyda Alpşen* (Roj newspaper).

19. David McDowall, *The Kurds, a Nation Denied*, Minority Rights Group, London, 1992, p. 44.

20. *Seyda Alpşen*.

21. Summary of the 'economic and differing viewpoints in Turkey' reproduced by permission of Ali Manaz, from a joint film proposal, *'The Kurds, Kizilbash and Communists'*, 1994.

7

Death by a thousand cuts:
sabotage of the enclave

In 1993, visiting 'Free Kurdistan' in northern Iraq after travelling through the oppressed Kurdish region under Turkish military rule came as a breath of fresh air. But the sense of exhilaration faded all too swiftly as evidence of the enclave's formidable problems impinged upon one's consciousness. As a result of the UN sanctions as well as the internal embargo imposed by Saddam on south Kurdistan, the economy was in ruins and the 'safe haven' in decay.

Although at the Khabur/Ibrahim Khalil border crossing the Kurds had introduced immigration procedures for entry clearance and established a public relations office, these facilities remained rudimentary and tentative, as if the Iraqi Kurds were always waiting to be reminded that in reality someone else was in charge. It was understandable.

The Kurdish enclave remained beneath the sword of the Turkish government. For as long as Khabur constituted the only lifeline to the enclave, the Turks could continue to impose distasteful conditions on the Kurdish administration. In exchange for keeping the route open, Turkey demanded the co-operation of the Iraqi Kurds in Turkey's war with the PKK.

Travelling with Michael Ignatieff and crew across Iraqi Kurdistan in the spring of 1993, it was clear that considerable headway had been made with the reconstruction of villages. Most of the rebuilding appeared to have been concentrated in Bahdinan. Projects beyond Mergasor and further south through Heran, Qala Diza, Sayid Sadiq and Halabja were fewer. Even so, it was heartening to see how in so many areas where recently only broken stones and dynamited concrete had lain in heaps across the fields there were now villages once again and the revival of rural life. Maize, wheat and rice crops were maturing, flocks of sheep and herds of goats grazed; the desolation of the Kurdish countryside was almost a thing of the past.

In the towns too there had been progress. A new Kurdish infra-structure had been created. There was a Kurdish police force, a security network, law courts and, of course, the parliament. The Kurdish-led administration was relatively inexperienced and, deprived of external political recognition and assistance, the mistakes it made would be both painful and costly to the Kurdish people.

In May 1993, Saddam Hussein abolished the 25-dinar note, the currency most in use in Kurdistan. Saddam gave the Iraqi people only five days during which to exchange their old money for the new Baghdad issue note. He promptly closed the internal borders with Kurdistan, as well as those with external states, cutting Kurdistan off from the rest of the country, and left the Kurds to watch helplessly as their money and savings were literally lost overnight.

That morning following this announcement the main streets of Arbil were chaotic with Kurds mobbing the banks to register their 25-dinar notes before the expiry of the deadline. The scene remained unchanged during the next four days. But after registering their old 25-dinar notes there was no guarantee of compensation. Chaos ensued. The abolition of the dinar note threw the economy into confusion and inspired the fear that other denominations currently in use might suffer the same fate.

The Kurdish parliament in session

The Kurdish parliament had been debating the possibility of using US dollars, Syrian pounds or even Turkish lira as a safer form of currency for Kurdistan. It continued to assemble in the former seat of Saddam's 'Autonomous Region' parliament in Arbil (Hewler). This was a multi-storey rough-cast concrete and stone edifice built in keeping with a style of architecture much favoured by the Ba'ath for its public buildings. The parliament building was set at a considerable distance from the main road, although highly visible from it. Surrounded by ornamental flower beds, it was intersected by a broad asphalt approach which swept up to the highly polished black marble steps at the main entrance. Immediately within the large double doors was an area for conducting body and baggage searches and depositing weapons. After security procedures had been completed a visitor could be admitted to the front foyer.

The parliament building was located within the old security neigh-bourhood, close to the headquarters of the Istikhbarat and Ba'ath party offices. Most of the security buildings had been torn apart by the Kurds during the uprising and the second wave of liberation, anxious to rid themselves of the ghosts of Ba'athist terror.

The 25-dinar crisis was just erupting when we arrived to follow the debate in the Kurdish parliament. In the modern assembly chamber the ministers soberly took their seats and started discussing how to tackle the dilemma. The influence and authority of the leaders of the two main parties, Massoud Barzani of the KDP and Jalal Talabani of the PUK, was still supreme, although the pair were not members of the parliament and both were in the United States at the time the monetary crisis occurred. Their hard-pressed ministers at home were convinced that their case would be pressed at the US State Department, because the leaders were there.

Parliament was in session. The first speaker cleared his throat and introduced his question: 'about the proposal of the parliament to open a bank abroad for the Kurdistan region'. The parliamentary speaker adjusted his microphone judiciously and replied:

> Mr Barzani and Mr Talabani are now there [abroad] talking with the UN about these problems, meeting with the Foreign Ministry and the American government, with European MPs and the UN. That is the situation at present. The Kurdistan government hasn't taken any further decision as yet but we are doing everything possible to counteract the Iraqi government's decision. The Ministers' Assembly decided to record all names and numbers of the 25-dinar note through the Ministry of Finance in all of our banks. The banks have been given special forms to record the quantity and precise numbers of the dinar notes, so as to block any currency coming in later from Jordan, Turkey or Iran, by those who might hold on to it and try to bring it into Kurdistan once the problem is resolved. Our compensatory measures will only apply to those Kurdish people who have lost their money, and whose names and currency note numbers have been recorded. That is what we have done to date. We hope that it will prove productive. We have also taken precautions with workers' salaries, and are considering how best to now administer the money in Kurdistan.

UN sanctions and Saddam's embargo

Because 'Free' Kurdistan was still officially part of Iraq, it remained subject to UN sanctions like the rest of Iraq. Turkey was able to refuse passage to any equipment or supplies not constituting humanitarian aid across its borders. In the isolated Kurdish enclave, the situation reflected a steady economic decline, coupled with increasing political intrigue, and social insecurity. The legacy of a century of political disease coupled with fresh economic hardship was to produce a virulent social illness which had already started to gnaw into the heart of daily life.

Part of the sickness stemmed from the widening gap between the powerful and the powerless and with this, the gap between rich and poor. While the upper class and the *nouveau riche* traders and profiteers were able to feast on meat and vegetables and drink imported spirits almost every night of the week, the poor could no longer find the cash to buy adequate supplies of flour and rice to feed their families. An unhealthy degree of corruption began to undermine trade in the markets; many unscrupulous merchants and smugglers, ex-*jash*, wealthy *aghas*, and opportunists from Turkey, Iran and other parts of Iraq were able to profit under the new Kurdish administration. Unlike the Ba'ath, the Kurds did not yet carry out executions for hoarding goods or raising prices. The merchants therefore felt little risk of punishment and duly operated with a free hand at the expense of ordinary people.

Part of the insecurity at this time also arose as a result of daily reminders that Saddam was still in power and unnervingly nearby. The blockade was weakening social and political relations between the Kurds, as intended. The government had cut the municipal electricity supply to Kurdistan. In Dohuk province, the towns of Zakho and Dohuk, and every point between, had been deprived of electricity since the onset of autumn. After February 1994, a small amount of electricity was supplied on an irregular basis by Turkey. Before that time, the power went on and off according to Baghdad's whim. Afterwards, the Turks played with it in the same fashion.

Ironically, most of the region's electricity is generated from within Kurdistan itself – from Dokan and Darbendikhan (not including the Mosul generator, which lies outside the liberated area) – but supply lines conducted it directly into the area still under Iraqi government control. The regime could therefore choose whether or not to resupply this power back to Kurdistan. The Kurdish administration needed to be able to re-route the supply from Dokan and Darbendikhan directly to their own towns in order to control the electricity themselves. But certain vital components required for the hydroelectric stations could not be obtained because of the UN sanctions. The result of the sanctions was widespread hardship affecting every aspect of people's lives in south Kurdistan; not only electricity but fuel, food, medicine and heating materials were in desperately short supply. Whatever got in was sure to be expensive.

Telecommunications by and large remained confined to individual towns; there were few lines between the cities and even fewer to the outside world. Satellite phones were rare, and so costly that only visiting foreigners, party officials and the wealthy could afford to use them. Kurdistan, in fact, needed to be separately connected with the European satellite network in order to end its isolation from the rest of the world. But three years after the Gulf war, there was not even a postal service; all international mail had to be carried outside by individuals and posted abroad.

Kurdistan possesses oil (although it has never been granted the right to it). Within the Kurdish area there are a number of wells; these fall within the area under Allied protection. Kirkuk itself is but one point on the broad grid which maps a subterranean oil lake running from Zakho to Chemchemal. This lake can be accessed from several other outlets aside from Kirkuk and Mosul. Yet all along Kurdistan has been forced to depend on Baghdad for fuel.

From October 1991 onwards, the Iraqi government charged Kurdistan five times the rate it charged the rest of the country for oil supplies. The government also refused to supply fuel of any kind in adequate quantities per capita of the population of the enclave. This problem could have been resolved sooner by uncapping those wells deliberately sealed off by the regime, installing filtration and pumping equipment and thereafter meeting the needs of the Kurdish region. Again, the main practical obstacle was the UN sanctions which prohibited the supply and transportation of vital equipment into Kurdistan. The politics of Kurdish oil are even more complicated.

Sardar Pishdari, an independent figure, had previously carried out extensive research into the oil venture. Pishdari was obstructed politically from being able to realise his dream of providing Kurdish oil to the Kurds, despite having brought several international experts on oil to Kurdistan. The delegates jointly participated in the opening of a number of the capped Kurdish wells and oil literally flowed across the ground. Finally, however, the Kurdish political parties presented the main challenge to Pishdari's endeavours; the parties wished to control the oil themselves, competitively rather than jointly on a national basis.

A simple airport might also have been built adjacent to the military airfields in use within Kurdistan. An airport would have made it easier for vital supplies to reach the people most in need, and would also have helped link Kurdistan with the outside world, making it less dependent upon its hostile neighbours. But the outside world showed little readiness to assist in Kurdistan's development and kept the Kurds living hand to mouth. In itself, this was as effective a tool as Ba'athist terror and torture in keeping the population subjugated.

The Iraqi army maintained its forces along the boundaries of the liberated Kurdish area, their tanks just in view of the population, firing off occasional rounds of artillery into Kurdish settlements or staging raids to pillage and destroy crops, keeping the inhabitants of the 'border' areas in a perpetual state of insecurity.

Life in Iraq had never been like this before. The standard of living in the region had been high. People had been able to prosper financially and to share the country's wealth. Most public buildings were well constructed and of sound design; the roads were good, as were communications. But this was almost completely destroyed during both the Iran–Iraq war and the Gulf war.

It was not, however, just general economic and administrative impediments that blocked progress. International political safeguards failed to materialise; there were no foreign financial packages for development or investment in Kurdistan; there were not even any regional agreements. Rather, there were only temporary understandings (memorandum of understanding or MOU) and an unsteady and inadequate supply of humanitarian aid, renegotiated every few months when sanctions against Iraq came up for renewal. The MOU was:

> based on the principle that humanitarian aid requires the consent of the sovereign state involved. This allowed Baghdad a significant say in setting the terms on which UN and NGO assistance is provided … The terms of MOU renewal have increasingly restricted UN and NGO access and freedom to operate. Under the April 1991 agreement and first renewal in December 1991, the UN theoretically had access to the whole country, and was permitted to establish sub-offices outside Baghdad. But the UNHCR failed in its efforts to establish such an office in Kirkuk, which might have allowed the repatriation of 150,000–200,000 Kurds who had fled that governorate during the uprising.[1]

There were also signs of increasing Western indifference as the situation in Kurdistan worsened. Of the entire aid budgeted for Kurdistan, 95 per cent benefited Baghdad and not the Kurdish region. The Iraqi government continued to profit from the exchange rate, and NGOs lost enormous sums of money. A better alternative would have been to buy supplies in neighbouring countries and send them to Kurdistan. If UN sanctions could have been restricted in application and waived in the unique case of the Kurdish enclave, Kurdistan would not have been kept dependent on humanitarian aid. As it was, sanctions affected the civilian population, not the regime against whom they had been imposed.

Large Kurdish cities remained host to thousands of refugee families unable to return to areas still under Iraqi government control. Hundreds of children were growing up in camps, compounds, and in temporary shelter in unhealthy environments such as the former security buildings. These children received no education at all and spent their days selling cigarettes, sweets, seeds, roots and wildflowers, shining shoes, foraging and begging. The same was true of the destroyed village areas.

The majority of children able to attend school sat in classrooms which lacked either air-conditioning in the stifling days of summer (temperatures can exceed 40°C), or heating throughout the freezing days of winter. Although education in the region was free of Ba'ath Party censorship and thereby culturally free, Kurdish schools lacked materials and used the regime's old texts, unable to find the money to reprint new books. No international funding had been allocated for education. As a consequence education at all levels was handicapped.

State terrorism and sabotage

The Baghdad regime paid terrorist agents between 1,000 and 100,000,000 dinar to deliver bombs, plant explosive devices, assassinate foreigners and perform other acts of sabotage. In 1994, the fee for killing a foreigner was $10,000 a head. Disaffected elements among the local population saw it in their interest to take advantage of Saddam's offers to disrupt the Kurdish administration. But as Kurdish security improved, local citizens began to inform against those behaving suspiciously. Saboteurs were often intercepted before an attack occurred. But not always.

After Arbil, Sulaimaniya is the second largest city in south Kurdistan. A bustling dusty metropolis, Sulaimaniya boasted an almost entirely Kurdish ethnic population of around one million people, swollen still further to one and a half million by the refugees from Kirkuk and the destroyed villages throughout the province. The main urban highways of Sulaimaniya were laid out in long straight avenues decorated with that peculiar type of sculpture and monument characteristic of Saddam's Iraq. Much of this was later either adapted to Kurdish purposes or desecrated. Among the monuments left intact was a large arch constructed of stone blocks erected at a major junction on the two-lane highway from Chemchemal into the city. This arch formerly displayed a cameo inset of the president; I remembered having photographed it when I first visited Sulaimaniya under Ba'ath control in 1989. After the liberation of Sulaimaniya the Kurds replaced Saddam's portrait with a bas-relief in black stone of Mulla Mustafa Barzani, with a portrait of his late son, Idris, killed in battle by government forces in 1987 on the reverse. (The Kurdish sculptor, Kosar Ahmed (23), who had made the relief and surrounding statuary, killed himself in May 1993 because of disillusion with the Kurdish regime. Even the statues would finally be destroyed in the rival fighting [*Hengaw*, May 1995].) Handsome, individually painted portraits of Kurdish patriots who fell as martyrs in the course of Kurdistan's long struggle watched over similarly prominent roadside sites throughout Iraqi Kurdistan. These were erected by each of the Kurdish parties and had become a source of competition between them, a reflection of the growing divisions within the Kurdistan Front as the respective parties began to vie for regional supremacy to the detriment of political unity.

Control of so busy a city as Sulaimaniya posed a considerable challenge to the parties as well as to the Kurdish administration. Trucks laden with explosives had just been intercepted when we reached town; one was carrying 50 kilos of TNT, the other 70 kilos. Kurdish security had intercepted numerous car-bombs and vehicles carrying TNT in the preceding months. These 'home-made' bombs – a mixture of TNT and shrapnel looking just like baker's dough and raisins – were rigged to air-conditioners, or stuffed into small plastic containers and attached to cars or the walls of buildings, to be triggered by remote control or detonated by timing devices. Faik Tawfiq, the KDP head of security in Sulaimaniya, retained a number of these lethal devices as exhibits in his office, evidence of the government's attempts to sabotage the enclave. Faik would produce these from locked cupboards, explaining the circumstances behind the capture of each item to enthralled audiences.

Another form of local sabotage had been the cutting, selling off or destruction of electric wires, power-lines, copper cable, road-making equipment, tractors and other equipment of value. Thousands of dollars worth of such goods were stolen and sold to Iran by the poor and the wealthy alike. While in Sulaimaniya, we sat in on the trial of two Kurdish men accused of stealing electric wiring – a serious crime given the economic and social stress in Kurdistan at the time. The case was conducted in both Kurdish and Arabic. On this occasion, the defendants were both acquitted on the basis of insufficient evidence. The judge might just as easily have made scapegoats of them.[2]

While Iraqi law was generally still observed in Kurdistan, articles passed by Saddam Hussein to terrorise the populace were being redrafted. The Kurdish parliament, in conjunction with international lawyers and consultants, sought to amend all laws which contravened fundamental human rights. According to Iraqi law, the Kurdish administration and all its supporters were guilty of treason. Any person proved to be supporting the Kurdish government could be punished with execution in Ba'ath-controlled Iraq.

The most conspicuous people in the new Kurdistan and those most at risk were the MPs, party leaders, prominent members of the main parties, their security and intelligence officials, and of course the NGOs and journalists working in Kurdistan. All these had a price on their heads. Simply to travel through town by car, to walk about in the streets or to wander through crowded places could prove fatal. Officials of the new Kurdistan were therefore surrounded by bodyguards; private cars were flanked by jeeps of armed peshmergas who accompanied them wherever they went. Prominent Kurds frequently went about in unmarked cars so as not to draw attention to themselves in the course of their every-day work. The Kurdish administration was especially vigilant when using the main roads in and out of town, or stretches of open highway where a hitman could stage an ambush.

In such a way Stuart Cameron, an Australian aid worker with CARE, was killed in January 1992, travelling on the Sulaimaniya–Chemchemal road. Cameron's movements had been observed by agents the day before his murder. Two months later, on 22 March 1992, Vincent Tollet, the co-ordinator of Handicap International, was shot dead in a similar attack on the road north of Sulaimaniya. Other people travelling in his vehicle were also injured. A spate of identical attacks was carried out on the personnel, offices and vehicles of most international organisations, including the UK Mines Advisory Group. Such attacks persisted throughout 1993 and by 1994 they had become so frequent that the UN guards asked for the Allied Forces to be recalled to Kurdistan to provide protection. Needless to say, the call went unheeded.

Iranian-sponsored sabotage

The steep rise of Islamic fundamentalism in Kurdistan was something quite unexpected before the imposition of UN sanctions. Iran, Saudi Arabia and Pakistan thereafter made concerted efforts through Hizbullah, as deployed in the Islamic Movement of Kurdistan (IMK), to gain a psychological hold over the Kurdish population, buying support with generous handouts of cash and carrying out bomb attacks on urban bookshops and in the universities, which stocked material considered hostile to the teachings of Islam. Women's groups, individual women and teaching staff in the schools and universities were also targeted.

Many poor families became dependent on the IMK simply to survive. Those who agreed to bear arms for the Islamic Movement were paid an attractive salary. Clashes between the Islamic fighters and the PUK began in December 1993. Before an agreement could be reached, 200 people had died.

This was something new for Kurdistan. In the past, religion had been a private and personal matter, and religion was largely kept separate from politics. While many peshmergas were strict and faithful Muslims who readily laid down their guns to observe the hours of prayer, the focus of their struggle had always been for their nation, not for *Jihad* (holy war) as with Hamas in Palestine or Hizbullah in Lebanon.

Iraqi Kurds who drove for us on various trips often took trouble to pray, even while driving. During the long working days when they felt it to be impractical to take time off, or they were unwilling to disrupt busy schedules, our peshmergas would recite their prayers silently to themselves without display, lips moving, eyes slightly narrowed, bowing forward over the steering wheel, reclining back again, bowing and reclining, as they mentally visualised the rites they would regularly perform when stationary. These Kurds would also pray whenever we stopped for food or rest. But they never discussed their religion, nor tried to draw attention to the fact that they were believers. Neither were we ever challenged to religious debate.

Yet the Islamic Republic of Iran had formally condemned the Kurdish administration as 'un-Islamic'. Iran issued regular warnings threatening further action over the 'godless and morally corrupt' situation in Iraqi Kurdistan. Like all Kurdistan's neighbours, Iran was equally determined to help curtail Kurdish freedom.

For several years the Islamic government had paid its agents handsomely to kill prominent Kurds belonging to dissident Iranian Kurdish parties. In 1993, a number of assassinations were carried out against Iranian Kurds in Iraq, Turkey and various European countries. The *pasdars* pursued Kurdish families deep into Iraq after attacking and destroying their villages in Iran, forcing thousands of Kurdish villagers living along the sensitive border area to evacuate their homes and seek sanctuary within the Kurdish enclave. Iranian intelligence similarly pursued political opponents of the regime in other foreign countries, where they were killed with letter-bombs, shot or 'disappeared'.

Given the inaccessibility of much of the mountain area where the Iranian Kurdish partisans were operative, Iran relied on heavy artillery and aerial bombardment. The latter proved devastating. Only after several waves of Iranian bombardment inside the 'safe haven' did the international community respond by issuing condemnations and warning Iran to desist. Kurdish sources alleged that the primary purpose of the Iranian attacks, like those of the Turks, was to undermine the *de facto* Kurdish state blossoming in Iraq. Air strikes were almost certainly carried out with the consent of the Iraqi government to penetrate Iraqi air-space. The raids occurred over an area of 180 miles, sometimes hitting Iraqi Kurdish villages, rather than the partisans' bases, which were not located in such areas at the time the attacks occurred.

The Iranian army subsequently took control of a six-mile stretch of territory in Kurdistan near Penjwin, and occupied it for a number of days before the Kurdish parliament took action. Representatives of the parliament called upon representatives of the Iranian regime to hold talks. The British and French governments were also called.

Kurdish partisans in Iran

The persecution and suffering of Kurds on both sides of the Iraq–Iran border served to bring Iranian Kurds closer to the Kurds of Iraq. The Kurdish Democratic Party of Iran (KDPI) had been the first Kurdish national party to be established in Iran. The KDPI achieved a historic victory in the founding of the Kurdish Republic in Mahabad in 1946, under Qazi Mohammed. A year later, with the withdrawal of Soviet support, the Kurdish Republic collapsed. Qazi Mohammed, his brother and cousin were hung in Mahabad's main square on the orders of the Shah. Qazi Mohammed still holds a precious place in the hearts of most Iranian Kurds, not only a hallowed martyr but a symbol of Kurdish hope.

Led by the late Abdurrahman Qassemlou until his murder by Iranian agents in 1989, the KDPI split in two following the party's eighth congress in 1987. Members opposing a number of issues contingent upon Qassemlou's leadership broke away under the leadership of Jalil Gardani. The breakaway faction adopted the name of KDPI–Revolutionary Leadership (KDPI–RL). Both factions continued to fight a guerrilla war against the Iranian regime and, until recently, against one another.

Following the murders of both Qassemlou and his successor, Sadegh Sharafkandi, by agents of the Iranian regime, the KDPI grew more determined in pursuing an armed struggle. A number of prominent members from both factions of the KDPI have been assassinated in the past five years. Both wings have continued to fight the regime militarily and are the largest of the Kurdish Iranian groups to have done so. Kurdish sources estimate that more than forty thousand Kurdish civilians and some five thousand cadres and fighters from the KPDI have lost their lives in the conflict to date. Approximately three hundred Iranian Kurdish villages have been destroyed. Losses on the government side have also been high, the *pasdars* being less familiar with mountain warfare than the partisans.

The size of the Iranian military presence was estimated at around two hundred thousand armed forces, comprising the army and the *pasdars*. They established more than three thousand bases across Kurdistan, and at the time of writing in 1995 still maintain control of the Kurdish region within Iran. Their bases are often quite small, being manned by groups of no more than thirty armed forces, machine-guns trained on the remaining Kurdish villages and main thoroughfares. But support is said to be waning within the army for the Iranian regime. Many Iranian soldiers chose to desert the army after having had a closer acquaintance with the Kurdish resistance. This has had a significant effect on the level and nature of aggression.

Since its foundation, the KDPI had been committed to the goal of autonomy for the Kurds in Iran. The party believed that autonomy offered the only solution to the Kurdish question in Iran, given the prevailing circumstances within the country and the attitude of the West. But they allowed that any change in this status quo could in turn affect their policy on the issue itself.

In 1993, the Iranian government began building a new military road in the mountains along its border with Iraq, the better to mobilise its army against the Kurds. Many were forced to flee to escape the escalation of violence in the area. The situation received virtually no mention in the press because of the effective blackout of reporting by Iran and the difficulty of access to the Kurdish region.

On 15 May 1993 Michael Ignatieff and I, together with crew, arrived to film the KDPI's political headquarters in Boleh, Iraqi Kurdistan, high on the slopes of Mount Qandil astride the Iraq–Iran border. Our visit coincided with a respite from Iranian bombing missions against Boleh and other targets in the area, including the KDPI–RL's base at Qala Seyda.

About thirty families still lived in the alpine village of Boleh at this time. On 13 March 1993, six Iranian warplanes had crossed the border and bombed this camp and a number of villages. Six people had died, several others had been injured and extensive damage had been inflicted both on Kurdish homes and on the KDPI's Azadî (Freedom) hospital nearby, run by Médecins du Monde and Aide Médicale Internationale. The Iranians used shells containing cluster bombs supplied by America. Several of these, which stood as high as a man, had been upended and fixed into the ground as both a memorial to the Kurdish martyrs and a testimony to Iranian intentions. Although the French medical teams in Boleh had escaped unhurt, one hospitalised patient had been killed and another partisan left permanently disabled; he was now bedridden and lived in a small cabin within the hospital compound.

We had already been given a tour of the KPDI's politburo, situated at the top of the road amongst tall trees overlooking the houses of the village. It was a well-established place; the KDPI had allegedly had a base there for the past twenty years. After sharing a meal with Mulla Abdurrahman, who was in charge at Boleh in the absence of Mostafa Hedjiri, the general secretary, we completed our tour of Boleh camp. Several KDPI partisans wore photographs of the late Dr Qassemlou and Dr Sharafkandi on their ammunition belts. The partisans took shifts to man a large anti-aircraft gun close to the hospital, its sights focused on the mountain tops nearby which constituted the border here with Iran.

The partisans explained how when the first Iranian attack had come, they had not even had time to operate this gun, so swiftly and unexpectedly had the warplanes swooped over.

But the KDPI generally appeared well organised. Several KPDI families were also living at Shewaraz, four hours' journey south, a mere stone's throw from the Iranian border. In practice this had proved an easy shelling distance for the Iranian government, which launched several punitory attacks on Shewaraz. The government had massed 100,000 troops along this border. Shewaraz was subsequently bombed on 19, 20, 22 and 30 June. The villagers we met in May were later forced to evacuate their homes and move deeper into the Kurdish enclave. Boleh was also bombed twice more on 18 May, only three days after our visit, a further three times on 27 May, and again on 28 May, 1 June, 14 June, 15 June and 30 June. The Iranian Kurds were evacuated. More than thirty other Iranian Kurdish villages were also regularly shelled and bombed after 19 April 1993; and an estimated ten thousand Iranian Kurds were forced into exile.[3]

In the Spring of 1993, when Iranian incursions into Iraqi Kurdistan began, the KDPI broke with their former policy of isolating their struggle from that of the Kurds in other parts of the homeland and supported the (Iraqi) Kurdish parliament. It was in their interests to do so, as they were no longer able to move about effectively inside Iran, having been forced to vacate their bases along the border.

In December 1993, Iran concluded a new security agreement with Turkey. In return for co-operation against the PKK, Turkey agreed to deny refuge to Iranian dissident groups, including the Mujahadeen Khalq, which derived its membership and support not only from Kurds and Persian Iranians, but also from Azerbaijanis and other minority groups which together make up the population of contemporary Iran.

Tehran Radio announced that a joint Iranian–Turkish security committee had agreed on a mechanism for anti-guerrilla action on their border at a meeting in Ankara the previous month. Turkish Foreign Minister Hikmet Çetin said the accord allowed Turkish observers to *watch* Iranian military operations against the PKK inside Iran. Iranian Foreign Minister Ali Akbar Velayati and Çetin said they hoped to meet again soon with Syrian Foreign Minister Farouq al-Shara in Turkey, in what would be the third such tripartite discussion.[4] Agents of the Iranian regime murdered a KDPI–RL cadre, Taha Kirmanj, in Çorum, Turkey on 4 January 1994 and on 18 January a letter-bomb badly injured Abubakr Hedayati, a KDPI committee member, in Stockholm, Sweden.

Turkey also conducted renewed aerial bombing missions across the border into 'Free Kurdistan', ostensibly 'pursuing PKK guerrillas', while causing death and injury to Iraqi Kurds and physical damage to the enclave. Typical of its two-pronged policy towards the Kurds and the West, in order to assuage Western opinion but also retain tactical leverage, Turkey assented to a further extension of Allied surveillance flights above the 36th parallel in Kurdistan operating from Turkish territory at Incirlik. It was thus able to maintain its own military and intelligence foothold in northern Iraq.

Within the ring of crocodile teeth

By this time, the Kurdish administration therefore faced not only the individual, but also the joint aggressions of the governments of Iraq, Turkey and Iran. Turkey always sought to justify its attacks on the enclave as pursuit of the PKK, while Iran did the same with regard to the KDPI and other dissident groups. Syria, on the other hand, although helpful to Iraqi Kurds generally, and logistically supportive of the PKK, remained enigmatic and unpredictable.

The British government, acting purely in its own interests, continued to warn the Kurdish leadership not to aspire to independence but to seek federalism within Iraq. The Kurds were urged to renegotiate with Saddam Hussein, also with the object of placating neighbouring Turkey, the intimate ally of NATO which, as a fellow member of the group, was privy to all Allied intelligence concerning the Kurds and the 'safe haven'.

Saddam, the victorious war criminal, was being allowed sufficient rope to slip back into the international community. The situation appeared lethal to the Kurds, at a time in their history when there was more than ever to lose.

Notes

1. Sarah Graham-Brown, *Middle East Report: The Iraqi Sanctions Dilemma – Intervention, Sovereignty and Responsibiliity*, pp. 6–7, No. 193, March–April 1995.
2. Part of this trial was filmed and shown in *Blood and Belonging*, BBC 2, 1993.
3. Chronology of Iranian air and land attacks in Iraqi Kurdistan, *Bulletin of the KDPI*, pp. 32–3, Paris, June–July 1993.
4. Reuters, Ankara, 20 December 1993.

8

The war of the colours

The enemy within

By 1994, menace and danger in south Kurdistan had become like a virus in the air, sensed but unseen, striking at random. As a foreigner, you were now advised not to walk or travel anywhere alone. But frequently, of necessity, you would; you could not find spare bodyguards to accompany you, nor would there be a vehicle available to travel in, so you would walk a few blocks alone away from the NGO neighbourhoods, through the crowded bazaars or across an open field to contact someone. Foreigners working in south Kurdistan could now *feel* the $10,000 price tag on their heads, a sum confirmed by the UN in Baghdad as the going rate which Saddam was offering his assassins to kill a foreign NGO, journalist, or even a member of the UN Guards.

Sunbathing off-duty in the high-walled rose garden of the UNGCI 'Danish House', Tom Olsen, the team leader for Zakho, explained to me that the UN had suffered 151 attacks against both their personnel and premises in the first four months of 1994, sometimes with fatal consequences. Iraqi agents had attacked one of the UNGCI minibuses within the Kurdish-controlled checkpoint near Arbil the previous month. Two Austrian guards were seriously wounded; one remained paralysed. Their bus had been sprayed by machine-gun fire from artillery hidden in trenches recently dug by the Iraqis inside 'Free Kurdistan' itself. The UN guards were dissatisfied with the security impasse and claimed they needed additional protection if they were to carry on. The guards knew they had become the prime targets of the regime. Many were eager to return home before renewing their contracts for a further term in Kurdistan. UN now stands for 'United Nothing' one of them laughed and the rest nodded their heads in grim agreement.

Black banners raised above the walls of NGO and Kurdish political party offices flapped grimly in the wind, reminders of the 'accidental deaths' of the MCC (Military Command Centre) helicopter victims a month before, and of German journalist Lissie Schmidt, friend of the

Kurds, assassinated along with her bodyguard by two Iraqi agents hired by the regime in Kirkuk. One of these black banners, suspended outside Zakho prison, read: 'In fact you get martyrdom for the sake of humanity and human rights.' Such was the gloom. I thought of Lissie with a weary sadness. We had often met up as our paths crossed in various parts of Kurdistan. Now my Kurdish friends were warning me: 'Don't be like Lissie. Be careful. Don't trust anybody.' But how could you be careful? It seemed nobody could take care of anything any more in south Kurdistan. The mood of hope had gone from the 'safe haven', and in its place I recognised desperation, violence and uncertainty as the West failed to tackle the political causes at the heart of the Kurdish conflict in both northern Iraq and Turkey.

By the spring of 1994, when I returned alone to Kurdistan, the 'unsafe haven' in Zakho was seething with intelligence operatives – agents from many hostile nations, neighbouring states with a stake in the future of Kurdistan. Cars with Turkish number-plates, or no plates at all, openly cruised the neighbourhoods of Zakho and Dohuk filled with Turkish plainclothes police – the MİT. Well-informed local people could tell you that the Kurdish Public Relations Offices were likely to be infiltrated by agents on the Turkish government's payroll during your visit.

On the roof of the Turkish Red Crescent's headquarters in Dohuk, armed gunmen maintained constant vigil, fingers ready on the trigger. The walls were reinforced by sandbags and the mood of the place did not suggest humanitarian benevolence towards the Kurds; it seemed more like a fortress ready to face a siege.

Sanctions and political turmoil

Saddam Hussein was to be congratulated for so effective a disruption as his imposition of the internal embargo upon Kurdish-controlled northern Iraq in October 1991. After three years, Kurdistan was literally starving to death. His plan was finally coming to fruition. As a further extension of UN sanctions against Iraq came up for renewal, it was certain there could be little improvement in the living conditions of ordinary civilians. There were deeply troubling political consequences. With so great an economic catastrophe hitting Kurdistan, most ordinary Kurds became desperate to survive. They could now understand, as Saddam had done all along, that freedom on an empty stomach was not true freedom. 'Free Kurdistan' had become a prison once again.

The daily reality had for months been one of increasing deprivation. There was virtually no employment and even for those few in work, wages were inadequate to support their families. The cracks in the economy grew greater as the gap between the rich and the poor further widened. Traders still profited from the double embargo, selling their products in the free market at prices that only the 5 per cent upper class could afford. The poor no longer ate meat or vegetables but subsisted on rice, bread, dates and potatoes.

With the Iraqi dinar at an all time low of D75 to the US dollar, families were lucky if they could earn 10 dinar a day – sufficient only for a half-kilo of rice or of runner beans. By this stage many families had been forced to sell every last item of furniture – even the doors and glass window panes from their houses – to feed their families for another month, another week, or another day. The few remaining NGOs in Kurdistan, including the UNHCR, UNICEF, WFP, Save the Children and Qandil, did not have the budgets to resolve the problem.

The Swedish health project, Qandil, was treating a monthly average of close on four hundred cases of severe malnutrition in babies and young children in a single clinic alone, seeing severe marasmus and kwashiorkor. With as many as between four and sixteen children in a single family, survival had become difficult. Virtually no birth control is practised in Kurdistan, for religious as well as social reasons, and a new baby arrives hard on the heels of the last. On the day I attended Qandil's supplementary feeding centre in Zakho, a total of 90 women and children were treated in a taxing six hours. Three other Qandil teams with doctors and health workers providing care to outlying Kurdish villages returned to the Zakho clinic to report the same problems. Mothers turned up at the feeding centre with pairs of twins wasting away before their eyes. Women's health was widely deteriorating, with goitre, protein and mineral deficiencies and anaemia becoming prevalent.

The situation worsened. In the spring of 1994 an estimated ten thousand Kurds fled attacks on their villages by the Turkish army to seek sanctuary in south Kurdistan (northern Iraq) and elsewhere. Turkish warplanes had continued their bombing raids across the border while ground forces intensified the campaign of destruction against Kurdish villages and wooded areas within Turkey. The aim of the Turks was not only to isolate the guerrillas from the Kurdish population, but to de-populate the whole of Turkish Kurdistan by forcibly driving out its inhabitants. (see chapter 9).

Political suicide in south Kurdistan

Kurdish political ties, which once derived primarily from tribal affinity to prominent families, allegiance to aghas (wealthy landowners) and to sheikhs (religious leaders), gradually evolved into widespread popular support for various Kurdish political parties or political movements, although the Kurdish 'clans' continued to exert a degree of political influence in the region.[1]

The Kurdish elections of May 1992, held in 'Free Kurdistan', left regional power divided 50/50 between the KDP and the PUK, and contributed to the decades' old divisions and rivalries between the two parties. After some months, local Kurds began to refer to the overt manifestation of internal tensions as the 'war of the colours', as the two main parties vied for ultimate political supremacy in Free Kurdistan – the green flags and green-painted buildings of Jalal Talabani's PUK competing with the yellow banners and paintwork of the KDP.

Background to internal war

When the Barzani movement and its rebellions were crushed by the Iraqi government with the help of British airpower in 1945, Mulla Mustafa Barzani had been obliged to withdraw to Iran. There he was very much perceived to be an agent of the British. The Russians who controlled the province of Azerbaijan held much the same view of him. For this reason KDPI leader Qazi Mohammed had not at first conferred a position of any importance upon Mulla Mustafa, but instead kept the Barzanis in a village on the border. Relations between the two were promoted for the sake of political strength and unity by Ibrahim Ahmad. Ahmad was head of the KDP's programme affairs in 1951 and went on to become secretary general in 1953–64. He held the office of KDP politburo branch secretary-general in 1964–70.

The rivalry between the KDP and the PUK dates back to this period. From the outset, the KDP comprised two distinct and largely incompatible elements: the progressive urban wing led by Ibrahim Ahmad, and the traditional rural tribal wing led by Mulla Mustafa Barzani.

The uneducated masses needed a folk hero, and Barzani had stood against the British army and fought so many wars that he had become larger than life. Realising this, the politburo helped make Barzani a figurehead and ended up becoming his victims. Seeking to then unify the Kurds under a political leadership the politburo came in conflict with Mulla Mustafa, who joined with the aghas and landlords and pushed Ibrahim Ahmad, Jalal Talabani and their supporters into Iran. The 90 per cent of Kurds who lived in the shadow of the Barzani myth did not comprehend the politburo's intentions – or indeed know anything about them; consequently, when the politburo members were driven to Iran, they were charged with trying to uncrown Barzani, the hero in the public mind, and were easily portrayed as traitors.

Barzani had become the obstacle to reform and the politburo used the Ba'ath to re-arm and follow the road of nationalism by going to Baghdad. In their attempts to reform the tribes they attacked the aghas who, as fellow feudalists, joined Barzani for protection. These were the same tribes which had expelled the politburo when their interests were threatened.[2]

The politburo returned to Barzani in 1965, but the chief sought to punish them for their recent disloyalty. Although escape plans were made the politburo's associates betrayed them and Barzani was made aware of their hiding place; they had little alternative but to flee to Baghdad until 1969.

After the collapse of the Kurdish rebellion in 1975, this essentially dissident group within the KDP felt that Barzani had failed the movement once again. One hundred and fifty thousand peshmergas had told Barzani they were still willing to carry on and fight, whether he wished to stay or to step down, so long as they did not surrender to Baghdad. Although Barzani wanted to avoid further bloodshed, he was also against any of his powerful commanders, such as Omar Dababa or Ali Askeri, suceeding him. He therefore sacrificed the Kurdish cause and threatened to fight the dissidents from Iran with Iranian support.

The PUK was subsequently formed in June 1975 from this group of disillusioned ex-members of the KDP, Talabani's 'Broad Line' (Hatî Giştî) and two other major groups, Komela Marxist-Leninist and Bizutnawayi Sosyalîst, the Socialist Movement. The PUK was led by Jalal Talabani, Ibrahim Ahmad's son-in-law and political heir. Massoud Barzani was invested with the leadership of the KDP in 1978. Massoud could have chosen to take things forward rather than accepting the political morass inherited from his father. When he failed to do this, the power contest between the KDP and the PUK went on until 1982, erupting once more in May 1994. There was no central power in Kurdistan, rather there were still one hundred little powers, the legacy of feudalism. Massoud continued to rally the feudalists.

Summary of the main players in Iraqi Kurdistan

The Kurdistan Democratic Party (KDP)

Led by Massoud Barzani, and strongest in Bahdinan, the KDP has retained a reputation for conservatism. It claims to respect the old Kurdish traditions but persists in striking up alliances with its enemy neighbours, all of which have betrayed the Kurdish liberation movement at any given opportunity. While Kurds generally acknowledge the political contributions made by Mulla Mustafa Barzani, the figurehead of the party, to the Kurdish movement, many also remember the dismay they felt when Barzani (influenced by his faith in Kissinger and the CIA) laid down his arms and and abandoned the struggle when he was defeated in 1975. His capitulation came at the moment of the Kurds' greatest power during the Kurdish revolution of 1970–75. At that juncture there had been an estimated one hundred and fifty thousand armed peshmergas fighting for Kurdish rights. With Iraq's subsequent signing of the Algiers Agreement with Iran, all the gains of the revolution were immediately lost.

Although at present there are only two Barzani family members in senior positions within the party – its leader, Massoud, and his nephew Nachirvan, one of the seven members of the politburo – sworn allegiance to Massoud Barzani is still a prerequisite of membership. The KDP's senior committee members claim to advocate the implementation of a democratic structure within the party. But many non-party members still accuse the KDP of being autocratic, arguing that Mulla Mustafa himself designated Massoud as his successor. He was not elected by the other members. Could a non-Barzani be elected to the leadership of the KDP?

In the Bahdinan region the KDP retains the majority of the Kurdish vote, while in the Soran region popular support is mostly for the PUK, with a third smaller section of the population split between the Communists, the Islamic Movement, Zahmet Keishan, the PKK and a handful of other parties and independents, as demonstrated both by the election results of 1992 and the internal fighting of 1994–95.

The Patriotic Union of Kurdistan (PUK)

Affiliations with the Patriotic Union of Kurdistan (PUK) and to its leader, Jalal Talabani, continue to derive from the urban classes of Sulaimaniya, Arbil (Hewler) and Koysanjaq. Many of its prominent members are wealthy business people, middle-class urban intellectuals influenced by the Arab nationalist movement, frequently anti-Communist in origin, and unemployed youths paid a basic wage to serve as *çekdars* (armed combatants). The PUK historically favoured military force to resolve problems and has regularly initiated armed conflict when in disagreement with other political groups. (The armed hostilities against the KDP in 1994–95 represent the sixth such round of internal fighting.)

For so long as Jalal Talabani, leader and creator of the party, continues to head the PUK the true extent of democracy within cannot easily be appraised. No internal party elections were held before 1992; politburo members were selected and appointed by Talabani himself. Talabani has proved to be a clever survivor. Despite the twists and turns of his career, he has remained firmly at the centre of control within his party. It is said among Kurds that no one can ever predict what Jalal Talabani will do next. A quick thinker, he is often called the Kurds' most successful diplomat. But his strategy has often outwardly involved the forging of short-term alliances that have perhaps not benefited the ordinary people of Kurdistan in the medium term. The PUK and the KDP attract a different type of supporter: the PUK's affiliates tend to appear more 'modern', less traditional in outlook and behaviour, urbanised.

The Iraqi Communist Party (ICP–Hizbi Shiyu'i)

The Iraqi Communist Party (ICP) drew considerable membership from the Kurdish population. Founded in 1934, it had been opposed both to the Iraqi monarchy and to British interference in the region.

Ismet Sherif Vanly, Kurdish writer and historian, summed up the ICP's position by explaining that the ICP had been opposed to the KDP's 'petty bourgeois Kurdish nationalism, its attacks on Iraq's "Arab king", its demands concerning "Kurdish oil" and its refusal to participate in "the common struggle" of the opposition parties'. The KDP in turn had criticised the ICP for its unhelpful stand on the issue of Kurdish national rights. But at the second congress of the ICP in 1956, the Communist Party changed its position and, in short, recognised the Kurdish nation.

Apart from the issue of 'Kurdish autonomy', the immediate goals of the KDP did not greatly differ from those of the Iraqi Communist Party or the National Democratic Party (NDP). The ICP and the NDP both set out to become mass parties and succeeded. The ICP had an entirely Kurdish 'Kurdistan section' and its leadership was ethnically mixed.[3]

The Iraqi government, the PUK and the KDP have all been in armed conflict with the ICP at various times. In 1973, twelve ICP cadres who had been students in Moscow had just returned to Kurdistan via Zakho when they 'disappeared'. At the time, the Iraqi Ba'ath government and the ICP were both coalition members of the National Front under the influence of the USSR. The Ba'athists had signed a pledge of 20–years' friendship with Moscow in exchange for arms and support. The ICP accused the KDP's Kurdish security police in Dohuk, the Parastin, of killing the twelve missing cadres. However, other witnesses present at the time recall how, although KDP military commander Isa Swar had been accused of the murders, the KDP's own internal inquiry concluded that the killings had been carried out by Ba'ath Party agents, also strong in the area at that date. This was also the moment when the USSR turned its back on the Kurds and openly supported the Ba'ath Party. The ICP rejected the Kurdish national movement and remained allied with the Ba'athists until 1979. The ICP went on to became a member of the Kurdistan Front in 1988. Twelve members of the PKSK were killed on 2 November 1995, near Koysanjak, by PUK militia.

In 1993 a group of communist intellectuals of Kurdish origin, including poet Rafiq Sabir, split from the ICP after criticising Aziz Muhammad's leadership. They formed the PKSK (Partîya Karî Serxwebûna Kurdistan or Working Party for the Independence of Kurdistan), which advocated post-Glasnost socialist reforms.[4]

The Kurdistan Communist Party

The KCP was established as a separate branch of the ICP and took its own decisions in the Kurdish region after 1993, although it remained allied to the mother party. It retained the support of many of its original Kurdish members and central committee leaders who refused to ally themselves with either the KDP or PUK following the elections of May 1992, sticking to their old political values despite the end of the Cold War and the collapse of the Soviet Union.

The Kurdistan Socialist Party (Iraq)

'When the revolution suffered its setback in 1975,' recalls Mahmoud Othman, former leader of the now disbanded Socialist Party, 'we cadres formed the KDP Preparatory Committee, as we had disagreed with Barzani's decision to end the revolution. We had been in Iran at the time and now returned to Kurdistan. In August 1979, we relocated in Syria and with a number of prominent supporters from the Kurdish Socialist Movement, one of the two main alliances in the PUK, we formed the Socialist Party.'[5] The party went on to become one of the eight main parties in the coalition under the Kurdistan Front in the 1980s. The KSP was led by the late Rasul Mamand after 1991 until it formed a joint leadership with PASOK for the elections in Iraqi Kurdistan of May 1992. Following the elections

it was expanded to include the KPDP and in August 1992 all three formed a new party – the Kurdistan Unity Party (KUP: *Partî Yekgirtîa Kurdistan*), which temporarily retained a three-member leadership body in lieu of a single leader. While both the KPDP and PASOK were dissolved after this unity, the KSP-I continued to operate under the leadership of Rasul Mamand, who had refused to join the KUP. The considerably smaller KSP-I was itself dissolved in December 1992, when Rasul Mamand joined the PUK as a member of its political bureau.[6]

Mamand's body was returned to Kurdistan from the UK in April 1994 after his death from heart failure. The funeral procession stretched from Zakho to Amadiya.

Kurdish Socialist Party (PASOK)

Founded in Kirkuk in 1975 after the defeat of the KDP by Kurdish intellectuals Ahmad Herdi, Sherko Bekas and Azad Mustafa, PASOK defended the ideal of a Greater Kurdistan. After its first congress it assembled a force of its own peshmergas and undertook armed operations in Sulaimaniya and Arbil, particularly within the universities. It joined the National Democratic Front in 1982 and the Kurdistan Front which superseded it in May 1988. After its 1991 congress, it changed its name to PDSK (Partîya Serxwebûna Kurdistan – Kurdistan Independence Party), joining the KSP and KPDP.[7]

The Kurdistan Popular Democratic Party (KPDP)

In 1979 Sami Abdurrahman (politburo member and foreign adviser to Barzani) also split from the KDP, taking his supporters away with him to form the Kurdistan Popular Democratic Party (KPDP). The breakaway occurred because of a personal power squabble between Sami and the late Idris Barzani, one of Mustafa Barzani's two most politically active sons. The KPDP remained independent until after the Kurdish uprising of 1991. In mid-1993, Sami Aburrahman rejoined the KDP along with his supporters.

In 1992, following the elections in Kurdistan, the situation had become polarised once more between the KDP and the PUK. The Socialist Party also split apart and its members mostly joined either the KDP or PUK. A small group remained unaffiliated.

The Islamic Movement in Kurdistan (IMK)

Since 1992, and clashes between the PUK and its members in Kurdish towns along the Iraq–Iran border such as Raniya, where it has a strong following, the IMK has grown:

> [It is] both politically and militarily, the third force in the region today. A Sunni Muslim movement, it was formed in 1986 during the Iran-Iraq war and is headed by Shaikh 'Uthman 'Abd al-'Aziz, its spiritual guide. Its

leadership cadres include former members of the Union of Religious Scholars (*Yekîtî Mamostayanî Îslam* ... established in 1971, its principal role being the promotion of religious awareness. It became defunct after the collapse of the Kurdish opposition movement in 1975, but was re-constituted some six months after the March 1991 uprising ...). Others are veterans of the war in Afghanistan. In the past three years, the IMK has boosted its membership levels in Iraqi Kurdistan where it has estab-lished its own infrastructure ...

Apart from the IMK there are several smaller Islamist political groups in Iraqi Kurdistan today. Among them is Kurdish *Hizbullah* (*Hizbullahi Kurdî*), ... led by Shaikh Muhammad Khaled Barzani (a cousin of Massoud Barzani) ... and Revolutionary *Hizbullah* (*Hizbullah Kurdî Shoreshger*) ... led by Adham Barzani.[8]

The Iraqi National Congress (INC)

The other main new group on the political scene since the Gulf war is the INC (Iraqi National Congress), formed in Vienna in June 1992. The INC is a body of Iraqi oppostion groups, both Arab and Kurdish.

The INC agreed upon a right of self-determination for the Kurds and sought US recognition as an anti-Saddam government-in-exile with the possibility of becoming established in northern Iraq. While [US Secretary of State] James Baker refused to go that far, the Iraqis' visit [to the US] elevated their relationship with the United States. Baker issed a statement that urged them to continue to unify in order to create a democratic, pluralistic government which lives in peace with its neighbours and cares for its people.[9]

Supported financially and politically by the Western coalition govern-ments and certain Arab states, the INC entered the international political debate on the future of Iraq at a time when Western governments were still encouraging the Iraqi opposition to overthrow Saddam. However, two years after the Gulf war, as internal divisions began to manifest themselves in Iraq, Western diplomats cooled off towards both the INC and the Kurdish leadership and encouraged a return to dialogue with Saddam while still keeping sanctions in place against the country as part of a two-pronged, and highly destructive policy. During the fighting between the KDP and PUK in 1994, the INC was encouraged by the West to play a mediating role in attempting to restore peace in Kurdistan and succeeded for a short while, until in December 1994 the PUK and KDP resumed fighting for supreme control of strategic areas of the *de facto* autonomy region.

The INC had its own army of some 20,000 men, many of them deserters from the Iraqi army who had remained in Kurdistan since the uprising, alert to the fate they would meet should they return to government-controlled areas of the country.

Other groups, including the PKK, calling for unity across Greater Kurdistan, originated outside Iraqi Kurdistan then built up a support base within. Some of these have considerable influence on the policies of Iraqi Kurdestan and are described elsewhere.

Outbreak of war between the KDP and PUK

The first of a series of clashes between the two parties finally erupted in Qala Diza during the annual commemoration of May Day, 1994.

A private dispute over property rights between a senior KDP official, Ali Hasso Mirkhan, and local citizens led to a violent quarrel which escalated into serious inter-party conflict. The regional PUK representative, Mam Jutyar, had advised Mirkhan, the complainant, to delay negotiations of his property claims until after the May Day holiday. However, this advice was ignored and an argument broke out. It is alleged that Mirkhan then shot Jutyar dead in a fit of passion, and tensions spread like wildfire between the two rival parties until the conflict took in the whole of Kurdistan.

On 2 and 3 May, the KDP and the PUK began to attack each other's bases and headquarters in Sulaimaniya, Raniya, Chemchemal, Halabja and Salahaddin. The conflict was also intensely felt in Bahdinan – particularly in the larger cities of Dohuk and Zakho. Here, the KDP preserved a majority and KDP members effectively surrounded, occupied and thereafter hoisted their yellow flags above the former headquarters of the PUK, who abruptly departed *en masse* to join their main strongholds in Sulaimaniya and Arbil. Although there was sporadic gunfire, it appeared that there were no serious casualties in Bahdinan province.

Although I witnessed the events as they took place in Dohuk and Zakho, information about fighting in the other areas of Kurdistan was difficult to obtain as the two parties sought to minimise the damage by denying the seriousness of the conflict, hoping to defuse further aggression. To have done otherwise would have been much the same as setting a match to a dry forest. This would not occur until some time later.

Just as during the Kurdish uprising in March 1991, the streets of Zakho swarmed with Kurds bearing arms. Portable cannons and RPG rockets appeared on street corners, with fighters ready to use them against their own brothers. Uneasy bystanders gravitated to the rooftops of the tallest buildings, ready to react to any development. Bands of youths formed noisy groups protesting and chanting slogans in favour of the KDP, trampling the signs and placards of the rival PUK underfoot in their wake. (In Sulaimaniya, Raniya and Qala Diza the reverse was true. The PUK took the KDP's buildings and popular demonstrations of this sort were in the PUK's favour.)

By the next morning, any painted sign in Zakho which had previously read 'PUK' had been altered to 'KDP' (in Kurdish, PDK (Partiya Demoqrata Kurdistan) – an easier alteration); even the green PUK flags had all been replaced by the KDP's yellow ones – a dangerous situation. Meanwhile, in distant Halabja, the Iran-backed Kurdish Islamic Movement once again entered the conflict. Several people died during the chaotic gun battles that ensued. Exact figures for the total number of casualties from this first round of inter-party fighting remained unclear, but estimates put it at around six hundred people.

PUK leader Jalal Talabani was abroad in Europe when the conflict began, and for a full month after the conflict had begun was unable to return to help restore calm. Talabani had refused to go back as Massoud Barzani failed to travel in person to receive him at the border – the one assurance which might have guaranteed his personal security and led to a stand-down between the two feuding factions at this precise point in time. KDP leader Massoud Barzani had, however, published a speech saying that although his party had been damaged by the conflict he wished to emphasise that nobody should take revenge for any casualties they might have suffered as this could only jeopardise the lasting stability of Iraqi Kurdistan itself. Barzani requested that all the KDP's armed forces should withdraw from the conflict at once.

While still abroad, Jalal Talabani sent the KDP politburo and Massoud Barzani a formal message urging Barzani to assume interim leadership of both parties and take control of the situation until he could return. But despite the show of unity, it was impossible for Barzani and the Kurdish administration to restore order.

A second and then a third round of intense fighting broke out on 19 May, again in the southern part of the liberated area in and around Koysanjaq, Haiba Sultan, Shaqlawa, Halabja and Khormal. Islamic forces joined the KDP against the PUK. The PUK's representative for Dohuk, Hassan Kwestani, was executed after being captured in a localised battle on the Choman–Haj Omran road on 17 May, allegedly by the IMK (Islamic Movement of Kurdistan), KDP, Kurdish Hizbullah and Iranian pasdars. The homes of ministers of the Kurdish Federated Parliament in Arbil were also attacked by rival factions.[10]

The gravity of the situation caused alarm in Western capitals as well as in other parts of Kurdistan. Western officials, including representatives of the British Foreign Office, exhorted Mr Talabani to return with haste to the area and warned the Kurdish leaders to heal their differences swiftly and make peace or face the consequences: withdrawal of Western political and humanitarian support. Kurdish intellectuals were equally swift to send messages to Salahaddin entreating Barzani and the PUK representatives to find a way to restore peace before the considerable damage already caused should become irreparable. Iraqi Kurdistan had effectively been divided into two mutually exclusive spheres of influence: Barzani loyalists in the north west and Talabani adherents in the south east. Such a situation was incompatible with Kurdistan's popular struggle to inaugurate democracy.

Iran urged Turkey to expedite a military intervention, believing that Turkey might be capable of striking the final death blow to the enclave and thereby easing the minds of the anti-Kurdish coalition. Iranian forces backed the Kurdish Islamic Movement while it occupied Halabja and bombarded the town with artillery from across the mountains. Saddam delightedly announced in the state-controlled press that the Kurds were incapable of administering their own affairs in the region, signifying that the ordinary people would prefer a return to Baghdad's administration.

Meanwhile the UN sanctions against Iraq were renewed on 21 May 1994 until the end of the year. There was virtually no change in the terms of the sanctions apart from a provision for Turkey to clean the Iraqi oil pipeline which passed through its territory and for some 30 per cent of subsequent oil revenues to be allocated to humanitarian aid for Kurdistan. But, as Sarah Graham-Brown explained in *Middle East Report*, 'Baghdad refused to use the one-time proceeds amounting to about $300 million ... insisting that it had the sole right to distribute these goods, unsupervised, in the northern enclave as well as in government-controlled areas.'[11]

An uneasy peace held in northern Iraq while the rival elements brokered an agreement via the INC (Iraqi National Congress) providing for all parties to return to their pre-clash positions. But all too soon, fighting broke out again. The death toll is still unclear. Tensions remained high in the 'peaceful' interval that ensued and again the main protagonists and onlookers simply held their breath and waited. The stage was set for Jalal Talabani's return and a final settlement. He was escorted back to Kurdistan on 1 June 1994, exactly one month after the fighting had begun.

On 30 June 1994, named the 'Black Day', an estimated twenty thousand Kurds participated in the funeral procession for Osman Qala Minowar, a KDP military commander for central Sulaimaniya. Trouble began when the procession reached Kawa Square and shooting broke out. Attacks by the KDP and PUK against each other's bases in the cities resumed on a sporadic basis. On 15 August 1994, these clashes intensified and focused on the city of Shaqlawa. The KDP traditionally celebrates its party anniversary on 16 August each year. Prior to this, KDP members had begun to decorate Shaqlawa and other towns with their yellow flags and banners preliminary to holding concerts and enjoying other peaceful celebrations. This display of their rival's 'colours' irritated PUK members; a PUK peshmerga shot and injured one of the KDP's members as he hoisted the yellow flags. This provoked the KDP into attacking the PUK's positions in Shaqlawa for the next twelve hours, until Massoud himself arrived in town and put an end to the fighting. From then on until mid-September 1994 there was a period of relative peace. Then the PUK prepared to attack and retake Halabja from the IMK and KDP with a force of some 3,000 peshmergas. On learning this, the KDP attacked Qala Diza.

Arif Tayfur, of the KDP's second headquarters in Halabja, warned: 'If the PUK attack us on one front, we will attack them on another where they have no forces in place.' The KDP were defeated in Qala Diza but retained control of Halabja with the IMK, on the basis that defence is more successful in such a situation than an attack can be. Fighting raged for three days in Halabja. It was so fierce that it was impossible to remove for burial the dead bodies sprawled in the streets.[12] Iran was simultaneously shelling Qala Diza with artillery from its positions on the border. Many civilians were killed; others fled to Sulaimaniya and Hewler. Following this carnage the warring parties appeared to have understood that neither side could be the ultimate victor and that war was costly both in terms of life and resources. The KDP and PUK began to organise 'normalisation committees' in the cities to restore one another's bases and allow the parliament to resume its work. In November 1994, the two warring leaders concluded a 14–point agreement. One of these stated that foreign relations would only be assumed with the knowledge of both sides and on the basis that Kurdistan was still an integral part of Iraq.[13] In order to allay the concerns of neighbouring countries the parties also resolved to inform the international community that the Kurdish objective was federation within a united Iraq, not separation.

But by Christmas 1994, the KDP and PUK were at war again. Sporadic fighting raged intermittently until the Turkish invasion of Iraqi Kurdistan on the eve of the Kurdish New Year, 21 March 1995, which seemed to bring the warring Kurds to their senses, if only momentarily. Both parties demanded the immediate withdrawal of the Turks, even though the KDP was accused of collaborating with Ankara at the time (see chapter 9).

Like caged birds

Perhaps it was inevitable that the many hardships inflicted upon the Kurds due to the double sanctions and political isolation would release the pent-up internal political tensions, dissent and hatred that accompany unsettled past scores and serve to keep people apart.

The KDP justified the war on the basis of their old conflict with the PUK dating from 1964 and for the PUK's attempt to remove Barzani's name. For their part, the PUK called the KDP 'international traitors' and counter-revolutionaries, the betrayers of Kurdish nationalism for party interests. (The PUK similarly maintained their own international links.) The neighbouring countries preserved their traditional anti-Kurdish coalition to exacerbate whatever internal tensions arose between the Kurds, exploiting divisions in line with their interests.

Kurdish society became divided into 'martyrs', 'traitors' and 'patriots'. It was impossible to remain neutral; neutrality itself was tantamount to treachery in the heated political atmosphere where the very survival of the Kurds as a people was at stake. Kurdish martyrs have always been revered by their fellows, and the meaning has always been a national rather than a religious one; the martyrs of Kurdistan die for the liberation of their country, not in order to win a ticket to paradise. This meaning is inherent in the very name peshmerga: 'one who faces death'. A pesh-merga expects to sacrifice himself for his people. Martyrs come from every walk of life, from every party, and have perished in their thousands for the liberation of Kurdistan; they are immortalised in the songs of the patriots, in books and on posters. The song for the martyrs is sung at countless Kurdish gatherings:

> *Ey Şehîdan (Oh, Martyrs)*
>
> Oh martyrs, oh martyrs,
> your name and deeds will never die
> You became our leaders,
> you defend us from behind, you stand before us
> you raised the crown of greatness upon your heads
> you repulsed the nation's enemy
> the tree of freedom will not grow
> until our nation is freed
> Oh martyrs, oh martyrs
> your name and deeds will never die.

The internal fighting eroded some of Kurdish society's most cherished ideals. Peshmergas had seen themselves as saviours of the nation and defenders of the Kurdish dream; now peshmergas were killing pesh-mergas. Human rights abuses became rampant and the political parties hung their heads in shame as Amnesty International catalogued the list of atrocities Kurds had carried out against one another in Kurdistan since the uprising of 1991.[14] Here were Kurds who had believed them-selves patriots, lovers of their country, lovers of freedom, lovers of Kurdistan (*welatparêz*), exposed before the international community as little different from Saddam Hussein.

In the five years of psychological and economic deprivation since the Gulf war, the slow leeching away of their hopes and dreams, Iraq's Kurds had grown mad. Frustration and inaction burned up their hearts and minds. Kurdish hopes had soared when the 'safe haven' had been created, inspiring the Kurds of Iraq to rebuild their broken land – and then the tap was slowly turned off. The West dithered and looked on ineffectually as Iraq suffered and fell apart. The hopes of the Iraqi Kurds withered; their society was left in utter turmoil.

Notes

1. See Martin van Bruinessen's comprehensive analysis of Kurdish society in *Agha, Shaikh and State*, Zed Books, 1991.

2. Interview with witness to events, former PUK peshmerga, painter Tahir Fattah, USA, September 1995.

3. Ismet Sherif Vanly in Gérard Chaliand, *People Without a Country: the Kurds and Kurdistan*, Zed Books, London, p. 150.

4. Faysal Dağli, *Birakuji*, Belge Yayinlari, Istanbul, 1994, pp. 297–309.

5. From a private interview with Mahmoud Othman, London, February 1995.

6. Dağli, pp. 306–7.

7. Ibid., pp. 306–7.

8. Amnesty International, *Iraq: Human Rights Abuses in Iraqi Kurdistan Since 1991*, 28 February 1995, p. 10.

9. Carnegie Endowment for International Peace, *Self-determination in the New World Order*, Morton H. Halperin and David J. Scheffer with Patricia L. Small, Washington, 1992, p. 43.

10. Sources include eye-witnesses, letters and the two reports on the situation by the KDP and PUK: *What Happened in Iraqi Kurdistan? May 1994*, KDP Research Department. June 1994; and *Iraqi Kurdistan: a situation report on recent events*, PUK Foreign Relations Committee, February 1995. Also Amnesty International, *Iraq: Human Rights Abuses in Iraqi Kurdistan since 1991*, 28 February 1995, pp. 129–30.

11. *Middle East Report* (*MERIP*), No. 193, March–April 1995, p. 6.

12. Eyewitness report, *Hengaw* newspaper, London, October 1994.

13. *Hengaw* newspaper, London, December 1994.

14. See Amnesty International, *Iraq: Human Rights Abuses in Iraqi Kurdistan since 1991*, 28 February 1995.

9

Turkey: only a military solution

Regional elections in Turkey: March 1994

Despite its claims to be a democracy, Turkey showed few qualms in the build-up to the March 1994 regional elections about lifting the diplomatic immunity of six MPs from the DEP (Democracy Party), one independent MP, Mahmut Alinak, and an eighth MP, Hassan Mezarci, representing the Islamic Fundamentalist Refah Party. Mezarci faced 20 years' imprisonment simply for criticising Turkey's secular founder, Kemal Atatürk. The Kurdish MPs who included DEP Party Chairman, Hatip Dicle, Ahmet Türk, Orhan Doğan, Sirri Sakik and Leyla Zana, were left to face the death penalty or lengthy prison sentences if found guilty under article 125 of the penal code for treason (i.e. threatening the unity of the Turkish state).

Five of the MPs had sought sanctuary for two nights inside the Turkish parliament in Ankara before being taken into custody by police on 4 March 1994 when they joined colleagues, Orhan Doğan and Sirri Sakik arrested earlier outside the parliament. The *Daily Telegraph* on 8 March 1994 reported that the MPs were shown on television 'being carted off like common criminals after surrendering to the Turkish police [which] has brought a barrage of criticism at home and abroad.'

Despite condemnation from the European Parliament in Brussels, Turkish Prime Minister Tansu Çiller responded that Turkey 'will not allow interference in our internal affairs. We shall share the truth with [Turkish] and world public opinion.' The Çiller government continued to refuse any dialogue with Kurdish democratic opposition groups, or reach any settlement with the PKK. Rather, it single-mindedly pursued a military option in response to the Kurdish problem – the policy of successive Turkish governments for the past 70 years.

The European Parliament urged the immediate release of the MPs and that Turkey recognise the right to autonomy of its Kurdish people.

The Foreign Ministry responded that the fate of the MPs was now 'in the hands of independent courts'. Western governments voicing their concern to President Süleyman Demirel were simply informed that the DEP deputies had links with the PKK. The DEP had withdrawn from regional elections scheduled for 27 March 1994 after individual candidates, supporters and would-be voters suffered harassment and intimidation from the Turkish military.

The eighteen Kurdish deputies originally elected were seen as a 'potential informal channel between the government and the PKK', John Murray Brown reported in the *Financial Times* (4 March 1994). One DEP MP had already been killed in 1993 and 54 local party officials murdered in south-east Turkey. More than seventy members of the DEP and its predecessor, the HEP, were murdered altogether; 320 of the candidates designated to stand in the elections were arrested. Twenty DEP offices were bombed; the rest were later closed.

The Turkish authorities warned local villagers likely to support the DEP that if they voted in DEP's favour their villages would be destroyed and the inhabitants killed. Sirri Sakik, one of the detained DEP MPs, argued: 'They just don't want to listen to us. They seem to want to execute us. If they think they will solve the Kurdish problem by hanging us, let them do it. But history will show us to be right.' (*Independent*, 4 March 1994.)

Although the MPs made a brief court appearance their pleas were not heard and they were removed to Ankara prison. They were also denied access to lawyers and visits from their families. (*Özgür Gündem*, 18 March 1994.) By April 1994, the state had forced *Özgür Gündem* to close in what amounted to a further attempt to silence the Kurdish opposition voice. In its place, *Özgür Ülke* (Free Country) went to press. On 15 May, its editor also was arrested.

From March 1994 onwards, an estimated four hundred and fifty thousand Turkish troops were sent into action in the Kurdish provinces to take part in the state's most brutal campaign to date. Its declared object was, as always: 'to finish off the PKK' – but the result was bloodshed and the slaughter of civilians.

The Turkish campaign took the form of an intensification of military attacks against the Kurdish population, resulting in a new mass exodus of villagers in the wake of the destruction which ensued. By December 1994, Turkish Prime Minister Tansu Çiller would announce a plan to build 'compound villages' for the hundreds of thousands of Kurds whose homes had been destroyed by her army, following the example Saddam had set for her with the Kurds in Iraq.

At the time of the elections, in the process of migration, many

Kurdish votes were lost. Others cast their votes in favour of the Islamic-based Refah Party. According to one UK/Ireland human rights mission monitoring the elections in Kurdistan:

> voting is mandatory in Turkey – though the fine is small … . Many DEP and PKK supporters had intended to boycott the election, and in some towns the total of abstentions and spoilt or blank papers was high: in Tunceli (Dersim) it was put at about 79%; in Diyarbakir about 50%. The 'winners' there, as in most of the region, the Refah (Welfare) Party took control with the votes of only a small percentage of the population. In rural areas, the (human rights) teams were told that villagers would be forced by the army to vote – in some cases for village guards standing for other parties (including the fascist MHP) with military backing … . All the discussions that team members had with Kurdish people confirmed that DEP would have enjoyed overwhelming support had it been able to field candidates. The majority of people said they intended to boycott the poll.[1]

There were some four hundred observers from Western Europe for the elections in Turkey. Their presence proved to be a considerable irritant to the authorities. Newroz (Kurdish New Year) was not celebrated openly since the risk of military reprisals was overwhelming. Those Kurds who chose to celebrate Newroz in Istanbul were attacked by police. However, village guards and the military organised mock Newroz celebrations in an ironic PR exercise planned to demonstrate Kurdish freedom to the Turkish public. In a bizarre twist, Newroz was pronounced a 'Turkish national holiday' although it is meaningless to the majority of the Turkish population.

Big Brother is watching

Two 'terminators' sauntered towards me through the crowded lanes of Istanbul's famous tourist haunt, the Kapali Çarşi, the Covered Bazaar. These were Turkish Security Police, kitted out in black and red 'action' uniforms introduced just a week before on the April 'Police Holiday': black bovver boots, padded shoulders, truncheons and handguns completed the look. Fifteen days before, the second of two bombs had exploded in the bazaar, killing two tourists and wounding 15 others. Now the terminators were everywhere.

One side-effect of the Kurdish anti-tourism campaign in the cities was that Turkish and Kurdish democrats were once more speaking in whispers whenever they discussed the current political situation. Old friends warned me: 'Even in Istanbul, people are disappearing in the night. Take care!' The telephones crackled, suddenly went dead; sometimes you could hear police radio interrupting your conversation. Nobody said anything meaningful on the phone any more.

Refugees from the villages destroyed in Kurdistan had settled on the outskirts of most big Turkish towns in areas where Kurdish shanty-town colonies (*gecekondu*) have mushroomed since the troubles began. In the large, relatively cosmopolitan city of Izmir several sizeable colonies of Kurdish evacuees had taken root. The Turkish Armed Forces had imposed a curfew on some of the larger ghettos. In Izmir's Kurdish quarters such as Cili, Camlik and Akincilar, visitors arriving by car were forced to surrender their identity documents at the entrance and supply full details of the address they intended to visit. Their documents were returned when the visit was over. Some of these colonies were identified as pro-Kurdish and their inhabitants were facing forcible evacuation by the Turkish authorities.

The present patterns of Kurdish migration to western Turkey are focused on areas with a history of Kurdish settlement. In Izmir, for example, Kurds from Dersim (Tunceli), Sivas, Erzincan and Erzurum went to join relatives of the same origin in Izmir's Çili. From other parts of Kurdistan they would flock to Buca or Karabağlar. In Diyarbakir, newly built and only partly finished tenement-style apartments housed the latest refugees from Şirnak, Lice and Cizre. For the first time this decade, thousands of families fled the destruction of their villages between Şirnak and Hakkari into south Kurdistan – the misnamed 'safe haven'.

The Turkish government commenced its annual spring-cleaning operation against the Kurds on 12 April 1994. It began by bombing the mountain areas near Mazi and Sivi in northern Iraq and followed this up by dispatching 5,000 special forces to occupy the border area and set up a post at Kani Masi in KDP-controlled Bahdinan. The army then turned its attention on all Kurdish villages which had refused to become village-guard villages to fight the PKK.

Kurds flee from Turkey into South Kurdistan

By 1 April 1994, following an intensification of Turkish military bombing of Kurdish towns and villages along the Turkey–Iraq border, thousands of Turkish Kurds began to cross into northern Iraq. Ironically, they were following the same difficult mountain routes trodden by Iraqi Kurds three years before in the aftermath of their failed uprising, but in reverse. But for these Kurds, flight from Turkey into the former 'safe haven' was no guarantee of safety. Operation Provide Comfort had always been restricted to protecting Iraqi Kurds from air and ground attack by Saddam Hussein. Turkey and Iran continued bombing within and beyond the territory designated as the 'safe haven' with apparent impunity, having killed more than one thousand five hundred Kurdish civilians from Iraq, Iran and Turkey in the area since the 'protection' operation began.

The refugees' flight across the mountains down to the lowlands of Zakho – a difficult journey lasting as many as six days – ended in Shiranish: a valley offering pasturing for livestock, with a clean water source but little else. There they stopped in their life-or-death flight from the Turkish army, set up rough shelters and simply appealed to the international community for assistance and recognition. The response was shockingly slow and inadequate.

On 18 May 1994, 50 Turkish warplanes attacked the tiny village of Zelê on the Iraq–Iran border, 130 km south of the official Turkish border, where the PKK had kept a base since the Kurdish war of 1992. It was the second such operation in six months and cost the almost bankrupt Turkish government around $40 million on both occasions – with little result. By the winter, there were over twelve thousand refugees from the destroyed villages around Uludere-Şirnak, living under plastic, thatch and canvas, dependent upon the meagre budgets of the few NGOs based in Zakho to assist the Iraqi Kurds.

From the outset, the Kurds from Turkey feared Turkish aerial attacks on the exposed camps in Shiranish. Their worst fears came true. In one incident in November 1994, Turkey dropped more than twenty-three bombs on the villagers in a single attack, prompting them to move away from the border to a new site near Derkar, some 15 minutes from Zakho township. In another attack, a village supervised by the Swedish health project, Qandil, was machine-gunned by a Turkish helicopter; two jets then flew over to mop up. A number of Kurds were out in the fields at the time of the attack and, taken by surprise, were unable to find cover. Two pick-ups travelling along the road came under fire and went off the road at a steep incline. Two children suffered shrapnel injuries, one woman was killed and several others were badly wounded in the attack.

Turkey had been bombing the area continuously since the summer, focusing its attacks on three main fronts. Shinan Keshan was bombed again in December, adding to the numbers of displaced people attempting to find their way down towards Zakho. Eleven villages on the Turkish side of the border and five on the Iraqi side of the border were destroyed. All the occupants fled into the Zakho area where they hoped – but were unlikely – to find the help they needed.

Neither the UN nor the Zakho-based Coalition Forces – the MCC (Military Command Centre that controls the movements of the coalition forces) – were now allowed to visit the border areas. This meant that the only information emerging, aside from intelligence and military reconnaissance, was that supplied by aid organisations who had witnessed the damage and casualties caused by the Turks. Their personnel were threatened and staff warned not to report their findings.

Because the MCC in Zakho has been manned by top-level military intelligence staff from France, Britain, America *and* Turkey, since summer 1991, Turkey has been able to obtain direct security information throughout its operations. At the same time it has succeeded in maintaining pressure on its coalition partners to remain quiet about Turkey's military activities in Kurdistan.

On a visit to the destroyed villages close to the border, one NGO spokesperson observed with concern that the corpses of dead Kurdish villagers showed signs of having been tortured and mutilated by the Turkish army which entered after the raids. The survivors fled either to western Turkey or into Iraqi Kurdistan.

Most of the 12,000 refugees from the Shiranish camps were moved to a large camp in Atrush by the end of the year. Although Shelter Now had obtained a contract from the UNHCR to start building medium-term shelters, the project would not be able to start until the spring of 1995. This meant that the refugees had to face the winter in tents. The delay had been caused by the UNHCR's inability to recognise the Turkish Kurds as refugees. As 'displaced people' they were simply not eligible for immediate international aid. The UNHCR had been reluctant to get involved in the plight of the Kurds from Turkey because of the status quo politics in the region, highlighting Western governmental compliance in Turkey's methods of combating Kurdish discontent. But by the end of 1994, more than two thousand Kurdish villages in south-east Turkey had been destroyed, resulting in more than an estimated one-quarter of a million homeless Kurds.

The Turkish army threatened to set up a buffer zone in the heart of Kurdistan, and to occupy both sides of the border. The MCC continued to turn a blind eye to Turkish assaults on the Kurdish region. But there were murmurs of American discontent. The *Air Force Times* ran an article entitled 'Is U.S. Intelligence being misused?' in its December 1994 issue. The article reiterated what I and other observers had known now for more than three years:

> When Turkish bombing missions – called special missions in the *Provide Comfort* lexicon – are being flown, the Turks ground coalition aircraft ... The result is that American, British and French planes are not flying even when they should be because of Turkish missions ... Because *Provide Comfort* is staged from a Turkish air base and Turkey is a member of the

coalition to protect the Kurds in northern Iraq, Turkish military officials are privy to virtually all intelligence gathered not only from the Americans but from Britain and France ... In an attempt to curb the attacks against Kurdish rebels for fear of hurting civilians, senior American military officials with increasing intensity have advised their commanders to avoid giving Turkish military leaders intelligence that could be used against the Kurds. But the Turks continue to have access to information from AWACS aircraft because of the presence of Turkish controllers and because AWACS data transmissions pass through Turkish ground stations on their way to American commanders on the ground. The Turks also review American and British reconnaissance aircraft data compiled during *Provide Comfort* flights.[2]

In April 1994, I had met the four colonels who spearheaded the MCC (British, French, American and Turkish), and pressed them about the welfare of the Kurdish refugees arriving from over the Turkish border. The Turkish colonel had scoffed, 'How do you know these people are Kurdish?'

When I furnished him with a considered academic answer, the American colonel showed me the door. Evidently here, too, discussion of the Kurdish problem was forbidden. The MCC was extremely nervous about the arrival of thousands of Kurds from Turkey in northern Iraq. It made Turkey's Kurdish problem more difficult to hide from the outside world. Turkey's response was to close the border to journalists.

Prime Minister Tansu Çiller attempted to bluff that the Kurds had been forced to flee into Iraq by the PKK as part of a 'ploy to affect international opinion'. The government claimed that the PKK had offered each family $1,500 to cross. Not only was this assertion ludicrous, but all the evidence was to the contrary.

These Kurds – young and old, men, women and children – unanimously reported that their villages had been shelled and destroyed by the Turkish army when they had refused to become state-paid militia against the PKK. Many had witnessed the slaughter of family members by the Turkish army and contra-guerrillas in the past months. They had also been subjected to a blockade of food, medicine and clothing; the governor of Hakkari had decreed that only the militia would receive provisions. The governor's assistant, Mehmet Çetin, when challenged by the Hakkari Human Rights Association branch chairman on the issue, defended his action on the grounds that provisions 'were being taken to the PKK'.

Almost the entire surviving population of Hilal, Şirîş, Taşdelen, Balveren, Mijîn, Salpaca, Nirwa, Kilba and other villages in the Uludere/ Şirnak region had found themselves camped uneasily across the border in northern Iraq. Several people, including small children, had been shot by Turkish Security Forces and village guards while they attempted to escape after dark across the treacherous, heavily mined mountain border. Arrests and torture were carried out at random as a further warning to those who had not yet managed to escape. As the campaign of state terrorism increased, so too did the murders of prominent Kurds from all walks of life: bodies of tortured and murdered lawyers, businessmen and newspaper workers were left, barely concealed, as warnings to their colleagues.

The show-trial of the Kurdish MPs

The DEP MPs were tried in the Ankara State Security Court, and the trial proceedings reported in detail by *Özgür Ülke* newspaper. These I translated into English and edited for the press and for publication. Almost none of the information appeared in the British press.

DEP Chairman Hatip Dicle, on trial for treason together with six of his colleagues, had warned the press that a just verdict might not be possible because of the Parliamentary General Council's own secret orders and directives. At the beginning of the defence proceedings, Dicle underlined that the MPs were simply being tried for bringing the Kurdish people's demands on to the agenda.

The MPs had been stripped of their diplomatic immunity by the Ankara State Security Court on 2 March 1994, taken into custody soon after and charged with treason; they were not allowed bail prior to the hearing. The trial of Hatip Dicle, Ahmet Türk, Orhan Doğan, Leyla Zana, Sirri Sakik and the independent MP for Şirnak, Mahmut Alinak, continued on 8 October 1994.

Hatip Dicle told how, during Newroz 1992, 14 people in Nusaybin were run over by army panzers, that assistance to the victims had been prevented and that a 16-year-old girl named Bîşeng Anik had died defending herself against rape in police custody. Dicle then asked rhetorically, 'Since the parliament and the country's president remained silent about these events, what should we have done? Even now a hearing ought to be convened for the murders of these 15 people [killed during Newroz].'

Dicle pointed out that the MPs were being tried for statements such as: 'the PKK is a side in this war', or that 'real proof was necessary of the state's intentions to solve the Kurdish problem' and that 'the armed struggle had taken on the dimensions of war'. However, he stressed that his suggestions for a solution to the Kurdish problem had been his personal views, and that they were not debated within the party; he emphasised that it was necessary that the guns be silenced and a two-way ceasefire proclaimed. He had also advocated that once the gunfire died down, both the constitution and Turkish law should amend all articles contradictory to the recognition of Kurdish identity. Dicle added that an open referendum was necessary for a fundamental solution to the problem. He observed further that his packet of suggestions was being exhibited as an offence and he was being tried on account of this with the death penalty in mind. Of the 19 items listed against him, 17 originated from speeches; the other two were for 'sheltering or assisting a member of the PKK'.

Speaking after Hatip Dicle, the MP for Şirnak, Orhan Doğan, dwelt largely upon the crookedness of the judicial system in Turkey and the errors made in its hearing of the case.

> In Turkish law there are 156 items covering the removal of diplomatic immunity. These were adopted to cover such crimes as corruption, avoiding tax, taking bribes or to prevent MPs profiting from transactions as middle-men, for giving their personal backing to contracts, and for taking a person's life for a political end. Of 22 people accused under the article governing separatism, six had been singled out. We were thereafter accused of 'separatism' and imprisoned. Yet, when we say that this is a 'political crime', you become uneasy.

The DEP MP for Muş, Sirri Sakik, explained in his speech how the previous year he had been in Muş when his village was burned down, but when he attempted to return he had not been allowed in. He had therefore made representation to the Governor and the military commander and finally, having received no response, to President Demirel who said he would take the matter up.

> After the President took the matter up, 23 more villages were burned down. Parliamentary Chief Minister Kamer Genç had also contacted President Demirel to voice his concern on the subject of the villages being burned down in Tunceli. 'God forbid!' I say now. 'Don't involve the President; the number will only go up further … ' We are being tried for our thoughts.

Mardin MP Ahmet Türk emphasised: 'We were not brought here after being arrested for carrying guns in the mountains. We were not arrested for throwing bombs in the city. We are here because we made our views public'. Leyla Zana supported his statement, saying that the official system did not permit variant views; those whose thoughts were different were labelled traitors. She recalled Coşkun Kirca's declaration that 'The Kurds in this country have only one right; the right to silence', and claimed they were bring tried for wanting peace and brotherhood and for articulating their views on the Kurdish question.[3]

The DEP MPs were finally brought to the stand for sentencing in Ankara's State Security Court on 8 December 1994. Although the court did not impose the death penalty on the MPs for their 'separatist' activities, the 15-year prison sentences imposed under article 169 of the Turkish Penal Code upon Hatip Dicle, Orhan Doğan, Leyla Zana, Selim Sadak and Ahmet Türk for allegedly sheltering or assisting members of the illegal Kurdistan Workers' Party horrified European trial observers. Sedat Yurttaş was sentenced to seven years six months, while Mahmut Alinak and Sirri Sakik were each given sentences of three years six months and heavy fines for 'separatist' propaganda. The trial was condemned as a farce; the defence had not been permitted to provide evidence or call witnesses in support of their case. The sentences went automatically to the Appeal Court, but Prime Minister Çiller stated in televised interviews broadcast later that day that she was satisfied that the trial was just and impartial, barely concealing her delight in the verdict imposed upon her opponents.

Amnesty International stated in its news service release of the same day: 'This judgement is part of a general attack on freedom of expression which is intensifying in Turkey. The number of people imprisoned or threatened with imprisonment for expressing their non-violent opinions is on the increase.'[4]

In the early hours of the morning of 3 December 1994, both the Ankara and Istanbul offices of the pro-Kurdish newspaper *Özgür Ülke* were bombed to the ground. The explosion in Istanbul was caused by a massive amount of plastic explosive packed into a parked car positioned outside the building. The attack represented another attempt by the regime to silence the Kurdish voice. However, the bombing failed to stop *Özgür Ülke* for even one day. With the help of colleagues from other newspapers, the daily succeeded in going to press the next morning carrying the story of the attack as its headline. Two weeks later a secret order to the Ministry of Defence was printed in the paper, alleging that Çiller herself was authoress of the plan to silence *Özgür Ülke* by such means. The newspaper was finally closed down by the Turkish authorities early in 1995. It was succeeded by *Yeni Politika* (New Politics) which would meet the same fate eight months later, to be succeeded by *Özgür Politika* (Free Politics).

The flight of the DEP chair and MPs into exile

Yaşar Kaya, the chair of the DEP and publisher of *Özgür Gündem*, was compelled to leave Turkey after being sentenced to four years' imprisonment by the Ankara State Security Court on 18 February 1994. He fled to Europe to seek political asylum.

He was charged with 'separatism' on account of a speech he had given in Arbil, south Kurdistan, at the congress of the KDP on 15 August 1993 and was released on bail pending further hearings. He claimed there was nothing in his speech specific to or against Turkey, nor any reference to territorial division.

The eight DEP MPs now in prison had been sentenced under special state security laws introduced under the Anti-Terror Law. Six DEP MPs, the DEP Chair, the former municipal chair and the Istanbul provincial chair had gone into exile having openly declared that they rejected the court's verdict as little other than a further attack on the right of the Kurdish people to democratic representation. 'For the past 37 years that I have been working on this issue I have had the misfortune of seeing the interior of 18 Turkish prisons and I am now banished to Europe,' Yaşar Kaya explained.[5]

The Kurdistan Parliament-in-Exile

The idea of establishing a parliament-in-exile evolved from the closure of DEP and the removal of all democratic political means of the Kurdish people and their elected representatives for resolving the Kurdish problem in Turkey. The DEP MPs in exile recognised how vital it was to continue the legal democratic struggle abroad.

The Kurdistan Parliament-in-Exile (Kurdistan Sürgün Parlamento) was established on 24 April 1995. It was intended to act as a representative of the Kurdish people, possessing a voice capable of helping to resolve internal disputes. The Kurdish groups represented included the Alevi Union, Keldani community, Kurdish Intellectual Union, Assyrian Federation, Islamic Movement, ERNK, TAJK and the DEP MPs. It also included Kurdish representatives from Russia, America, Canada and Australia and had contact with representatives from all the parliaments throughout Europe. 'We are also committed to co-operation with the Federated Parliament of South Kurdistan,' Yaşar Kaya told me, 'even though KDP's continuing relations with Turkey are understood to be detrimental to the greater welfare of the Kurdish people.'[6]

While HADEP attempted to continue the struggle for democracy in Turkey, the DEP MPs took their seats within the Kurdistan Parliament-in-Exile.

Turkey invades Iraqi Kurdistan: Newroz 1995

On the eve of Newroz, 20 March, the Turkish government undertook its most massive military operation in 70 years, a bigger operation than the invasion of Cyprus. This time, the assault was launched against Kurds

beyond the Turkish border. Staged by 35,000 ground troops backed by
F-16 jet fighters, paratroopers, tanks and helicopters, the Turks thrust
deep into Iraqi Kurdistan, seizing a strip almost 30 miles long and 140
miles broad, and occupying Zakho. Although the invasion was a flagrant
intervention of an internationally protected area under Iraqi Kurdish
control, the attack had the prior consent of the Allies, foremost among
them the United States. The Operation Provide Comfort forces ceased
operation rather than protecting the Kurds on the ground at the time of
the invasion.

The Turkish assault, allegedly aimed at 'wiping out' the Kurdish
liberation movement, immediately resulted in civilian arrests, abductions
and casualties among both Iraqi and Turkish Kurds. Turkish soldiers
carried out house-to-house searches in Zakho, Derkar, Hizawa and in the
camps approaching Shiranish. Although the UNHCR began the evacuation of civilian Kurds three days after the invasion, there were con-
spicuously few men among the 2,000 refugees first airlifted into the
overflowing camps at Atrush. Understanding that any male was a
potential target for the Turkish soldiers, non-combatant Kurdish men
had gone into hiding.

The previous week, 30 civilians had been killed in the conflict (predominantly Kurds who had fled the destruction of their villages in
Turkey), 50 others had disappeared and more than 250 people had been
wounded in riots in the Gazi quarter of Istanbul – further evidence of
the ethnic, political and religious tensions arising from the Turkish
government's policies. Turkish police are generally recruited from the
fascist supporters of the MHPs (Grey Wolves). In this incident, the
mainly Alevi[7] left-wing Turkish and Kurdish residents of the shanty-
towns rioted after the torture and death of an Alevi civilian in police
custody; he had been arrested for a minor criminal offence. Shots had
been fired by unknown assailants into an Alevi teahouse where customers
were watching a football match on television, killing two people. In-
censed, those involved marched upon the police station. The police
blocked the roads and called for reinforcements. The angry crowd threw
stones at the police, who then fired shots at the protesters. The whole
episode was filmed. Hayri Kozakçioğlu, former Super Governor of the
Kurdish State of Emergency region, appointed governor (Vali) of Istanbul in August 1991, lost control over the violence. The government and
press laid the blame on Kozakçioğlu. Most interestingly here, speaking
in his own defence, the governor replied that he had asked for additional
support from the gendarmes but that this had failed to materialise as all
the gendarmes had been sent into operation in the Kurdish region.

The subsequent assault on Iraqi Kurdistan just days after the Gazi riots was intended to deflect attention from the troubles within the country and to improve the government's ratings among the Turkish population. The assault, however, had clearly been planned months before when Turkish tanks were first positioned along the Turko-Iraqi border. Journalists other than those resident in Turkey had been banned from crossing into Iraqi Kurdistan from Turkey since September 1994. In this way, Turkey continued to impose a high level of control over information emerging from the area. Only NGOs and journalists with Turkish accreditation were able to respond to international inquiries from the enclave.

Western governments were initially reluctant to condemn the Turkish invasion, because of Turkey's membership of NATO as well as its role in the now cynically named Operation Provide Comfort. However, alarm bells finally began to ring after the third day of attacks when the UNHCR was obliged to assist in the evacuation of Turkish Kurdish refugees. The airlift and evacuation by road using convoys of local minibuses was a precaution, removing the vulnerable from the path of the Turkish army.

> Mohammad Hassan, 34, of the village of Hizawa, near the Turkish border, said: 'They have come to oppress us just like Saddam Hussein did.' Mr Hassan, a teacher, said Turkish troops raided Hizawa on Tuesday, rounding up men for interrogation and seizing their weapons. 'They began hitting them with their rifle butts and whipping them with plastic tubes, demanding what they knew about the PKK.' Six of those detained, all of them Turkish Kurdish refugees from south-east Turkey, are reported to be missing ... Officials of the KDP ... said at least 10 villages were hit after Turkish aircraft began bombing the region north of the town of Al-Amadiyah ... An Iraqi Kurdish official said: 'The situation is very tense here. People want the Turks to go home.' But he failed to mention that the Turkish military is acting in co-ordination with the KDP. Mr Massoud Barzani, the KDP leader is believed to have secured promises of help in his battle for control over northern Iraq with Mr Jalal Talabani's Patriotic Union of Kurdistan in exchange for co-operation (*Daily Telegraph*, 24 March 1995).

The aim of the Turkish cross-border incursions has consistently been to undermine the Kurdish administration of northern Iraq at the same time as hunting out the PKK. By supporting the KDP against the PUK, Turkey has severely damaged inter-Kurdish relations. Iraq also took advantage of the invasion, not only to condemn Turkey, but to launch renewed attacks on the enclave itself. The Iraqis bombed Kurdish-controlled areas outside Arbil and Sulaimaniya, pushing inside as far as the Arbil ring road.

As international condemnation intensified the Turks came under increasing pressure to withdraw. European foreign ministers said that the incursion must end immediately. The United States was initially more sympathetic, 'saying it recognised its fellow NATO member's need to deal decisively with terrorists of the Kurdistan Workers party' (*Daily Telegraph*, 24 March 1995). But only two days later, US Defense Secretary William Perry warned Tansu Çiller against setting up a permanent, Lebanon-style 'security zone' in northern Iraq. 'We cannot accept a permanent extension of this effort,' said Perry. 'We have been assured by Turkish officials that they will finish it quickly.' He added that he was 'very concerned' at reports of the bombings of Iraqi Kurdish villages (*Sunday Telegraph*, 26 March 1995). But according to Turkish Foreign Minister Murat Karayalçin, 'Turkey could not let the PKK control northern Iraq, whatever international pressure Ankara might face' (*Guardian*, 27 March 1995).

Although Tansu Çiller assured Western leaders that the Turkish invasion would be of limited duration, and that Turkish forces would leave once the PKK had been 'eradicated', the Turkish military commander in control of operations, General Kundakci (known to the Turks as Kundakci Pasha) claimed otherwise, stating the army would remain in northern Iraq for as long as necessary, perhaps for up to one year.

As foreign opposition continued to mount, Turkey was obliged to start moving its troops from the area. Although they resisted for a month, by the end of April 1995 the first 23,000 troops were on the move back across the border. This left an estimated 12,000 Turkish troops still inside northern Iraq, attempting to maintain a presence in the area. Turkish army sources claimed to have killed 555 guerrillas, taken 13 prisoners and lost 61 Turkish soldiers with 185 wounded. (*Hürriyet*, 3 May 1995). This the PKK refuted, claiming they had few losses. The PKK claimed that guerrillas had inflicted heavy casualties upon Turkish forces, attacking the troops even as they retreated (*Kurd-A*, 3 May 1995). The latest military campaign failed once again. The country had to bear the enormous cost of 2 trillion, 800 billion Turkish liras – around $US 65 million or £47 million (*Hürriyet*, 3 May 1995).

Undismayed, on 5 July 1995 3,000 Turkish troops again invaded northern Iraq, pressing 15 km south. As a result of Turkish bombing of villages on both sides of the border, in addition to a number of civilian casualties among both Turkish Kurds and Iraqi Kurds, 20 villages were abandoned and 3,000 Iraqi Kurdish civilians fled the Turkish army in the mountainous area north east of Arbil.

Fighting again erupted between the PUK and KDP around Shaqlawa at the same time, and renewed tensions caused shockwaves throughout the region, breaking the ceasefire and leaving more than a thousand dead. The total number of victims of the internal war now exceeded 5,000.

Relations between the KDP and the Turkish government were set back by the Turkish invasion, which was condemned by the KDP's Ankara spokesman Sefin Dizayee. The KDP had looked favourably upon a deal under discussion with the Turks to establish a border presence to oppose PKK operations, planning to deploy 20,000 peshmergas and build new forts and police lookouts, in exchange for US $30 million. This figure was bargained down to $20,000 before the talks bogged down. Turkey refused to pay.

US-sponsored peace talks screened by Turks

Talks between senior representatives of the KDP, PUK, INC and US State Department officials to put an end to the internal fighting finally got underway in Dublin on 9–11 August 1995.

Robert Deutsch, the recently appointed director of Northern Gulf Affairs in the US State Department, issued identical letters of invitation to the PUK and KDP leadership, offering US mediation to bring an end to the war of attrition which had first erupted on 1 May 1994. Although the KDP exhibited some initial reluctance and sought to present its own demands, the leadership finally gave its consent for preliminary talks to go ahead. The PUK had already accepted the US offer 'unconditionally'. There was to be an 'open agenda', although the talks would take place behind closed doors and would be barred to the press.

The KDP delegation was led by Sami Abdurrahman (former leader of the KPDP), accompanied by Hoshyar Zebari, (the KDP's most senior London representative), Jewher Namik Saleh (former speaker of the Iraqi Kurdistan parliament), and Muhsin Dizayee (Massoud Barzani's aide and the grand old man of the KDP, being virtually a contemporary of the late Mulla Mustafa Barzani). The PUK delegation was led by Jalal Talabani's senior aide, Noshirwan Mustafa, joined by the PUK's US representative, Berham Saleh, Fuad Mahsoum (former prime minister of the Iraqi Kurdistan parliament) and Sa'adi Pir (MP in the federated parliament and former minister of agriculture). The INC delegation was headed by its chairman, Ahmed Chelebi, accompanied by Tawfiq Al-Yassuri and Hani al-Fakiky. Subject to the successful conclusion of the first rounds of talks, a summit was to be sought between the PUK and KDP leaders.

The US-initiated talks followed further serious clashes between the PUK and KDP in the last week of July 1995 in which a further 200 people were killed, bringing the total number of casualties in the internecine conflict to an estimated five thousand people. The US, perturbed by the growing influence of Iran on the *realpolitik* of the region, urged an immediate ceasefire and warned the two Kurdish parties against pursuing negotiations with Baghdad or allowing Iranian infiltration via the Islamic Movement of Kurdistan, the KDP's ally. The US also proposed that the Dublin (Drogheda) peace talks should attempt to resolve the issue of the allocation of government revenues in south Kurdistan, controlled by the KDP since the seizure of the customs post in Zakho (a monthly revenue amounting to some $100,000 from Iraqi oil illegally exported to Turkey and dues collected on incoming humanitarian aid); and the demilitarisation of Arbil, the seat of the non-functioning Kurdish parliament and capital of south Kurdistan.

Turkey had been exerting pressure on both parties to seek a reconciliation with Saddam. An envoy from Baghdad had visited the enclave that same week. The Turks also continued to impose Ankara's authority upon the region by the use of force, as with its massive military invasion of northern Iraq in March 1995 and the lesser incursions in July, with the backing of Washington.

According to the KDP office in London, a 'last-minute decision' was taken allowing representatives from the Turkish Foreign Office in London to attend the peace talks. This boded ill for the Turkish Kurds in the overall picture. The issue of the PKK's presence in south Kurdistan was discussed in confidence. The final lines of the official press release from the table stated that 'all of the above points will be carried out within the territorial integrity of Iraq ... these points will also take into consideration the legitimate security concerns of Turkey.' (INC/KDP/PUK Press Release, Drogheda, 11 August 1995).

The talks were convened with the support of Britain. Jeremy Hanley, minister of state at the Foreign Office, had dispatched a strongly worded letter warning the Kurdish leaders that 'continued internecine fighting would jeopardise support for the safe haven' (*Financial Times*, 27 July 1995). From mid-July both Iraqi government forces and the KDP had shelled PUK-controlled Arbil. The PUK had thereafter attacked the Rawanduz area north of Shaqlawa with a force of several thousand peshmergas. Civilian casualties and disruption to the provision of international aid in the region had raised the concern of the UN in Baghdad. Jewher Namik, one of the KDP delegates to Dublin, was quoted as saying: '[we] believe the Kurdish experiment has failed and that the Kurds should settle for whatever terms they can get from Saddam' (*Financial Times*, 27 July 1995).

But even as the delegates sat down to talk on 9 August, two of Saddam's closest aides, married to Hussein's daughters, had defected to

Jordan, where they were swiftly granted political asylum. The news of the surprise defections prompted the Kurdish delegates to take the peace negotiations more seriously and terms were agreed for finalization at an 'imminent date'. Their implementation, however, would prove more difficult as all revenues under the control of the parties dating from the commencement of fighting in May 1994 were to be accounted for.

Meanwhile, US officials sped to Amman to quiz the defectors, with the express intent of accessing vital information on Iraq's secret military programme and Saddam's personal security from the former minister of military industry, General Hussein Kamel al-Majid and his brother, Saddam Kamel al-Majid, former head of the president's bodyguards.

Reporting on developments, David Hirst observed that Hussein Kamel 'ranks as number five on the list of high officials it [the INC] wants to see indicted by an international tribunal for crimes against humanity. It charges him on eight counts including mass executions and torture, and the use of chemical weapons against Kurdish civilians. It wants a tribunal to investigate his brother on two such counts' (*Guardian*, 12 August 1995).

Western statesmen speculated that the defection of two of Saddam's top aides, the sacking of his half-brother Watban Ibrahim Hassan in May, and the demotion of his cousin, Ali Hassan al-Majid ('Chemical Ali') in July, taken together, suggested a 'narrowing of the president's powerbase' (*Financial Times*, 11 August 1995). With such unprecedented developments rocking Iraq, the Kurdish delegates and Iraqi opposition assembled in Ireland understood that conditions in the north of the country might be altered by events beyond their control. The two warring leaders risked losing their fragile grip on Kurdistan altogether should they fail to forge a workable peace in more than words.

As Saddam swayed and the West speculated on the possibility of his ultimate collapse, the president artfully played his cards. Granting access to the UN's special monitor, Rolf Ekeus, to the long sought-after information on Iraq's military capabilities, he sought to discredit the defectors, accusing General Hussein Kamel al-Majid of having withheld information the UN had demanded – data affecting the lifting of economic sanctions. By this act, Saddam shored up his position and put the ball firmly in the court of the UN.

As a snub to Turkey and its collaboration with the rapid reaction forces, Saddam also closed down his embassy in Istanbul and expelled Turkish officials from Mosul and Turkey.

Turkey's 'Special Research Report on the Eastern Problem' (Doğu Sorunu Teşhisler ve Tespitler)

In July 1995, a special report was published on the 'Eastern Problem' (a well-used euphemism for the Kurdish problem) by the Turkish Trade and Commerce Union (TOBB). It was written and researched by a team under the guidance of Professor Doğu Ergil from the political studies faculty at Ankara University and colleague of Yalim Erez, the president of the TOBB and, interestingly, the original sponsor of Tansu Çiller's candidacy for the premiership. Encountering the backlash, Erez commented: 'This report does not reflect the view of the Turkish Trade and Commerce Union. What is important here is that the facts and errors in this research are debated.'

The report produced shockwaves in Turkey, it being the first time that such a report had been undertaken and made public with the object of finding a political solution to the Kurdish problem. Perhaps a brave first step, the report was considered by the pro-Kurdish quarter, including Hasip Kaplan, lawyer for the now banned DEP party, to have shown a 'very serious lack of information about the government's decade-old policy of violence and repression pursued in the south east. The report investigates PKK violence but it does not give any space to violence carried out by the government. This issue involved the PKK on one side and the government on the other. From this perspective it is not a just enquiry. Nor is it healthy.'

The pro-military lobby, including the Super Governor Ünal Erkan, claimed that the report was incorrect and had only taken in the view of 2,000–3,000 people in three or four provinces: 'According to this report 50% of those consulted were related to the PKK. There are millions of people in the south east. It is not possible to claim that 50% of their relatives are connected with terrorism.'

Interior Minister Nahit Menteşe claimed that the report did not reflect the facts, saying that it advocated a federal solution to the problem and that they would certainly not give permission for such a thing. 'What the PKK wants first anyway is autonomy, after that federation, and then finally to establish an independent Kurdish state. The report has shown too great a support for federation. Such a thing is definitely not possible in Turkey' (quoted from *Hürriyet*, 8 August 1995). Televised debates on the subject of the report, however, reflected 58 per cent public support.

Although recently 22 articles of the Turkish Constitution were amended, article 8 of the Anti-Terror Law has not been superseded nor has there been any real outward improvement; changes remain cosmetic.

Six of the DEP MPs still in prison after 18 months (August 1995) viewed the amendments as inadequate:

> For the people of Turkey life is no different even after these changes. There is nothing new on the horizon for either Turkish or Kurdish people ... Although in principle we support Turkey's application to join the European Customs Union, without Turkey first abandoning the policy and practice of violence and repression inflicting terror at all levels of society, and without a democratic solution to the Kurdish Question (the main source of all the problems in Turkey) its admission to the EU would serve to condone state terrorism officially ... This issue is of great concern to us' (Letter signed by the DEP MPs sent to the head of the Socialist Group of the European Parliament, 14 August 1995).

KDP: a legitimate target of the PKK?

PKK leader Abdullah Öcalan announced on the 15 August 1995 that his party would open a new battle front against the KDP on account of its collaboration with Turkey. This would be understood as the party's second *atilim* (advance), the first *atilim* having been on 15 August 1984 when the PKK reacted decisively to Turkey's *imha politikasi* (policy of annihilation) against Kurdistan by undertaking armed struggle. The PKK's first attack against KDP targets in south Kurdistan began on 26 August 1995 and rapidly escalated. The KDP attacked the refugee camps in Atrush. Turkey applied to the UN in New York to close the camps, arguing they had been infiltrated by the PKK and weapons discovered there. The UN representative in the region refuted this.

The second round of peace talks between the rival Iraqi Kurdish parties took place in Dublin in mid-September 1995 but stalled over the issues of the PUK's demilitarisation of Arbil and of the means to an equitable distribution of revenues from the Ibrahim Khalil customs post which was under the sole control of the KDP. Underlying these issues were tensions aggravated by Turkey's manoeuvres to commit the two parties to its war in the south against the PKK. PUK spokesmen claim to have been privately courted by Turkish officials, who promised to resolve the PUK–KDP conflict if the PUK would agree to fight alongside the Turkish military with the KDP to crush the guerrillas. The PUK declined. But Sami Abdurrahman (M.M. Abdurrahman, the KDP's foreign relations official, said he did not agree with PUK claims that 'Turkish demands for the talks to concentrate more on Turkey's security concerns had hurt the peace process' (*Turkish Daily News*, 27 September 1995). The KDP allegedly informed the PUK that they would never see a penny from the Ibrahim Khalil customs post; the PUK responded by warning that Hewler (Arbil) would not be demobilised.

Sami Abdurrahman was reported by the *Turkish Daily News* as having declared: 'We could overcome the PKK easily if we had arms and ammunion. The ammunition especially is important because we do not wish to use up our ammunition in fighting the PKK and then end up in a weak position if we are attacked by the PUK' (*TDN*, 27 September 1995). Abdurrahman later denied having made these remarks to the Turkish press.

The fundamental mercenary character of the conflict had become self-evident. Armed support was no longer based upon the principle of political support for the KDP so much as upon salary. These fighters were not all peshmergas, they included *çekdars* (armed people), literally, mercenaries.

Meanwhile, Iran and Syria complained to the KDP that while Turkey had insinuated herself as a party to the peace talks their own representatives had been denied access and their interests ignored. The KDP sent delegations to Damascus and Iran to apologise for the political slight.

PUK leader Jalal Talabani, in London during October 1995 for discussions with the Iraqi opposition, the British foreign ministry, PUK committee members and the press, agreed to meet me for an interview. Relaxed in an autumnal suburban setting and clearly in good spirits, he drew out two chairs for us at the dining table to talk politics. I asked him about regional relations and the PUK's position. The KDP had aligned itself with Turkey against the PKK. The PUK had accepted to secure the borders of the region under its control with Iran against attacks from within by the KDPI.

As far as the KDPI goes, there is no revolution now in Iranian Kurdistan, there is no uprising; it is finished. While in Turkey there *is* an uprising, there is fighting in Dersim, Elaziğ, Ağri, Mardin, Diyarbakir, Hakkari, Van. Every day the Turkish newspapers tell us there is some kind of fighting, some kind of confrontation. In Iran there is nothing. Some people escaped from Iranian Kurdistan and came to Iraqi Kurdistan; they must respect our laws. If they want to leave, if they want to go back to their country, they are welcome – we will open the doors. But it is impossible to host them here, allowing ten people to attack Iran and then come back to the same base. Which world state will permit such a thing? Even if Kurdistan will be liberated, if there is an independent Kurdistan, it cannot turn itself into a base for this. While each one [i.e. each organisation] is busy with its own part they must respect the interests of the other. Iran cannot of course permit them [to attack]. Like Turkey it will interfere. We, the PUK, cannot fight against Iran, Turkey and the KDP at the same time. We are surrounded. The main Kurdish movement deserves support. Iranian Kurdistan is quiet. (Excerpt from a private interview with Jalal Talabani, 23 October 1995.)

Chaos in the Turkish coalition government

On 20 September 1995, following the breakdown of talks with CHP partner Deniz Baykal, Prime Minister Tansu Çiller handed her resignation to President Demirel after four years of coalition rule. While Baykal pushed for fundamental changes in Turkey's approach to its problems, Çiller sought to pursue the same policies until the end of her term in November 1996. When asked by President Demirel to form a new government Çiller took steps to gain support, which resulted in the unexpected formation of a minority government backed by the extreme right-wing MHP, Milliyetçi Haraket Parti, the Nationalist Action party of Alparslan Türkeş and Bülent Ecevit's DSP (Demokrat Sol Parti), Democratic Left Party, which offers little evidence of democratic socialism and is characterised by narrow Turkish chauvinism. 'The 1991 parliament that produced a centre–right coalition with the Social Democrats promising to "turn prison walls into glass" has delivered one of the oldest, most right-wing and narrowly nationalist administrations,' observed Hugh Pope of the *Independent* (7 October 1995). (In this spirit of chauvinism the government sent letters of complaint to the Nobel Peace Prize committee objecting to its nomination of Leyla Zana, while seeking to invalidate her candidacy by labelling her a 'terrorist'. Leyla Zana had never employed violent means to deliver her political message of rights for the Kurds.)

Prime Minister Çiller's reactionary move alarmed moderates throughout the country, who perceived in the initiative a dangerous reversion to the fascism behind the violent clashes of the 1970s and the military coup of 1980. Alparslan Türkeş (who sought to bring Turkey into the Second World War on the side of Germany and is the leader of the Grey Wolves) refused to consider any option but a military one: a 'strategy that has only escalated a Kurdish insurgency that broke out in 1984 and has killed more than 17,000 people' (*Independent*, 7 October 1995).

Fortunately for the population, the minority government was defeated by a vote of no confidence in parliament. Çiller momentarily floundered, but was rescued through a surprise reconciliation with former coalition partner Deniz Baykal after she agreed to dismiss the Istanbul chief of police. This was one of the issues which had caused the rift in the coalition in the first place. The coalition restored, Çiller turned her attention once more to pursuit of Turkey's membership of the European Customs Union (EU). Deniz Baykal swiftly departed on a foreign tour aimed at improving the government's image abroad and its chance of success in finalising agreement with the EU. There was talk of a possible release from prison of some of the Kurdish MPs, of improved human rights and of changes to article 8 as preconditions of Union membership.

Despite the manoeuvres of politicians, the war in south-east Turkey (with its second front in northern Iraq) became increasingly ugly. In their invasion of northern Iraq in March 1995, Turkish soldiers had mutilated the bodies of seven Iraqi Kurdish shepherds whom they had captured in Sarsang and then executed after amputating their fingers and genitals, gouging their eyes and slashing their bodies with bayonets. Film shot in evidence by the KDP soon after the murders occurred was broadcast on MED TV, the Kurdish satellite station, on 6 October 1995, coinciding with a relatively minor invasion of south Kurdistan by the Turkish army. Prison sentences of 15 years were ratified against MPs, Leyla Zana, Hatip Dicle, Orhan Doğan and Selim Sadak on 26 October 1995. Ahmet Türk and Sedat Yurttaş were released.

The generals intended to inflict maximum damage on the Kurdish resistance before winter hindered access to the mountains and the few remaining villages. They took advantage of the conflicts between the KDP and PUK, and the KDP and PKK to weaken the Kurdish national movement. The divisions within the movement allowed the enemies of Kurdish nationalism – Iran, Iraq, Syria, Turkey and the Western governments – to preserve their regional interests. Ordinary Kurds endured unthinkable conditions while Kurdistan's problems were predominantly overshadowed on international agendas by those of Bosnia, and the Palestinian and IRA peace processes.

Notes

1. *Stop the War in Kurdistan* – report by mission headed by Lord Avebury to Kurdistan, 19–29 March 1994, published by Kurdistan Information Centre/Kurdistan Solidarity Committee, London.

2. Vago Muradian, 'Is U.S. Intelligence being Mis-used?', *Air Force Times*, USA, 12 December 1994, pp. 20–1.

3. Özgür Ülke, *Dicle asks for a Referendum*, 8 October 1994.

4. Amnesty International, *Turkey: Kurdish Deputies Sentenced to Long Prison Terms*; AI Index EUR 44/WU/20/94.

5. From a private interview with Yaşar Kaya, February 1995.

6. Ibid.

7. The Kizilbash were originally predominantly Turkoman followers of the Safavi dynasty which propogated wildly eccentric shi'i ideas (though there were almost certainly Kurdish tribal followers of the Safavis too). How Kurds became Kizilbash is a matter for surmise: the Kizilbash theology probably incorporated Zoroastrian ideas (possibly already embodied in some eccentric form of Shi'ism). It is known that Kurdish and Turkoman tribes merged – some Kurdish tribes lost their 'identity' as Kurds and *vice versa*, and it was probably by this process that many Kurds embraced Alevism (which embodied a strong strain of folk religion as opposed to formalised Islam). (*Source*: David McDowall, personal communication.)

10

Kurdish women: identity and purpose

It seemed important, if a woman chose to tell me her story, that I should reproduce it as closely as possible to the way in which it was narrated so that the tone of the narrative would be hers rather than mine. Most of the stories told here are narrated in the first person, except that of the women of Barzan, whose saga of mass tragedy is a shared one. This story in particular required an introduction to the circumstances of their awful fate.

The other stories originate from all four main parts of Kurdistan. They cover a number of issues: women's relations within the community, within the political movement, within the home, the family and within personal relationships. They are all true stories. I have changed only the names of particular individuals and places to protect the narrators. In some instances, I have added commentary as background to some of the important issues which the stories themselves raise. Far from being unique to the narrators, these are issues which have bearing upon women's sense of identity throughout Kurdistan.

Daughters in the family

In traditional Kurdish society, as in other patriarchal societies, the ruling male elite – whether secular or religious – restricts the development of female identity. Women are not encouraged to realise and express their own power and independence. Instead, a woman may be killed for exerting her will, for choosing a man to marry that the family has not selected – or of whom they disapprove – for having a love affair or sexual relationship, for eloping or being discovered in a compromising situation or for joining a political party. Punitory killings are carried out by a woman's father, husband, brothers or other male relatives. There is no trial, simply a death sentence, often brutally carried out.

Since the Kurdish uprising, more than one hundred women in south

Kurdistan have been murdered by their fathers or male relatives on such grounds: Nigar Mohammad Haji Bapir was put to death in Raniya on 10 June 1992 by her father for wishing to marry a man of her own choosing. In Arbil, in August of the same year, three women were killed, the first by her father; the second, who was pregnant, was viciously attacked and killed; and the third was killed in Arbil's marketplace. In November of the same year, again in Arbil, at the Kawaskok Camp, another woman was killed by her father.

In February 1993, a woman was shot to death by unidentified persons in front of her two children in Bazian Camp. A month later, on 19 March, Dilkash Sadiq Mohammad was shot several times while in her own home in Barika. She was only 16 years old. Less than a week later, a woman named Pakshan was shot dead by her husband in Sulaimaniya. In May 1993, Amina Abdullah was killed by her father for wishing to marry somebody he disapproved of; and in Halabja, a woman named Ayshe was killed and her baby injured.

The Independent Women's Organisation, established in 1993, complained of these killings, confirming statistics to a Kurdish correspondent of the London-based *Hawkar* newsletter and commenting: 'It is a disgrace that of the 105 members of the Kurdish parliament, only two are women. It confirms that the female point of view is not being adequately expressed in the Kurdish Assembly.'[1]

Such 'traditional' behaviour as the killing of women for impropriety is not the mark of a civilised society. It demonstrates a fundamental lack of humanity and empathy. It is discrimination on the basis of difference, of gender. Physical and emotional abuse of others, whether male or female, is the mark of the beast in society, not of humanity.

According to Dr Tahire Koçtürk, the strong need to control women can be traced to a phenomenon which is older than Islam, the honour ethic. This is based on the belief that women cannot be trusted to protect their chastity in the best interests of the patriarchal society. The duty is given to the male relatives of the women.'[2]

Koçtürk also quotes the Islamic law:

Men have authority over women because God made the one superior to the others, and because they spend their wealth to maintain them. Good women are obedient. They guard their unseen parts because God has guarded them. As for those from whom you fear disobedience, admonish them and send them to beds apart and beat them. Then if they obey you, take no further action against them (quote from the Quran, 4:34; Dawood, 1974).[3]

Men sanctioned their own power and aggression by all manner of means, but the ultimate sanction has been religion: the Crusades, *Jihad*, various other 'holy' or despotic wars were justified by the religious books and the laws which were passed by ruling men. Saddam Hussein is a prime example in modern times of how both power and the abuse of power can be sanctioned by appealing to Islamic scripture to justify various actions.

The monotheistic nature of Yahweh, of God and of Allah in the scriptures of the Torah, the Bible and the Quran is not articulated in feminine terms. Nor are there female prophets. The angels too have male names. The authors and messengers who wrote and delivered the scriptures were male. But this is turned about in the great religions, so that male superiority is considered to be God's creation, as Muslims believe the Quran to be God's word and Mohammad but his messenger. Religious intolerance, the renaissance of the *fatwa*, and prejudiced religious scholarship may even make these statements dangerous to utter.

Islam perfected the segregation of human society. It created two worlds set apart from each other: the world of free, dominant men, and the fettered, passive, world of women:

> Islam's firm insistence on moulding the personalities of men and women in opposite poles, reflects the need of a patriarchy to protect itself from some imagined threats from women. 'Be careful about the rights of women,' said Mohammad on his deathbed, 'for they are prisoners at your hands.' The phrase conjures the image of a war between genders, with women being taken as prisoners, by men.[4]

From early childhood, young Kurdish girls, like girls in other Middle Eastern and Judaeo-Christian societies, are taught to feel ashamed of their bodies and told that a woman must submit to her husband, and must not show too obvious an outward pleasure in the act of physical love (despite the Quran's emphasis that a woman has the right to sexual gratification and that failure of a husband to provide that gratification is sufficient ground for divorce). She is repressed and confused. Often she is neither able, nor permitted, to ask about her body or about sexual matters, nor to express herself freely. She is restricted from learning to experience life and human relationships in their subtlety and complexity in the way that a boy can, lest she be labelled a whore and dishonour the men in her community.

Women are made to feel psychologically inferior because they are not encouraged to be self-reliant, to believe in their own abilities, or to strive for success in some professional or vocational field as a priority over or alternative to marriage. For a woman, marriage ought to be the first priority; a woman's *raison d'être*. But to defend his own honour and reputation a man may renounce or shame his partner, even in front of the community, with impunity. He can divorce his partner if she fails to live up to his expectations as a virtuous wife, a good mother and housekeeper. He may bring a second wife into the home, or as many as four wives, under Islamic law. Polygyny for men is justifiable on religious grounds. A woman is less than a whole person:

> Islam quantifies the inequality between men and women: in a court of law, the testimony of two women is equal to that of one man. In marriage she is equal to one-fourth of a man.[5]

Aspects of female biology, such as menstruation, become *haram*, unclean. A man must not have sexual relations with a menstruating woman. Women are not only physically, but also psychologically, shunned once a month for the duration of their fertile lives when not bearing children. A euphemism frequently employed by men of a menstruating woman is that she is 'sick'.

Much of women's history has been written with the blood of the womb – in menstrual pain and isolation, childbirth and self-sacrifice in defence of the human family. But while the birth of children should be the culmination and product of love, it is often the outcome of rape, of lust and of the brutality of warring men.

Kurdish women, like Muslim women elsewhere, often unwittingly reinforce negative social customs misnamed as their own 'traditions'. They are deeply caught up in unconscious social behaviour. They may satisfy their negative feelings about their social condition by indulging in cruel and damaging discussion about other Kurdish women who have been indiscreet. When women's gossip of this nature travels as far as men's ears, the resultant scandal can destroy the lives of all but the most powerful women. The male relatives in the family may even justify having a woman murdered as punishment for the shame associated with gossip about female romantic or illicit indiscretions, as illustrated above.

For a woman in Kurdish society to remain unmarried is tantamount to being rejected by the community as not good enough, not beautiful enough or too old. 'Too old' can be anything over 25. Worst of all three is to be 'not good enough', morally unfit, a woman of 'experience'. In keeping with the custom of most patriarchal societies, it is unacceptable for a woman to have more than one partner except in the case of the death of a first husband, where it is considered appropriate for a woman to remarry. Even so, many women choose not to do so lest they jeopardise their reputations, and hence their honour.

This 'tradition' of inequality between the sexes, of using a woman and her sexuality as a substitute for the honour of the individual members of the society, does not build a just and healthy community. It deludes and corrupts the hearts and minds of men and distorts the personalities of women. This is not the justice, kindness and freedom which Kurds claim to care about. Kurds who cling to 'traditions' like these as being 'Kurdish' do not yet understand what human freedom is. These are not Kurdish traditions. They are the customs of patriarchies, which suit men and have been sanctioned by men through the power of the state and of religion in many countries in the world. But men are deeply conditioned into living in accordance with the old convention of 'honour' which makes of women its victims, or its 'heroines'.

Brutal regimes terrorise and subdue their citizens into submission as a means of controlling them; must men also perpetuate violence against women as proof of what they perceive to be their superiority?

For a woman to enter the Kurdish political arena has traditionally been extremely difficult. The PKK has been one of the first parties to have succeeded in attracting large numbers of women into its political ranks as well as into its armed struggle, where women have their own army. The following stories look at various aspects of women's lives: those who chose to pursue a political path such as in the story of Nermin, who became a PKK guerrilla fighter like many young women of her generation from Turkish Kurdistan and Syria; women struggling against the constraints imposed upon them professionally and personally by feudal society, as with Nazdar and those who are particularly brutalised by the central governments at war with the Kurds; the most vulnerable members of their society such as with Amina and Sirwa in Ba'athist Iraq.

These are all women whom I have spent time with, coaxing their stories from them with as much tact and sympathy as possible to spare them pain as they probe some of their most difficult, or even most meaningful, experiences.

The widows of Barzan

After the collapse of the Kurdish revolution in 1975, the inhabitants of some 1,800 villages in the Barzan and Mergasor region, predominantly members of the Barzani tribe, were taken away by Saddam's forces to the south of Iraq. There they endured until 1978, when they were moved back north to Kurdistan and installed in detention camps at four main sites: Diana, Beherke, Harir and Qushtapa. The Iraqi government euphemistically named these places 'model villages'. They each numbered around 50,000 inhabitants. Most of the villages in the Barzan region were then destroyed.[6]

During the Iran–Iraq war, the Iraqi army suffered serious casualties at Haj Omran on 22 July 1983 following the incursion of Iranian forces into Iraqi Kurdistan. According to one Kurdish report on the affair, Saddam paid a visit to the front at Rawanduz to launch a counter-attack against Iran. Unable to dislodge the Iranians from their positions, Iraq claimed that the KDP had helped the Iranians take Haj Omran. Admitting the Iranian advance on television, Saddam Hussein held Massoud and his brother Idris Barzani personally responsible. Not being capable of reaching those it had accused, Iraq unleashed its hatred and wrath on 8,000 Barzani Kurds living under its own protection.[7]

On 30 July 1983, the Iraqi army surrounded the four camps and took away all males between the age of 10 and 80 years old. They were taken to Baghdad, Najaf and Kerbala, where Saddam paraded them as captured Iranian POWs before relocating them in another camp near the Jordanian border. In September that year, three of Mulla Mustafa Barzani's sons were arrested and executed.[8] Nothing has been heard of the rest, despite the fact that on 24 May 1988, the Preparatory Committee on Disappearances in Kurdistan presented their findings at the 24th session of the United Nations to the Working Group on Enforced and Involuntary Disappearances. The committee had earlier compiled a list of 2,280 of the 8,000 names of the missing, recounting the circumstances of their removal.[9] A resolution was passed to investigate the case and demand that the Iraqi government provide an official account for the disappearance of the 8,000 Barzani Kurds. Again, in May 1988, all the remaining males in these four camps aged 5 and above were taken away by the Iraqis. In the Karadagh region, near Sulaimaniya, all males aged between 10 and 80 years old were forcibly removed and placed in army trucks heading south.

But it was in 1983, a decade ago, that most of the women of Barzan became 'widows'. Lacking conclusive evidence of their spouses' decease, they have continued to live in a state of desperate hope that some day they will see their sons, brothers and husbands again, unsure as to whether they were executed, or whether they are still alive somewhere. Year in and year out they continue to hope that their men will one day return, for while there is still doubt, they are unable to mourn or begin new lives. Remarriage is a complicated issue. These women have become 'living martyrs'.

In 1988, when asked about the missing Barzani males, Saddam made a television announcement in which he declared they had been sent to 'the engravers' (in other words, the cemetery).[10] But the bodies have still to be located.

Left without men to work for them, the widows' economic circumstances are extremely harsh, as the men customarily bring in the income. These women and their unmarried daughters are sometimes exploited by outsiders. Some have been forced into prostitution in the towns near their camps to obtain the money to survive. Those who fall pregnant find themselves in a desperate situation. Morally ostracised, they are viewed as having brought further shame and suffering upon the extended community. With a bankrupt Kurdistan, mass unemployment and no social security system, it is no small matter to provide for thousands of Barzani widows.

Barzan women living in Qushtapa camp, Arbil, who had suffered the consequences of having relationships with men outside the tribe, or outside marriage, told one correspondent in summer 1993: 'Many women believe that in such circumstances killing is the only way to purge what they call "unclean hearts". A doctor working in Qushtapa says he knows of at least twenty such incidents in the past few years.'[11] Women are still being murdered by their families for 'sexual impropriety'. Females are not permitted by the society to stray into compromising relations.

The green fields surrounding Barzan village rippled with blood-red anemones. Many houses had been built over the old ruins and people were everywhere. On getting closer, however, you saw that almost all the inhabitants were women. This was a disturbing confirmation of the tragedy that had overtaken the Barzani families. As beautiful as the location of Barzan village happens to be, it is as if a dark cloud keeps the place in shadow.

Two grey-haired women sat on the doorstep of a newly rebuilt house looking out over the village. Both were dressed in black. The women wore their hair hanging in two long locks at the front, the rest tucked under the black hoods of their chadors in keeping with the style for women of their age in this area.

We approached the pair, hoping they would talk with us. Baby white rabbits scattered as we reached the steps which led to their front porch. An attractive young girl of about 14 years of age, dressed in a purple and white floral dress, came out of the house and stood smiling in welcome. Dr Lokman, an English-speaking doctor from Dohuk in charge of health care for the villages in and around Barzan, accompanied us. He knew the families here and his presence made it easier to call upon a household. The girl in the purple dress slipped inside to fetch refreshments and reappeared at once with a tray, offering glasses of orange cordial. The two women looked to be in their late forties or fifties. But it was difficult to know; suffering had doubtless aged them beyond their years. The women spoke in short anguished sentences, searching their memories for words which could begin to describe what had happened. 'Last autumn, I came back to Barzan. It used to be much better before. Once there were many people here. We had our flocks and herds to live off; we had our homes, our families and our possessions; now there is nothing left – no houses, no people, no animals, and no life.' Five men from her family had been taken and not heard of again.

'We don't know anything about what happened to our men,' she explained. 'They were all taken away by the government. We are low in spirits but we have some hope left. We are still waiting for God to bring them back safely … I had four sons. At the time they were captured, the youngest was 10 years old, the next 15, the third about 20 years old, married with two children, and the eldest was 25 years old. He was also married and had four children. We don't know why they were taken.

'It happened very early at about five one morning. Those who were awake had already got up to pray. Others were still in bed. The army came and surrounded our village. Saddam's soldiers commanded everyone to come outside and then they rounded us up and took all the men. Whoever was awake was taken first, then those still sleeping were sought and taken from their beds.

'The government saw us as their enemy. They wanted to evict us and force us to go into camps. Of course we didn't want to go. But what could we do? They made us leave our homes and villages. After that, we had to live in the camps they'd built for us.

'One time, they came to the camp we'd been moved to by night, and surrounded us as before. They rounded up any men who were there, even those who were sick or injured, even those who were mad, even those whose two eyes were blind. The soldiers tied their feet with animal tethers and dragged them off. No one was left, no one at all. By God, there was not an adult male left in the village old enough to slaughter the chickens. They took everyone and just dumped them into lorries and went away. Year after year, we women were left to wash the bodies of our dead and guard the camps ourselves.

'How can we forgive those who did this to us? We can never forgive them. They destroyed our homes, they destroyed our lives. Who could forgive them? We'll keep on hoping to see our men again for as long as we live.'[12]

Tears filled her eyes. She didn't try to wipe them away. She looked far into the distance, not seeing us any more.

Middle East Watch and Physicians for Human Rights, documenting evidence of genocide against the Kurds, believe:

Most, if not all, those who disappeared during Anfal were murdered by Iraqi security forces ... Surviving Kurds – women, children and the elderly – were transferred by truck in a state of great hunger and privation from forts to areas of southern Kurdistan. By tens of thousands they were dumped in camps which lacked food, water, shelter or medical attention. These camps were simply empty land watched by guard towers. Many died there; those who survived did so with the help of essential supplies brought into the camps by Kurds from neighbouring towns.[13]

One eyewitness to the forcible removal of Kurdish men from these camps told how: 'From the 22nd to the 29th of July 1983, we could tell from the passing of long lines of military trucks, armoured vehicles and fighter planes towards the north, that unusual events were taking place ... We, the inhabitants of Qushtapa camp, had no reason to fear, simply because we were civilians who had not acted against the regime. Some of our young men had been taken to be trained in government military camps, and the rest were preoccupied with our daily work to support our families. We did not expect any mass retaliation for what was happening at Haj Omran ... On July 30th my wife woke up as usual at four o'clock in the morning for the morning prayer and to prepare breakfast for us. That morning, I was awakened by my wife shaking me vigorously. She looked horrified and said, "Our camp is encircled by Iraqi soldiers, we are inside a ring of armoured vehicles."'

Soldiers then entered the camp, firing their guns and breaking down doors. The Kurds ran away to hide, but were ferociously beaten and dragged away once discovered. There were about 20,000 inhabitants in this camp and it was in an uproar. But by 11.30 that morning, the witness recalled, there were no men left between the ages of 12 and 80, except those who had successfully concealed themselves from the rampaging soldiers in ovens, barrels or any other hiding place. The narrator managed to escape that same night, and walked for the next four days through the mountains to safety.[14]

We wandered slowly back along the dirt lanes between the houses towards the orchards of broken trees, wild flowers blooming around their roots. I sat down on a large boulder on the green hillside overlooking the former stone terraces of the Barzan vineyards. No one spoke. Saddam's forces still lurked just a few miles away, leaving the widows to wonder if the soldiers would return and once more destroy everything that had been built.

Sirwa's narrative of the Halabja massacre

'It was 13 March 1988, and Iran had begun shelling the outskirts of Halabja. By the next day, the noise of the bombing was closer and a few shells hit the town itself. News reached us that Iran had killed a number of Kurdish people in these attacks.

'At that time I was a teacher, busy preparing papers for examinations. The exams were set for 16 March. Everybody had been working hard for these exams and our minds were focused on them. Although there had been some disruption in the school because of the shelling, I was going to go anyway to get exams over with for my students.

'One of my colleagues, Pari, was in the final month of her pregnancy. She left us on 13 March saying how happy she would be to see us at her home after the baby was born. We were delighted for her, and even the Iranian bombing did not affect our spirits. Pari kissed us affectionately and left the school.

'The night of the 15th, things in Halabja were very unstable. We saw that many peshmergas from the PUK and from the Islamic Party led by Mella Ali had come into town. This was something very unusual as the Ba'ath Party who had been entrenched in our midst and the senior Ba'ath officials of the *Amn* (Security) and Munazama (Ba'ath Party Political Headquarters) were nowhere to be seen, nor had we heard that any of them had been killed. They must have been pre-warned of Saddam's intentions and left. Only ordinary Iraqi army conscripts from the tank forces remained in position to defend the area against Iran. They were hungry and their morale was low.

'It was a warm spring evening and people were outside. We were talking with the peshmergas about developments. They spoke of liberating Sulaimaniya and other parts of Kurdistan, telling us, 'Now you are free in Halabja.' But they had only their Kalashnikovs, no heavier weapons. The people were surprised by this and didn't know what to believe.

'I felt anxious and was unable to sleep because of the highly charged atmosphere around us. You could feel that something was about to happen. I had returned home that evening at 11 p.m. after listening to the news and had gathered up my valuables: my jewellery, money and identity papers and those of Kamal, my husband. He and the rest of his family with whom we lived felt the same apprehension.

'On the morning of 16 March, I asked Kamal if he thought I should call in at school as it was the day for the examinations. I thought perhaps the students would be arriving to sit their test. Kamal did not like this idea as we could see that the peshmergas were still in town and that there were no government officials about. The sound of shelling from Iran was still close.

'I set off for school anyway as it was near our home. It was a bright sunny day but everyone in the street seemed tense. Many women had begun to collect their belongings and assemble their families as if they were getting ready to leave town. I didn't see any of my students or any of the other teachers.

'By the time I reached school a large padlock had been fixed to the outside gate. I returned home quickly feeling disappointed that so much work had been in vain and put my papers aside. Iranian bombs were falling just a few kilometres away. I felt very restless and wanted to understand what was going on. My family lived several hours away in Sulaimaniya and I began to fear that I might not be able to see them again. I decided to visit a friend with Kamal to find out if anyone was planning to travel to Sulaimaniya.

'When I arrived at my friend's home two of my friends were also there. They said that nobody had been able to leave for Sulaimaniya because Iran had been bombing the road. Others had tried to head for the border with Iran but the peshmergas had prevented them from going any further, repeating that they were now liberated in Halabja and must remain there. Several people had gathered in my friend's house because there was a bomb shelter there. Most of the houses in Halabja had cellars or shelters as the war between Iraq and Iran had been going on for a long time. After an hour conferring with these friends, Kamal and I returned home. The shutters of the shops were all closed now and the markets were empty. Groups of people were standing around outside their houses trying to decide what best to do next.

'It was still quite early in the day, around 10 a.m. But now there were so many Iranian *pasdars* and peshmergas in the streets, it looked like a kind of procession. They were all armed and seemed ready to fight. Some were riding mules; some mules were laden with weapons. This was the first time I had ever seen the *pasdars* up close and I was frightened. When we arrived home, my mother-in-law had already cooked lunch and we sat down to eat. Everyone had seen the *pasdars* in town with the peshmergas. As soon as lunch was over, I went outside with my sister-in-law to wash the dishes under the garden tap, as there was no plumbing for running water in the kitchen. The family were inside drinking tea. I heard the sound of planes approaching. At almost the same moment, the bathroom adjoining the garden was struck by a bomb from above. There were perhaps as many as eight planes overhead. But because our house had been hit, the air was suddenly filled with dust and I couldn't see a thing. I could only hear the sound of dishes breaking and my husband

and his mother crying out to us in alarm from within, knowing we had been near where the shell struck. I covered my eyes, and crouched in the corner of the garden until the dust settled. As the air cleared, the planes also receded. I could see that other parts of town had also been hit. As we had no bomb shelter of our own we decided to leave the house. One of our neighbours across the street had a shelter. We went straight there. We saw that two or three other houses in the block had also been destroyed by the bombs.

'Many of our neighbours had already gathered in this shelter. Their eyes were full of fear. Some had brought blankets, lamps, and candles and some had bread with them. Others had brought their valuables. There was a clamour of voices, and people were blaming the peshmergas for bringing in the *pasdars*, and turning Halabja into a war zone. Now the planes began to come over every few minutes, bombing incessantly.

'Down in the shelter we huddled together in a corner, motionless and silent, our heads buried in our laps, until the sound of the planes had gone. There were nearly a hundred people down there all trampling on each other and the air was suffocating. Small children were screaming and crying; everyone was calling out to everyone else. Suddenly bombs began to rain down on the house overhead. Across the entrance to the shelter from the stairs there was no door, only a blanket. Our shelter filled with dust and chips of flying concrete. Some of the people got up to see what had happened: the house had been destroyed by a bomb. And the planes were still coming over non-stop. They came so fast and hard there was no time even to change our places. They flew very low and purposefully, roaring over us. We believed that this time Saddam meant to show us no mercy.

'Suddenly, we began to smell something very peculiar, rather like household gas. But there was something different about it too. Soon it began to affect our breathing. I had heard that Saddam had used chemicals in Karadagh not far from Halabja. I had even read that if attacked by chemicals you should immediately soak a piece of cloth in water and cover your face with it. These thoughts came to me in a flash at that moment. People had started coughing. I asked my husband to bring water quickly. Someone near me said the smell was probably only gas leaking somewhere in the house. But my husband did as I'd asked anyway and returned to the shelter with a large bucket of water. He told everyone to soak their blankets and clothes in it and went out again to fetch more.

'After half an hour we decided to try to escape from this shelter even though the planes kept on coming, bombing the town from every direction. Outside, everything had been transformed. This was no longer the place it had been. Houses were in flames. Fires had been ignited from the oil and exploding gas released by the shelling. People were running through the streets, coughing, desperately covering their faces. I too kept my eyes and mouth covered with a wet cloth and ran in the direction of a shelter we knew which lay beneath a large public building away from the centre of town. As I ran, I caught sight of a man lying on the footpath gasping for breath. We knew he was affected by the chemicals but were unable to stop and help him. A little further on we saw an old woman who already lay dead, past help. There was no sign of blood or any injury on her. Her face was waxen and white foam bubbled from the side of her mouth.

'The shelter we sought was below one of the government offices. Everyone in the immediate vicinity had also gone there thinking it would offer better protection from conventional aerial bombing. There were about 500 people already there when we arrived; none of them knew anything about any chemical attacks, nor had they smelled anything like gas in the area. In the shelter there wasn't even space left to sit down. It now occurred to me that my handbag with all our valuables inside had been forgotten back at our house. My husband insisted on going back to retrieve it as we didn't have a penny with us and were now considering making a run for the border. When he arrived back at the crowded shelter with the bag, Kamal told us that he'd seen as many as a dozen people lying dead in the street. Upon entering our house he'd also found that all the hens, the rooster and the turkeys we kept were lying dead across the ground. Now we were sure that chemicals had been used this morning against Halabja. I looked up at my husband and saw that his lips, his entire face, was deathly white.

'The planes could be heard again approaching at great speed. As they flew down close above us we heard the sound of shells being dropped. Almost at once we began to smell the gas. "These are chemical bombs. Our area was hit by them before we came here. We have to leave here now!" we warned the others. But some were unwilling to believe such an incredible idea and replied, "This building is very strong, we are safest here." They didn't think that chemical gas was really being used against us, nor that it would easily penetrate this shelter.

'I suspected that the government's plan had been to make us think that this was just conventional bombing so that people would try to hide themselves in such shelters as this one and would certainly be killed once chemical gas was used as well. Within minutes, people began coughing and gasping for breath. Others had begun to vomit. We got out quickly. By now it was about 6 p.m., but as it was springtime the sky was still light. Outside the building we found a tap with a hose attached to it. Kamal immediately began to spray our faces with water. We were calling back and forth to each other, asking, "What do you feel now? Are you all right? What is happening?"

'I was starting to get dizzy. I couldn't catch my breath. And I was so terrified that my legs would hardly hold up any longer. Although we saw a few peshmergas who indicated which way to go, we didn't notice any *pasdars* now.

'It was then that I found out that Pari, my friend from school, had been killed in the first wave of bombing. Her husband and son had just left the room where she was sitting when the bomb struck. Her husband had been unable to rescue her from the rubble. Taking their small son with him, Pari's husband had quickly run away to a different part of the city to try to save themselves. But there too, within one hour, the bombs had begun to fall. They were chemical bombs. Nobody at all survived.'

Exodus from Halabja

'Kamal and I now headed for a village which lay a little way from Halabja. Along the way, we met an old woman and her son. The son was begging his mother to carry on with him, but she clearly couldn't walk any longer. She was urging him to go without her because she had been blinded by chemical gas and couldn't see any more. The two of them had been in the shelter with us. I too had begun to feel a sort of haze stealing across my eyes. Nothing seemed steady. My husband said his eyes had also been affected. His face was still utterly white. We held hands to try and keep walking but every time either one of us stumbled or fell, the other would also fall down. Slowly we went forward in this way, stumbling and getting up, falling and carrying on again.

'We reached green fields now. There were a number of townspeople around us, some helping those who'd become ill, others awkwardly carry-ing relatives on their backs, clutching what few belongings they could manage. The elderly and disabled faced the greatest difficulty. Some had to be left behind in Halabja if there was no one who could bring them. We were half-blind ourselves, wailing, crying out to one another to keep in contact.

'It had begun to get dark by the time we reached the village around 8 p.m. In front of one of the houses we came upon a man in his sixties lying on his back on the grass. Three of his sons were frantically trying to resuscitate him, pumping his heart and massaging his hands, fighting through their tears to keep him alive. But it was no use. Finally, they had to abandon him and carry on themselves.

'We gently stepped over the man and went in search of water inside the house. We bathed our eyes and drenched our faces and went out again. The sky had become dark. The air was fresh and cool and we could feel it helping to clear our eyes. I was wearing a light dress and had nothing else to put on against the chill night air. Then I caught sight of Ronak, a friend from Halabja who had just reached the village with her husband. I knew she suffered from asthma and when I spoke with her I became worried. Although she had been able to bring some medicine with her, she was crying, saying she couldn't make it.

'Then suddenly the planes came back in the direction of Halabja. We fled up into the foothills outside the village, about five kilometres beyond Halabja. When the planes began bombing we could see around us bright as day. We watched the flashes of light made by the falling bombs, saw fires breaking out and smoke billowing above the rooftops. Then we pressed on again, looking for the way to the Iranian border, each following the other, hoping we were going in the right direction. From four different routes, the Kurds were streaming out of Halabja heading towards Iran in search of safety.

'Night was setting in now and the air was growing colder. Because we were at a higher altitude out in the fresh cold air the effects of the chemical gas grew less, but we were still helpless against conventional bombs. After taking only short stops to rest we would carry on walking again, desperate to reach the border. My husband and I were holding onto each other by the hand. It was black out and we were unable to light the way for fear of attracting the attention of the planes.

'And then I tripped and fell into a large pit, its sides jagged with rocks and sharp stones. Kamal and Ronak also fell in after me. Ronak struck her forehead against the rocks. At the time no one could see how serious her injury was. Ronak simply said that she felt dizzy. We helped wrap her head in a scarf as she complained of the pain, begging us to leave her behind. But we got her back up onto her feet and forced her to carry on.

'Some people on that difficult journey tied themselves together with lengths of cloth from the men's *shittik* (cummerbunds) so as not to lose one another, there were so many people stumbling through the darkness. We had not thought to do this but instead relied on staying together by calling out to one another by name as we walked.

'A small cluster of people had stopped just in front of us. They were shouting and weeping. There had been an accident. A youth had fallen into a deep well. The boy's sister had also fallen but had been caught in time. Now their mother was refusing to leave the place, crying hysterically, begging people to help rescue her son from the well. But down in the well all was silent. It was impossible to hear or see the boy as the well was so deep. Perhaps he was unconscious or dead already. The crowd was urging the woman to leave the well and carry on without her son, and she was begging them to stay and try to get her son out. But it was impossible. At last she consented to leave, weeping bitterly.

'A little further along in the darkness, a woman was giving birth. She lay beneath some blankets which some strangers had provided but had only one old woman with her. They were crying out for someone to help deliver the baby. In any other circumstances it would have been shameful for a man to do this, but here there was no choice. A kind man helped to bring the unfortunate baby into this world. After the baby was born they went looking for something sharp enough to cut the cord and could only find a piece of rock. It was terrible. There was great confusion and people were shouting that the child was a symbol of bad luck. The poor mother was deeply distressed and downcast with shame.

'And so we walked on until we could not walk another step. It must have been about 2 a.m. before we stopped again. A few people had begun to light fires along the way. After less than half an hour beside a fire we felt we must move on or our legs would not respond at all. Ronak had become faint and was out of breath, pleading with us to leave her. Other sick and elderly people were also begging to be left so as not to burden the rest by holding them back. Children had already died along the way.

'We were now very close to the Iranian border at a point where the river Sirwan flows into the neighbouring valleys. We heard the occasional sound of mines exploding. People were killed. We could not see where they were. From now on we had to move in single file very cautiously, placing one foot in front of the other on the narrow path we followed, afraid that one false move would see us stepping on a landmine, or tripping over to fall into the rushing river.

'We were still calling out one another's name to remain together. I called to my husband and he called back to me. Ten minutes later I called again. This time there was no answer. Reluctantly, Ronak, her husband and I carried on together with one of my husband's brothers who was also just behind us. The four of us walked on thinking the others must still be close by, or that at least we would find them as soon as it became light. We wanted to get across the river before daybreak as the river marked the border with Iran and, as we believed, safety.

'But now again, we could hear the growl of planes off in the distance. We were afraid they would find us once it grew light. But as it happened we did not reach the river until 6 a.m. The river was in full flood from the spring rains and melting snow, and the path down to it was steep and slippery. Some people slid on the path and tumbled screaming into the churning waters of the river only to be swept out of sight by the current.

'On the further side of the river we could now see the *pasdars*. They had already made a rough bridge for people to get across the water. When I reached the river bank the woman ahead of me had stopped half way along the bridge. She was screaming hysterically that she had lost her husband and five children in the chemical attacks and had just the small baby which she held in her arms. She cried that she had lost so much she no longer wanted the one child left to her. Suddenly, in a fit of passion, she threw the small bundle into the river before anyone could get to her. Some of the *pasdars* managed to get hold of her before she had the chance to cast herself off the bridge after the baby. We never saw her again. Perhaps the unfortunate creature succeeded in putting an end to her own tragic life.'

The Sojourn in Iran

'I crossed the bridge into Iran. There were many *pasdars* along the riverbank gathered in anticipation as the people of Halabja continued to flee in their thousands towards the border. We had just begun to feel relief at having reached a point of safety when we saw the Iraqi planes return. Just before they got to us I saw them dropping bombs on the Iraqi side of the river where I believed my husband must certainly have been as I had still not found him. Then, almost at once, the planes continued on until they were right above the bridge. The *pasdars* returned fire with anti-aircraft artillery. I could hear two different kinds of sounds as the bombs dropped – conventional explosions and another sound which accompanied the special chemical shells. At once there was a strange smell in the air. Instinctively, Ronak and I covered ourselves with a blanket. After a short while, I lifted a corner of the blanket to see what had happened as I could hear people screaming and crying out with fear. To my astonishment all the *pasdars* around us were wearing gas masks.

'The mountainside before us was steep and the ascent was sharp, so that climbing was slow and difficult. We had only gone a short distance when again the planes returned and bombed. This time people began to feel a burning sensation beneath their skin even in places where the skin was not exposed. I was affected too, and Ronak's general condition was deteriorating. One of the *pasdars* removed the scarf we'd tied around her forehead. Now I realised how severe her injury had been. A deep gash slashed Ronak's brow almost to the bone. There was little time to treat her here and the *pasdars* gave her basic first aid, freshening the bandage, before we moved on again. Many people had started to become ill because of the latest chemical attack.

'When we reached the top of the mountain we saw the *pasdars* were gathering the sick and wounded into army jeeps to take them to hospital.

People were desperate to leave and were pushing one another out of the way in the hope that they would be taken first, screaming and shouting in panic as the planes kept on coming, even though they were now invading Iranian airspace. Some of the *pasdars* were filming this scene with video cameras.

'I managed to get Ronak and her husband onto one of the jeeps and although I wanted to go with them, the jostling crowd made it impossible. We were separated. Now I was alone and felt very afraid. I was sick and weak, and thought that my husband and the rest of his family must have been killed. Life lost all meaning for me at that moment. I didn't care if I should also die there. I waited in that area for another two hours, hoping to catch sight of someone from my family, as there was a steady stream of people still arriving from across the bridge below. Some were saying that if we went with the jeeps it would be easier to find those who were missing later on. This seemed logical to me so at last I too decided to go on.

'The journey took nearly four hours. Our eyes streamed, burning from the effect of the chemicals, and our eyelids became stuck together. Many children were crying with fright as they felt their eyes becoming glued shut. The burning sensation under my skin had also worsened. We were desperately sick and people had started vomiting. It seemed that everyone had lost someone, was looking for a member of his or her family, separated in the confusion. Some of my fellow passengers died in the jeep alongside me.

'Finally we reached the town of Bakhtaran. The local townspeople were watching us as we passed by their shops and drove through the streets of the town. Some were distressed at our condition and wept at the sight of us with our faces swollen, black and blistered from the chemicals. A few put packets of bread or apples and other kinds of food into our vehicles; others were wary of us, wondering if we were going to prove a further burden to them and merely looked on without expression.

'The *pasdars'* jeeps unloaded people at schools vacated on account of the emergency, others at the hospitals and health clinics. As we were still wearing the same clothes, the chemical phosphates which had saturated the fabric were continuing to permeate our bodies. But it was not until we were taken to the *hamam* (public bath) the next day, where we were able to wash, that we understood this. All night we had remained in our clothes, getting sicker, not even able to sleep as we lay on the bare concrete floors of the classrooms, crying away the night in mourning for those who'd died or those who'd become lost to us. There was no way out. We were utterly helpless. The *pasdars* had locked us up in the school.'

Sirwa was reunited with her husband a month later. Kamal told her how the *pasdars* had allowed himself and some other families to return to their homes in Halabja after three days to retrieve a few possessions which Iran had been unable to provide them with. But upon arriving in Halabja they had discovered that all the most valuable household items – electrical appliances, televisions and furniture – had been stolen, and that little of value remained. Undisciplined elements within the Kurdish resistance were also implicated. The structure of most of the town's buildings, however, was still intact.

Kamal and Sirwa's tea still remained on the living room floor as they'd left it, their glasses half-full. After allowing this brief foray back, the *pasdars* quickly reassembled the people to return to the camps with what possessions they'd managed to retrieve. On the fourth day, Halabja was attacked again and retaken by Saddam as soon as the chemicals had dispersed. The townspeople would not see Halabja again for three years.

Why Halabja?

I met Sirwa and Kamal in London. They had left Kurdistan at the end of the failed Kurdish uprising of 1991, and fled with thousands of others across the border into Iran. After remaining in Iran for a further year, they had reached Britain and applied for political asylum. From there they continued to watch developments in their homeland with sadness and concern. They were trying to start a new life. Sirwa's chemical burns had left no facial disfigurement. To look upon this couple, so outwardly confident, one would never dream they had lived through so horrific an experience. One evening over dinner, as Sirwa finished telling me her story, Kamal explained why he thought Halabja had been bombed with chemicals.

Kamal was convinced that Halabja had always been in an unusual position. Situated as near as it was to Iran, it had always been subject to influences from Iran. At the same time, it had always had a fervently patriotic Kurdish element. The pro-Iranian and the pro-Kurdish elements historically represented the two opposite poles of opinion in Halabja. During the period before the uprising of 1991, when Saddam's government had been in control of all Kurdistan, Saddam had considerable difficulty controlling Halabja or subjecting its inhabitants to the will of the state. The Kurds in Halabja had been able to preserve a sense of their independent identity.

After the revolution in Iran, the new virulent fundamentalist form of Islam was exported into neighbouring Kurdistan, particularly the adjacent towns such as Halabja, Qala Diza and Raniya. For an element of the

Kurdish population opposed to the Ba'ath government the resurgence of fundamental Islamic values provided an attractive and meaningful alternative. There was a noticeable change in the behaviour of ordinary people. Outwardly, from around 1980 onwards, many of Halabja's women began to adopt Islamic dress. For the first time, head scarves were seen in the schools and on the street as women covered up. Women like Sirwa who had a deep sense of their Kurdish identity resisted the trend, observing an increasing division in the society around them even as they continued to go to work bareheaded, dressing in modern Western-style clothing, quite at ease with open necklines and short sleeves. Kurdish dress in this part of Kurdistan had always exhibited the female form with pride, favouring styles which enhanced the curves. Wearing Western dress came naturally to them.

During the Kurdish revolution of 1974–75, when the KDP had good relations with the Shah, the Kurdish towns along the Iraq–Iran border were virtually liberated from all government control as the peshmergas moved with comparative freedom back and forth between the two states.

After Mulla Mustafa Barzani's death and the emergence of the PUK, the PUK had by 1982 struck up an alliance with Iran against Baghdad. The PUK, KDP and Socialist Party all took the side of Iran against Iraq in the liberation of Halabja and had headquarters there. Iraq warned the occupants in radio broadcasts that every means would be used against them should they continue to support the 'Persian enemy' (the infidels). Six months before the assault on Halabja chemicals were used against several places, including Belissan, Karadagh and villages in Bahdinan. Several hundreds were killed in these early attacks. Thereafter, the Kurdish movement knew the Iraqi government was likely to employ chemicals against them.

Saddam had few qualms about using chemical weapons against Halabja. The Kurds were siding with Iran against him; Halabja had shown sympathy with the enemy. The Kurds had allegedly agreed to take Halabja for themselves, with Iranian back-up, in their struggle against Baghdad; but under the agreement, the *pasdars* were not supposed to have entered the town. Halabja had been unfaithful to the central government even in times of peace, and in Saddam's view it was not to be trusted. The entire population of 70,000 people therefore constituted a dispensable enemy and Halabja was conveniently hidden from the eyes of the world on the warfront.

Saddam attacked Halabja with a variety of chemical weapons and accused Iran. He printed lavish propaganda booklets which were distributed from Iraqi government offices throughout the West, reproducing photographs of Halabja's waxen-faced dead and still blaming Iran.

Western countries which had backed Iraq during the war had supplied Saddam with the ingredients necessary to manufacture chemical weapons in the first place; hence there was little outcry from them at the time. Although the chemical attack was widely reported, Western leaders did not consider it sufficiently heinous to warrant imposing international sanctions on Iraq. In fact, cynically, Western trade credits to Iraq were doubled.

Although Halabja had been hit with chemicals, little damage had been done to its physical structure by the few conventional bombs dropped by the government beforehand. But now, Halabja was made to disappear from view altogether. The regime went back in, dynamited the town to rubble, bulldozed it over and declared it a closed military area. It was Saddam's intention that no one should ever return to these Kurdish border towns to cause further trouble to the regime. Qala Diza, Sayid Sadiq, Penjwin and every other Kurdish town in the area met the same fate. It was not until the Kurdish uprising of March 1991 when civilian Kurds returned to their former homes in the forbidden areas that they saw with their own eyes the full scale of Saddam's twisted revenge. Little remained.

Nazdar's dream

'My husband, a well-educated Kurd from Kurdistan in Iraq, believed that women were intellectually inferior to men and claimed that this was scientifically proven. He said that men were not just physically more powerful, they were superior in every respect.

'Dilshad did not come from a religious background, and professed to be a socialist. It was not until after we'd been married for six months that I began to understand how a self-professed socialist like him could integrate such an attitude towards women with his political values. In fact, it is very easy for Kurdish men to possess such an outlook. The way we are brought up at home in Iraqi Kurdistan encourages sexism.

'A male child is doted upon by both parents. Sons are treated differently from daughters. Boys never have to do housework or prepare food. They don't have to serve. But girls are brought up to serve men from the beginning. Boys go out with their fathers and adult men. They are always treated in such a way that they come to understand that they are the ones who will be in charge in later life. It is their voices which will be heard and obeyed. Their sisters remain in the house, or go out with other female members of the household to work, or to visit relatives and friends as part of a family group. They do not go out with boys and men.

'Girls attend upon the visitors, even waiting on young male cousins and the sons of their parents' friends. They are supposed to be quiet and respectful and fetch and carry without complaint. They are not encouraged to have independent views, or to desire any kind of life other than that of being a good wife and mother. If they are educated and have qualifications as teachers, nurses or even engineers, they should still be good wives and mothers, married well before they are thirty.

'A young Kurdish boy sees his mother and sisters behave in this traditional way. He has authority over his sisters, who, following the example of their mother, will dote on him and their other brothers. The girls will listen to the males, always putting the boys before themselves, even letting the men eat before them at mealtimes. A girl who doesn't conform, who flaunts herself or who speaks out of turn, soon gets a bad reputation and is ostracised by the community.

'It is the women and girls who do all the menial work in the home. In the villages it is usually the women who go out to fetch heavy loads of firewood and water. You rarely see a man offering to help a woman, or taking a heavy load from her back to carry it for her in rural areas. Instead, they sit around smoking and drinking tea, watching the world go by, seeing women working as part of the natural order of things.

'A man has absolute freedom to do whatever he chooses, but a woman is expected to stay home awaiting her husband and his friends at any time of the day or night, cooking whenever visitors arrive, bringing tea and refreshments at all hours. She is a servant on duty every hour of the day, every day of the year for the rest of her life. Only women whose husbands are rich or politically powerful have an easier life.

'Very few of us seem to break out of such a way of existence. A woman's meaning in life has been predefined as someone who serves her father, her brothers and, later on, her husband. She derives her fulfilment from carrying out this role to the best of her ability such that the men in her life are satisfied with her performance. She must be a good cook, a good housewife, always sweet-natured and dutiful, utterly faithful to her spouse and, of course, she must try to look beautiful.

'In our part of Kurdistan, physical beauty is extremely important. In the big towns, women wear a lot of make-up; they can spend hours doing their hair and their faces. This is the way women are supposed to express themselves, to use their freedom and creativity. Any money they have is spent on clothes, jewellery and cosmetics.

'On special occasions, such as weddings and Newroz, husbands will go and choose some fabric for their wives to make themselves new dresses. Our fabrics are very colourful, sparkling with gold and silver thread and decorated with thousands of sequins, lace or beads. A Kurdish man likes to see his woman shine like a hundred stars because he knows that she shines for him alone. She is his possession and he wants to be proud of her in front of other men.

'I was educated in Iraq and later in the West. I mixed socially with women from other societies and their way of looking at the world interested me. Foreign women were horrified when I told them my husband believed it was scientifically proven that women were inferior. Not only did he believe this, he treated me as if this were so.

'I was expected to behave according to the role model, without complaint. He became extremely angry and irritated if meals were not cooked to coincide with his arrival home. If the meals I made were not dishes that he really enjoyed he would simply ignore his plate and stop talking for the rest of the evening, and sometimes even for the next day or more. He would put me down in front of his men friends if we were sitting together. I was not allowed to laugh with them, or show any interest in what they said lest this was interpreted as a sign that I was being forward and was, therefore, sexually available.

'Dilshad rarely expressed any affection to me in public. He walked with me, his hands at his side in the traditional way, and never joked or smiled with me out in the street. Even at home, he reserved his affection for times when he was physically aroused. He said little to encourage me, or cheer me up if I was sad about something, or if I needed intellectual stimulation.

'I began to lose confidence in myself after I had been married to him for three or four months. I felt as if I had no future, aside from serving him to the standard he demanded. Whenever I failed to meet those standards he would cut off all communication with me. As a way of coping with this, I began to read political books and books written by women. These gave me back some of the strength I possessed before my marriage, together with a sense of innate self-worth.

'I decided I had to do more with my life than simply remain a Kurdish housewife. I wanted to attend Kurdish political meetings, but the men in our family and in my husband's family were against women going to meetings. They only took their wives and daughters to Newroz parties or weddings, rarely to political events or to the annual congress of their party. Very few Iraqi Kurdish women were able to go to such meetings. Rather, we were supposed to join women's groups and remain segregated, writing newsletters in keeping with the themes and the tone established by the men, but never challenging them.

A friend of mine was a supporter of the international women's liberation movement. She had been imprisoned by the Ba'ath regime because her brothers had become peshmergas and had gone to the mountains. She began to write political poems while she was in prison and she somehow survived the torture, rape and terrible things they did to her. She told me not to lose my self-respect.

'I began to resent the way my husband treated me. I lost my respect for him because he wanted me to be his servant and not his equal. I tried to discuss equality, but he simply humiliated me, sometimes by physically overpowering me and stopping me from talking by making love. But it wasn't really love, he was just trying to prove that I was weak and that he could do whatever he wanted with me.

'If I became upset and cried he would leave the house. If I got angry or shouted he would become coolly furious and would not speak with me for days. I was not allowed to behave in any way except in a manner that showed him that I placed his wishes before mine. I was not allowed to argue, to complain, to ask him to change, or to insist that he do anything that I wanted. Our marriage was unilateral. And then I went home to visit my family, and I realised my mother and my sister behaved exactly as my husband's role model demanded. I screamed at them and asked them what sort of a life they had enslaved themselves to. I was told I should be ashamed of myself. Where was my honour? I replied that I had decided to become a doctor of medicine. I would go back to university and go on to medical college. They told me that women doctors were little better than prostitutes and that everyone knew what went on in the student hostels. It would not be right for a married woman. They advised me to give up this ridiculous idea and have a baby instead. That would put an end to my restlessness, they explained.

'For the next five years I cut off all contact with my family and I qualified as a doctor. I was able to help other people and I earned their respect. I was confident and, most important of all, I respected myself once more. Even my husband began to change when he saw how I had developed and that it was difficult for him now to upset or dominate me. I no longer contested any issues about sexual equality with him openly. I would let my actions speak for me. It worked. We had a child. It was a girl. I wanted to name her Ronak, which means 'light' or 'enlightened'. We named her Jiyan, which means 'life'.

'I wonder what sort of life Jiyan will have when she reaches womanhood. Will she be able to live the kind of life she wants as a person, as a free human being, or will the pressures of our society prove too strong? Perhaps she will be content to accept a traditional life like my mother and sister, happy to assume the role which Kurdish society has prepared for her.

'And what sort of father will Dilshad become – a dictator whom she fears, or a mentor to guide and understand her? Perhaps by that time, I will have been able to prove to him by my example that women, although different from men, are still equal; that these differences constitute our strengths, not our weaknesses. Our society once accorded women such a place. Islam and years of political repression have steadily eroded the rights we once enjoyed. Our struggle from now on must be to liberate our Kurdish women if we hope to liberate our society and flourish as a healthy nation.'

Amina: 'Government by rape and execution'

Amina, the daughter of a well-known Mullah, was studying medicine at Sulaimaniya University in south Kurdistan when she was unexpectedly abducted by the *Mukhabarat*. Amina had left university with two girl-friends at midday, but each had gone her own way home for lunch. The car which had been tailing them stopped alongside Amina and two members of the *Mukhabarat* seized her by the arms and dragged her into their car. Amina was gagged and blindfolded. Someone struck her. Before long the car pulled up outside the headquarters of the *Amn*.

When Amina didn't appear at home later that day her family visited the police station and then went on to *Amn* to ask if anyone had seen her. No one told them anything.

After three days in Sulaimaniya prison, Amina was interrogated and accused of supplying the peshmergas with medical supplies. Neither Amina nor her relatives had any connections with the Kurdish resistance, being a strictly religious family not involved in political activities. Although Amina denied the charges brought against her, her captors refused to release her. Instead she was blindfolded once more and taken by car on a long journey. She later learned that she had been taken to Kirkuk.

Amina was now subjected to torture in Kirkuk Prison. Sometimes the torturers heated a metal rod and burned her between her toes; assailants jumped on her back and kicked her in every part of her body. Her fingernails were pulled out one by one. Her head was shaved and she was stripped of her clothes.

But she was not to remain in Kirkuk. Another terrifying car journey followed and Amina was abandoned in Abu Ghraib Prison on the outskirts of Baghdad. Here she was thrown into a cell with fifteen or so other women prisoners. The gaolers brought food once a day, with a single litre of water per person intended for drinking as well as for washing. Because of the heat inside, there was never any water left over for cleaning themselves. Like her fellow prisoners, Amina soon caught lice. All the women were kept completely naked, locked in cells which had but a single tiny window, no bigger than a child's head, high up in the wall.

Several months passed. Amina was now taken to a separate cell. This was little more than a tiny closet. A prisoner could neither stretch out full length nor move about freely in these cells. Amina was left in solitary confinement in the cell and given nothing but a bucket to serve as a toilet. The guards came once a day to collect it.

They also came and took Amina from this small dark closet for two hours each day, when she would find herself with three or four others in a room especially designed for torture. Amina and the other women would be suspended upside down by the legs and beaten till their flesh was cut and bleeding. Sometimes the torture would be performed by men, sometimes by women – most of the women torturers were Sudanese, paid by the Ba'ath government to do this job. The torture would go on in various forms until the victims collapsed. Then they would each be dumped back in their closets. Amina saw girls as young as 10 and women as old as 60 treated like this. Some had become pregnant; others had already given birth to their illegitimate children. For all, rape was automatic. Children born in the prison as a result of rape were left with their mothers for the period of breast feeding. Then they were removed. It is believed that they were later brought up in special schools to serve the regime – trained to become professional killers, or carefully moulded for careers in the security or armed forces.

Many women were taken out of their cells never to return. They were blindfolded, then led out to a courtyard and placed before a firing squad. They were threatened that unless they confessed to the crimes they had been accused of, they would be executed. Most had nothing to confess. Execution was completely random.

Two years passed. One night, the guards burst through the door of Amina's cell. She was immediately blindfolded. She awaited her execution. But instead she was trussed up once again and thrown into a car. Another long journey began. Just as in the cell, so too in the car she was left stark naked. At last the car pulled to a halt. Amina was thrown out into the street. For a time she was too afraid to remove the blindfold to see where she was. Hearing the buzz of traffic and the calls of taxi drivers announcing their destinations, she realised she must be in a public place. Amina raised her blindfold. It was just before dawn. She found herself lying naked on the side of the road. Her thin body was cut and bruised.

Confused, she waited for sunrise. Then she shuffled over to one of the taxi drivers who was calling for passengers travelling to Sulaimaniya. Those who saw the young woman, her pale head shaven to a stubble, dismissed her as mad. Not only was she naked and filthy, she was also covered in cuts and sores.

No one troubled themselves to stand in her way when Amina boarded a minibus bound for Sulaimaniya. The vehicle collected other passengers and started to move off. The passengers began to gather up their fares to pass down to the driver. Amina found herself sitting beside an old man with a grey beard. He asked her to pay up too, thinking she was probably one of the mad women who lived out in the streets. Amina replied that she had no money; she had been in prison until that morning. The guards had thrown her out in the road.

Some of the other passengers began to listen. As they listened, they realised that the girl was not insane. Some women, weeping at her tale, took off items of clothing which they didn't need for Amina to put on and cover her nakedness.

When the bus pulled into Sulaimaniya, the old gentleman asked Amina where her parents lived. She gave him her address but said she didn't know if they were still alive or not. The old man advised her to go home with him first and promised to see if her family were still living at their old address.

Amina didn't know whether to trust him or not. In prison she had been threatened that if she told anyone what had happened to her they would bring her straight back. The old man told Amina he had a wife and daughters waiting at home and swore to help her. Then they walked home together. Amina ate, bathed and dressed in one of the daughter's clean clothes. Then the old man set out again to look for Amina's family.

He found them still living at the address Amina had written down for him. But Amina's family were also wary. The *Mukhabarat* had called at their house almost every day after having abducted the girl. The *Mukhabarat* had said that Amina must have run away to join the pesh-mergas. Then they had interrogated the parents extensively at their headquarters. After several months spent like this, the family had still had no word of Amina's whereabouts and wondered if their daughter might have eloped. There seemed to be no other explanation. But the truth was much worse.

When the old man appeared on their doorstep they were sure he had been sent there by the *Mukhabarat*, the description he gave them of Amina was so different from the daughter they had known. But the old man swore that what he said was true and that it really was their daughter who was waiting for them at home with his family. Amina's parents reluctantly agreed to go with him. But because the old man's house was near the *Amn* building, they didn't want to go inside. The old man, also afraid of *Amn* observing him, urged the couple to trust him and follow him indoors.

When Amina caught sight of her mother and father she was overcome.

Her mother fainted at the shock of seeing her. The old man's family, who had also gathered in the room, wept with the rest as Amina and her family embraced.

Not until after the Kurdish uprising did Amina tell anyone else this story; she was always terrified that the *Mukhabarat* would again come for her.[15]

Nermin and the guerrillas

'I was born in Afrin, a town in northern Syria populated mostly by Kurdish people – there are around thirty thousand Kurds living there. Although my family wanted to name me 'Nermin', Kurdish names are illegal in Syria, I was registered under the Arab name of 'Najma' instead.

'My father has two brothers who live in Qamishli, a Kurdish town, close to the Turkish border. In fact, near Qamishli the border runs right through the heart of a number of Kurdish villages, dividing our families between two countries. It is difficult to visit one another because we don't have passports and the border itself is heavily mined, and over-looked by Turkish military watchtowers, spaced every two kilometres or so. There are places where we are able to cross the river to reach Turkey, but this is also very dangerous as Turkish soldiers are liable to shoot at any sign of movement. Anyone who is caught or killed in this way is taken by the Turks, who will always say they've captured a PKK guerrilla. Whether the person is dead or alive, it is the same thing for them.

'My cousin, Bahar (pseudonym), the daughter of the younger of my two uncles, left Qamishli to join the PKK three years ago. A lot of Syrian Kurds are with the PKK now because we have no rights here. Sometimes we get news of Bahar from members who travel in and out of Syria. They told us that she had been injured in a guerrilla attack on the Turkish military in Nusaybin at Newroz, but that she is well again now, as her leg wounds were only superficial.

'Bahar went to train in the PKK camp in the Bekaa valley in Lebanon for 15 months before being sent into Kurdistan. There were hundreds of other Kurdish girls and women there also training to be guerrillas. Bahar sent us a letter from Bekaa saying that she was very happy and she was treated just the same as the men were. Bahar explained that in the PKK, there was no discrimination against women. They all call one another *heval*, 'comrade'. This was very important for her.

'I am 23 years old now. My father has arranged for me to marry one of my uncle's sons from Qamishli next year, but I am thinking of going to join the PKK. Because Ibrahim is Bahar's brother, perhaps he might also like to go and join the guerrillas. None of us who feel Kurdish can be happy here with things the way they are under President Assad's government.

'I would like to fight for a free Kurdistan, to travel and get to know my country better. Some friends have told me that the party can arrange for me to receive training and join Bahar. Because I have studied French here, I may go to France before I leave for Kurdistan, to improve my grammar and undertake political study at the same time. I am not ready to be married and have children, even though it is normal for girls my age to start a family.

'The PKK really attracts me because I can see that this party offers us a different way of life. Even if I die, I will die with honour. What is it to be a housewife in comparison with this, always living under a shadow, never really knowing what life might have been like had we been able to choose our own political future?'[16]

I met Nermin by chance in one of the PKK camps near Zelê almost a year later. Gone was the shy, hesitant young graduate with her pale make-up and lipstick, her black high-heeled shoes and straight, knee-length skirt.

Nermin had cut her black hair short like a boy's. She wore baggy khaki trousers (*shalvar*) and a khaki tailored jacket, like the other guerrillas. She had developed a new confident manner and evidently did not miss seeing her daily reflection in a mirror. Instead, she saw herself reflected in the eyes of her comrades and recognised herself as the person she had chosen to become. Nermin was proud and content. She lived her struggle with passion. Ibrahim, her betrothed cousin, had not joined the party with her, but had gone into business locally.

I spent that night with the women in their tent. They stayed up working by lamplight, copying various political texts and writing pages of notes before settling down on the ground. The floor of the big tent was covered with blankets and canvas, and the women finally stopped working in the small hours of the morning and pulled their rough covers over themselves to sleep.

The lamp burned all night long. By dawn they were active again, putting a smoke-blackened kettle onto the portable gas-tube fire to boil water for tea, disappearing alternately through the flap in the tent down to the nearby brook to wash. Our breakfast consisted of rounds of flat bread baked in the camp which the women kept stored in a hessian sack. This they consumed with incredibly sweet black tea. Hand-rolled cigarettes followed soon after.

One girl had remained sleeping: '*Heval, heval, rabe, rabe*!' (Comrade,

comrade, get up, get up!) they called, rocking her gently until she opened her eyes and pulled herself together.

For Nermin and her comrades, the PKK offered the possibility of both personal and political achievement, and a worthwhile sense of self-sacrifice. If there is to be sacrifice, they believe, it must to be a sacrifice for their country and beliefs, not just for another master occupying their house.

In his book about the new nationalism, *Blood and Belonging*, Michael Ignatieff uses the term 'master in your own house' in the sense of being in control of your nation and hence of yourself. He asks if the Kurds will ever truly be masters in their own house, commenting: 'Statelessness is a state of mind, and it is akin to homelessness. This is what a nationalist understands: a people can become completely human, completely themselves, only when they have a place of their own. The longing for this is too strong to be stopped by (state) terror.'[17]

This is what I know Nermin and the other *heval*, the comrades, felt deep in their hearts. There was no discrimination between men and women, rich or poor. They were all equal members of the community of believers. They felt that they were living life to the full, and for once embracing their real identity in that great quest to be masters in their own house, to have a country of their own, as near or as far away in time as that country might be.

One of the guerrilla women had written a moving poem for Berivan, one of their fallen comrades. More than any narrative, this poem communicates the feelings of the PKK women.

Karnveli Hill

Dedicated to the martyr Beritan,
by a woman guerrilla and friend, signed S.T.

I am angry and resentful, and a bit weary,
I have fought this awesome pain, and
my heart is pregnant with screams
like a song of unrequited love

The heart in my young body
rages with a stormy yearning,
Take the kettle from the fire
roll a cigarette from the tin

You smoke Muş tobacco, I know

like threads of carpet silk.
How I love these mountains
whose savage virgin beauty

we have honoured with our guns,
these mountains which have shielded us
like a mother's womb,
from the sword of Turks and Arabs

and Persians, hanging over us.
It is our fate, this passion
which locks my hands like twin volcanoes
over the barrel of my gun

The childlike hands are gone
the silken strands of my hair
the more the women fight
the more beautiful they become.

You may not say it, but I know
my pen does not tell of struggle
Abidin must draw the lasting
pictures of this struggle

Life is one, the struggle is one
the path is one, the comrades are one
and as I vow to follow in your path
to death, I shout your name

Martyr Beritan!

(*Karnveli Hill, the Southern War*)
25 October 1992[18]

Notes

1. *Hawkar*, Oct–Nov 1993, p. 4.
2. Tahire Koçtürk, *A Matter of Honour: Experiences of Turkish Women Immigrants*, Zed Books, 1992, p. 56.
3. Ibid., p. 54.
4. Ibid.
5. Ibid., p 51.
6. *Progress Report* on *the Missing 8000 Kurds in Iraq – United Nations Adopts the Case*; compiled by the Preparatory Committee on Disappearances in Kurdistan, London, May 1988, p. 10.
7. Report by a Preparatory Committee, *Eight Thousand Civilian Kurds Have Disappeared in Iraq – What Has Happened to Them?*, London, November 1987, p. 8. Names of the missing are given on pp. 17–56.

8. Ibid., pp. 8–9.

9. Ibid. Also from a letter from Jawad Mella to the Working Group on Enforced or Involuntary Disappearances, Centre for Human Rights at the United Nations, 23 May 1988. The Preparatory Committee on Disappearances in Kurdistan, *Progress Report on the Missing 8000 Kurds in Iraq – United Nations Adopts the Case*, pp. 9–11.

10. Faysal Dağli, *Birakuji*, Belge Yayinlari, 1994, p. 48.

11. Claire Pointon, 'The Mother of all Tragedies', *The Times Magazine*, 13 March 1993, p. 21.

12. In Islamic law (*shari'a*) only males should kill livestock for food. A male must have reached the age of puberty before it is considered *helal*, clean, for him to do so.

13. Interviewed in *Blood and Belonging*, BBC2, 1993.

14. Preparatory Committee Report, November 1987, appendix, pp. 14–16, anonymous witness.

15. Two years later, Amina married. She lives in uneasy peace in Sulaimaniya.

16. It is important to remember that while all Kurdish political parties, excluding the Islamic Party, work towards offering women an equal role with men, in practical terms it is only with the PKK guerrillas that Kurdish women lead the same life as the men. The Kurdish parties originating in Turkey do attempt to promote sexual equality and all address women's issues. Hundreds of Kurdish women in Turkey are active as politicians, journalists, lawyers, doctors or nurses, writers, singers, students and workers within these political movements, as discussed in previous chapters. The same is less true of the women in south (Iraq) and east (Iran) Kurdistan. Syrian Kurdish women (west Kurdistan) who wish to fight for the Kurdish cause also join the PKK in large numbers as other Syrian Kurdish parties cannot yet provide equal opportunities for women within a social framework which remains dominated by Arab nationalism and Islam.

17. See Michael Ignatieff, *Blood and Belonging*, BBC Books/Chatto, London, 1993, p. 161.

18. *Anthology of Contemporary Kurdish Poetry*, Kurdistan Solidarity Committee and Yashar Ismail, London, 1994, pp. 47–8.

11

The international community and the Kurdish question

Kurdish identity in the diaspora

The Kurdish diaspora numbers around one and a half million Kurds: refugees, migrants, second and third generation citizens. Half a million Kurds live in Germany alone, with approximately fifty thousand Kurds each in France and the Netherlands. Around twenty thousand Kurds live in Britain, Sweden, Austria, Switzerland and the United States. In Belgium and Denmark there are an estimated ten to twelve thousand Kurds; presently close to ten thousand Kurds live in Australia and Canada. In Norway, Greece, Spain, Italy a further three to five thousand Kurds reside. Smaller numbers of Kurdish families live in almost every country in the world, including the Czech Republic and Slovakia, Finland and Japan. Of all these, 85–90 per cent come from Kurdistan in Turkey.[1]

Lacking a national passport, they are deprived of the security that comes with a recognised identity. In other words, without a nation state of their own even their essential nationality has been denied to them. This continues to be a major cause of instability and unrest.

It is a political matter of the most extreme urgency that the Kurdish people be accorded 'formal recognition as a separate ethnic group of immigrants living in the EC in order that they can be granted the same rights as other immigrant groups ... to stop the double marginalisation they presently experience in the European Community as well as in Turkey, Iraq, Iran and Syria'.[2]

Kurds travelling as Turks, Arabs or Iranians on papers issued by these governments feature on immigration statistics solely by these same descriptions. As a consequence, no separate figures are available for the Kurdish population of Western Europe and other countries. Not only has Kurdish origin been masked prior to leaving Turkey, Iraq, Iran and Syria, it is also hidden from the moment of arrival on foreign soil. Even during the processing of asylum applications, or other immigration procedures, no separate status is accorded nor statistic retained for Kurdish applicants. Kurds are identified as nationals of the country in which they were reduced to minority status after 1924. Since that time, repression and persecution of the Kurdish people as minorities in each of the aforementioned countries has resulted in tens of thousands of refugees. 'While those from Iraq were at the centre of international attention, those from Turkey, Iran and Syria remained almost completely anonymous ... Research has shown that this highly disturbing political dimension has to be taken into account when considering the life-situation of Kurdish migrants in Europe.'[3]

Turkey, Iran, Iraq and Syria are all developing countries and caught on the negative side of international trade balances and relations of production. This has resulted in enormous rates of inflation, extreme poverty and never-ending spirals of economic decline, on top of the already unbearable costs of military expenditures in warfare against Kurds and neighbouring countries. These processes are not new but have intensified over the last 30–35 years.[4]

Of all four countries, Turkey is the only one which derives a considerable percentage of its gross income from tourism. The Kurds have campaigned for a boycott of tourism to Turkey claiming that 'every tourist dollar becomes a bullet to kill a Kurd'. But even operations against tourist targets have had little impact in dissuading ever-increasing numbers of European holidaymakers from selecting the West Coast resorts of Turkey as the destination for their summer vacations. While Turkey is being marketed as a 'paradise' by the government at enormous cost in its advertising and PR campaigns, the east of the country has become a 'living hell' characterised by destruction of the way of life, devastation of nature and slaughter of its native population. But few tourists ever get to see that part of the country.

Western governments have adopted different strategies towards the respective Kurdish groups, contingent upon their policies towards, and relations with, the individual central governments of those countries from which the Kurds originate. In this way, for example. American policy towards the Kurds of Iraq is quite unlike its policy towards the Kurds of Turkey. This observation applies equally in the case of other NATO countries and the EC.

As Turkey is a member of NATO and signatory to a number of European conventions, including the Treaty on Security and Cooperation in Europe, it has always been allowed considerable licence in its 'handling' of the Kurdish question. Turkey and Greece were the largest recipients of NATO military aid under the 'cascading' agreement, within the terms of which old and excess NATO weapons are donated; while other such aid is through 'direct sales and, increasingly, by joint production agreements between Western and Turkish companies to manufacture weapons wholly or partly in Turkey to enable it not only to produce weapons for its own requirements but also to become an arms exporter and start developing a high-tech industry of its own.'[5]

With a total of around four hundred and eighty thousand personnel, Turkey possesses the second largest armed force in NATO. The majority of the land army is stationed in north-west Kurdistan in addition to the Gendarmerie, a force of about seventy thousand whose main task is internal repression. According to the Stockholm International Peace Research Institute, Turkey's military budget was about $2,500 million annually during the 1980s but rose sharply at the end of the decade, reaching $3,870 million in 1991. Between 1987 and 1991 the main suppliers of major weapons were: USA – $3,953 million; the former West Germany – $1,549m; Netherlands – $237m; Italy – $125m; France – $22m; UK – $10m (*SIPRI Yearbook* 1992). In 1993, Turkey was the main recipient of conventional arms, mainly from the United States.[6]

Arms to Turkey to fight 'terrorism'

Despite hiccups in the supply of arms and other forms of economic aid owing to Turkey's consistent failure to observe human rights, Western governments have continued to treat the Kurdish problem in Turkey as one of 'terrorism', following Turkey's own line. In a resolution presented to an international conference on north-west Kurdistan, held in Brussels on 12–13 March 1994, the London-based Kurdistan Human Rights Project in conjunction with the Frankfurt office of Medico International determined that:

> The concept of terrorism has been abused by Turkey in an attempt to legitimise these weapons transfers, which are in reality used in military operations against organized armed groups fighting the agents of the Turkish state. States supplying weapons are a party to this abuse of the concept of terrorism. The United States should also apply the principles of its Foreign Assistance Act and also stop all military and economic aid to Turkey until Turkey fulfils the human rights requirements of the Foreign Assistance Act.[7]

The Kurdish problem in Turkey has been marginalised on the international agenda into a war between the Turkish armed forces and 'the separatist Marxist guerrillas of the PKK'. This attitude entirely fails to recognise that the guerrillas are the disaffected youth of the villages, towns and cities of Kurdistan and other parts of Turkey. They are popularly supported by at least 80 per cent of the Kurdish civilian population.[8]

Despite the PKK's offers to find a solution through peaceful political processes the Turkish government has rejected every initiative, vowing instead to 'finish the "terrorists" militarily'. In seeking to impose a final military solution, Turkey has been supported by the United States and fellow NATO and other European countries. Criticism of Turkey has arisen only when embarrassing proof of Turkey's use of NATO weapons against civilian Kurds emerges. For short periods thereafter, the countries involved in supplying weapons to Turkey may make a show of temporary suspension of aid, as in the case of Germany, or, as in the case of the USA, may reduce its level of military aid in percentage terms – both responses proving insufficient to alter the status quo. Other countries with a lesser interest in Turkey, such as Sweden, Switzerland and Norway, imposed bans and cancelled arms supplies to Turkey altogether during 1992 in case they were used against the Kurds.

More recently, the Turkish Ministry of Defence has been busy promoting its forthcoming '2nd International Defence Industry and Civil Aviation Fair' (IDEF), scheduled for September 1995. The IDEF invitations included the offer of payment of 'all necessary accommodation expenses' by Turkey to participating delegations.

In the first IDEF, held in 1993, the following companies from Britain featured among the international exhibitors: British Aerospace, BAe Defence, BAe Commercial Aircraft, BAe Corp. Jets, BAe Royal Ordnance Division, Defence Export Services Organisation, DTE Directorate of Test and Evaluation, GEC Alsthom Paxman Diesel, GEC Marconi Ltd, GEC Marconi Electronics, GEC Marconi Combat Systems, GEC Marconi Naval Systems, GEC Marconi Radar and Control Systems, GEC Marconi Sonar Systems, GEC Marconi Underwater Weapons, GEC Plessey Avionics, Marconi Defence Systems Ltd, Pilatus Britten Norman Ltd, Vosper Thornycroft Ltd, Yarrow Shipbuilders Ltd, Jane's Information Group, Raychem Ltd and the Defence Manufacturers Association. Exhibitors from virtually every country in the world took part (*source*: IDEF information).

Among the existing suppliers of arms to Turkey from the EC we can note: Augusta (Italy): helicopters and training equipment; Marconi (Italy): computerised communications systems; Aerospatiale (France): satellite communications; Thornson CSF (France): mobile radar; GIAT (France): guns for armed infantry and fighting vehicles (AIFVs); NFK (Holland): cable for TAFICS communication system; Philips (Holland): artillery, shell fuses, Stringer missile parts; CASA (Spain): transport aircraft.[9]

Responses to Turkey's invasion of northern Iraq

After the first six weeks of the operation, Turkey's invasion of south Kurdistan had cost the country £47 million (Reuters, 28 April 1995).

In reaction to the incursion, the Council of Europe's 34 member countries approved a resolution to suspend Turkey's membership of the European Council 'unless it showed significant progress towards a withdrawal from Iraq prior to the 26 June 1995 European Union summit. Turkey's membership of the Customs Union was also put on hold creating an anti-European backlash in the Grand National Assembly. The Council also called for a peaceful solution to the Kurdish problem and democratic reform of Turkey's constitution and laws. [But] Turkish officials responded with customary nonchalance behaving as the "injured party", and responded that its parliamentary delegation in Strasbourg "will no longer take part in activities and will refuse all cooperation".' (Reuters, 27 April 1995).

At the height of the invasion, Sir Peter Ustinov, writing in the *European*, condemned the 'moral flexibility that "justifies" the Turkish invasion of Iraq' and recommended that 'all military adventures against neighbouring territories should be roundly condemned not treated selectively according to national or business interests, or even those of security'. Ustinov observed further:

> the United States is once again playing an equivocal role, perhaps because its own habit of armed intervention into the affairs of its neighbours – as witnessed by its actions in Grenada, Panama and Haiti – hardly allows it to qualify as a moral mentor to the Turks. Rather, the US seems to say: 'Do what you have to, but do it quickly. Meanwhile I'll stand by the door and warn you if there's any sign of outraged world opinion. (*European*, 31 March 1995.)

Germany, as Turkey's closest ally, also found itself compromised by the Turkish invasion and was embarrassed into condemning it as reports began to be heard of civilian fatalities in the course of Turkish attacks on Iraqi Kurd villages.

> Although Mr Kinkel (the German Foreign Minister) and Douglas Hurd, the Foreign Secretary, want to avoid isolating Turkey, a country vital to NATO's southern flank, they have warned the Turks that they could scupper the ratification of Turkey's customs union agreement with the EU ... Germany, an important supplier of military equipment to Turkey, froze grants of DM150 million (£67 million) last week ... Although the gesture was largely symbolic because the bulk of German military supplies had already been delivered, it reflected Bonn's mounting concern about a lengthy Turkish presence in northern Iraq (*Guardian*, 4 April 1995).

Arms to Iraq

In a similar fashion, the West had also primarily backed Saddam Hussein during the Iran–Iraq war despite his regime's evident disregard for human life. Weapons and credits were still being supplied to Baghdad even after the Ba'ath government's systematic attempt at genocide of the Iraqi Kurds under the Anfal campaign and its use of internationally prohibited chemical weapons.

As far as Britain was concerned, Saddam was to be supplied with military equipment for as long as the government could get away with it. The Scott Inquiry was set up in November 1992 under Lord Justice Scott to find out if British ministers had overstepped their own guidelines in the five years before the invasion of Kuwait. It was asked whether they had been morally correct in issuing immunity certificates. The investigation arose out of allegations against three British businessmen from the Matrix Churchill company, which had been supplying machine tools to Iraq. The three were accused of breaking a ban on the supply of arms to Iraq. In the trial, which lasted eleven months, evidence was heard that implicated the British government all the way to the top. Indeed, the trail led beyond senior government ministers to number 10 Downing Street as former Prime Minister Margaret Thatcher and Prime Minister in office John Major were individually called upon to defend themselves. Intelligence officers sat in on the private sessions of the hearing. After 400 trial hours and 200 witnesses, 200,000 pages of documents and 166 public and closed sessions, the final report of the Scott Inquiry was considerably delayed before being made public. The main findings of the investigation were:

1. There was a breach of published guidelines by ministers who knew that equipment was to be used for military purposes by Iraq.
2. They approved deliveries to Jordan and Saudi Arabia knowing that they would be diverted to Iraq.
3. The ministers changed their own guidelines without telling the public.
4. The ministers were involved in a conspiracy to pervert the course of justice.
5. UN forces were put at risk by the export of arms to a government which had used chemical weapons against its own citizens. Ministers and civil servants undoubtedly abused their trust and deceived the public. There is no guarantee that similar abuses are still not being committed. (*Source*: public meeting on the Scott Inquiry chaired by Denis Healey (Labour), 29 June 1994.)

John Pilger, reporting in the *New Statesman & Society* (11 November 1994), observed:

> As the Scott Inquiry and numerous disclosures have confirmed, Britain was secretly, illegally and duplicitously supplying both sides in the Iran–Iraq war ... In the case of Iraq, it is now known that a vast supply network was operated in Britain throughout the 8–year war, largely by the security forces and other secret arms of government, such as the International Military Services (IMS). The role of the Foreign Office in safeguarding the 'economic prize' of Iraq was to lie.

Despite protestations that they were unaware of what was going on, both British prime ministers would have had routine access to each week's Thursday survey of intelligence, the 'Red Book' and information from MI6 and JIC reports. The prime minister and all senior cabinet ministers in Whitehall are aware of this. What is more, the export credit guarantee department also receives information on the arms trade. The government quite clearly knew about the use to which machine tools would be put, and Iraq's priorities. Matrix Churchill and Sheffield Forge Masters knew how to manufacture the late John Bull's 'Supergun'. Bull had been looking for someone to sell it to and Iraqi agents were looking for suppliers for local manufacturing capability. At the time in question, France was the main supplier of arms to Iraq (and is eager to become so again). According to Denis Healey, 'the Americans were also in it up to their eyes'. This is confirmed in disclosures appearing in Alan Friedman's book about President Bush's involvement in arming Iraq.

In 1994, a former aid-worker with the Kurdistan Reconstruction Organisation and self-designated 'friend' of the Kurds, British adventurer Stephen Crouch, was involved in establishing the Iraqi British Interests Group (IBIG), and as its director-general receiving pay-offs to the sum of £500 each from British businessmen. The payments were made in exchange for facilitating trade contacts with officials in the Iraqi government, such as Riyad al-Qaysi (Iraqi deputy foreign minister) with whom Crouch boasted a close acquaintance, to pursue deals of mutual advantage, despite the UN sanctions. Needless to say, the IBIG was one of those whose voices were heard most loudly in calling for the lifting of sanctions against Iraq.[10]

Turkey, Germany, France and Russia were also particularly eager for UN sanctions imposed on Iraq to be lifted from as early as 1992 for the resumption of what had always proved to be a profitable trade. Turkey played a two-handed game, politically divided over support for the USA on one hand and regional co-operation with neighbouring Iraq (against the Kurds) on the other. Again, in Denis Healey's words, 'third world countries resent arms control being imposed upon them by well-armed nations with nuclear capability (and for example, the United States supplying Israel). These countries are now making their own arms' (Scott Inquiry public meeting, 29 June 1994).

Criminalisation of the Kurdish community in the West

In 1993, Germany became the first European country to ban a Kurdish organisation, the PKK, on its soil and to bring charges against PKK members. A few months later France followed Germany's lead and also banned the PKK. In both countries, associations run by the party's supporters and sympathizers were raided, goods confiscated and occupants arrested. All Kurdish community associations allegedly linked with the PKK in Germany were closed. When the pro-PKK Kurds opened new associations and brought out new publications, the German police again went in, seized all Kurdish merchandise and arrested those in charge. The mainstream Turkish press, particularly *Hürriyet* and *Milliyet*, covered the developments in full as the ban hardened. Headlines appeared such as 'The PKK's Mask has fallen', 'The Ban on the PKK won't be Lifted', 'Call from the Police for Collaboration'. The latter article revealed:

> The German Police Organisation has called on citizens of Turkish and Kurdish origin to collaborate with them in a decisive campaign of intervention against PKK terrorism. Claiming they will not permit the further expansion of PKK terrorism, police officials commented that 'Our success in this intervention against this particular organisation will allow us to assist those who are threatened or attacked'. Frankfurt has recently become a stage for serious clashes between PKK supporters and police and tight security measures were put in place. Police officials claimed they had not granted permission for a PKK demonstration. The police carried out spot searches of anyone they considered suspicious and checked their vehicles. 30 people who had gathered suspiciously in Hauptwache Square were subjected to a spot identity check and arrested. (*Milliyet*, Frankfurt, August 1995.)

In other European countries, particularly Britain and Belgium, Interpol and the national intelligence agencies (Scotland Yard's Special Branch, MI5, MI6), police and immigration officers have been less overt in operation but have revealed that they share the view of Germany and France.

Mrs Stella Rimington, appointed as the new head of MI5 in June 1994, gave a Dimbleby Lecture in which she declared that the Kurds posed an 'increasing threat of violence' in Europe (18 June 1994).

According to an article in the *Financial Times* (22 November 1993) Britain has built up particularly strong links with Germany's domestic intelligence agency, BFV. The BFV is known to exchange information with the Turkish intelligence services (MİT) on what they call Kurdish 'separatists'. The Turkish police liaise with their European counterparts, including Britain. In an article headed 'MI5, Special Branch and the Criminalisation of the Kurds in Britain', writer Stephen Long explains:

> the European Liaison Unit of the Metropolitan Police Special Branch coordinates information distribution between European Union police and intelligence organisations. It was established by the Labour government in 1976 and has functioned as something of a European headquarters for combating 'terrorism'. It relays information from one European police force to another and services requests for data on, for example, would-be immigrants and asylum seekers ... In 1991 Germany proposed the establishment of a Europol. It was incorporated into the Maastricht Treaty ... The programme for criminalising Kurdish communities who overwhelmingly support the PKK was devised by the TREVI group of European Home Office Ministers as well as senior police and intelligence officers. TREVI is an acronym for terrorism, radicalism, extremism and violence. It is not accountable to any European body or Parliament. The development of Europol will supersede TREVI. However the TREVI programme against the Kurds uses the European Liaison Section at Scotland Yard and it is still functioning.[11]

Although neither the PKK nor other Kurdish associations had been prohibited or raided by police in the UK, by the end of 1994 prominent Kurdish political figures began to be arrested in the small hours of the morning, snatched from their homes or where they stayed as guests and thereafter detained at Her Majesty's pleasure as constituting 'a threat to national security', or under the Prevention of Terrorism Act (PTA).

The European representative of the ERNK (PKK political wing), Kani Yilmaz (Faysal Dunlayci), was arrested by police on 26 October 1994 a short distance from the House of Commons, where he was to address a parliamentary meeting on the issue of the peace process in Kurdistan. He was initially detained as a 'threat to national security', and it emerged soon after that the German government sought to extradite Yilmaz from the UK, accusing him of being responsible (as the ERNK's European representative) for acts of arson allegedly carried out by the PKK in German cities. There was no evidence linking him to any such activities. Labour MP John Austin-Walker, who had issued Yilmaz with the invitation to the House, criticised the British government for its hypocrisy, commenting:

[Kani] was set on by about a dozen officers of the Metropolitan Police and carted off to Charing Cross police station and subsequently served with a deportation order. When Jack Straw and I challenged Michael Howard as to what the reasons were – we were told he was a threat to national security. One of the wonderful pieces of British Law is that if the Home Secretary says someone is a threat to national security he doesn't have to give any reasons for the deportation ... You are not given the reasons why you are a threat to national security ... As far as we can see, the only allegation against Kani is that he is associated with the PKK and the German government regards the PKK as a terrorist organisation and for that reason is seeking his extradition ... There you have it, someone who is wanting to discuss a peace process, who wants to meet parliamentarians from this country to influence the peaceful solution to a war of genocide in Turkey, comes here on a peace mission and finds himself in Britain's maximum security jail.[12]

On 25 July 1995, the Magistrates' Court at Belmarsh Prison where Kani Yilmaz remained in detention accorded the German government the legal right to pursue extradition under the terms of the European Convention. Yilmaz's barrister immediately filed an appeal with the High Court on the grounds that Yilmaz could not expect a fair trial were he to be extradited to Germany. Ending their protest outside the British Home Office, 3,000 Kurds clashed with British police outside Victoria Station upon learning this news and staged an angry sit-down demonstration in the middle of Victoria Street, blocking all traffic in and out of Victoria for the next seven hours before finally dispersing. A number of other arrests, detentions and the denial of the right to travel abroad also occurred in the case of individual asylum seekers, including recognised political refugees, those with exceptional leave to remain, and even non-Kurds supporting the Kurdish cause.

Numbers of Iraqi Kurds with political refugee status, or exceptional leave to remain (ELR) returning to Europe after visits to northern Iraq via Turkey have been detained for several hours and questioned by immigration officials at the port of entry about the PKK: did they have any contact with the PKK? Who had they seen while in transit through Turkey? With whom did they reside in the UK? Which organisations were they in contact with? And so on. Again, these procedures are evidence of systematic attempts by foreign governments friendly with Turkey to support Turkey in its strategies of non-reconciliation and non-dialogue with the PKK as an organisation outlawed by, and within, Turkey. It is also an activity based upon a tactical differentiation between the various Kurdish groups and treatment according to their political sympathies.

It is generally easier for Iraqi and Iranian Kurds to obtain full refugee status throughout Europe. Despite the scale of the war in Turkey and the comprehensive reporting of human rights violations in the Kurdish provinces, it has become exceptionally difficult for Kurds from Turkey to obtain official recognition as persons suffering persecution and therefore entitled to international protection under the UN convention of 1951 on refugees. This is despite the fact that Kurds in Turkey are persecuted on the basis of their ethnicity in Turkey and that this persecution has not an individual, but a racial basis.

On 14 December 1994, despite the fact that a unanimous resolution was passed by the European Parliament on Turkey, individual governments failed to respond. In items 7, 8 and 9 the Parliament:

— calls on the Council of Europe to urge Turkey to embark on a process of dialogue in order to seek a democratic solution to the legitimate aspirations of its 15 million citizens of Kurdish origin, thereby removing a source of tension and conflict which is threatening peace and stability in the countries of the region and Western Europe;
— calls on the Member States not to deport Kurdish refugees who have fled from Turkey; instructs its president to forward this resolution to the Council, the Commission, the Member States, the Turkish Grand National Assembly and the Turkish Government, the Council of Europe, the UN Secretary-General and the Secretariat of the CSCE. (DOC/EN/RE/262/262821.)

Not only was there no positive reponse, in the UK only 5 per cent of all asylum seekers, including those from Turkey, were being granted full refugee status by the Home Office. Conditions adversely affecting the welfare of Kurdish refugees grew worse, and the threat of deportation increased. According to figures supplied by Winston Churchill MP in the form of a written parliamentary answer, between 1992 and 1994 45,655 claims for asylum were refused. During the same period there were 5,150 removals from the UK (including voluntary and forced removals). Despite these figures the government has 'come under attack from the political right ... for being lenient on immigration and especially for not enforcing more deportations' (Anti-Deportation Campaign Report circulated to Kurdish and Turkish refugee community associations, London, April 1995).

The Kurds were invariably afraid for their future safety. The strain had even begun to tell on their children. Schools across London phoned the refugee community centres with reports of distressed children having broken down in class, saying 'Daddy is being sent back to Turkey. What is going to happen to us? Will we be sent back too?' Some heads of schools offered to write letters of support for such families to enable them to remain in the UK on compassionate grounds, but 'compassion' was becoming an increasingly alien concept to the Home Office.

Even more disturbing was the prospect presented when the Metropolitan Police announced that they were forming special police units to investigate 'Turkish terrorists' in London and locate illegal immigrants. Some of these were taught Turkish in order to carry out their additional 'immigration duties', being better equipped thereby to identify Kurds from Turkey in the UK 'illegally'.

This created enormous suffering among Kurdish families whose applications had been refused. Refusals being in the majority, the situation promised to escalate out of control. The Home Office's statistics alone were sufficient evidence of the British government's new policy to keep down refugee numbers on a number-based consensus.

Kurdish unity: a threat to Western interests in the Middle East?

Since the Gulf war of 1991, the US has publicly supported the Kurds of Iraq on humanitarian grounds and called them 'good Kurds'. The Kurds of Iran have been ignored and the Kurds of Turkey branded 'terrorists', and likened to the IRA by Jeffrey Archer. The Allied protection flights over northern Iraq hypocritically 'protected' Iraqi Kurds but ceased their surveillance missions whenever Turkey warned of an impending cross-border operation to pursue Turkish Kurdish rebels. The continued coalition presence in northern Iraq maintained Allied access to regional intelligence to which Turkey also had full access, as I have previously mentioned. This intelligence was put to use in locating Turkish Kurd targets for Turkey's bombing raids.

While Turkey played a leading role in the affairs of northern Iraq after March 1991, its policy towards the Iraqi Kurds was one of the main causes of the fighting between the PUK and the KDP which first came to a head in April 1994. The Kurdish fighting gave Turkey the excuse it sought to invade northern Iraq in March 1995, as well as providing its Western allies with further reasons for failing to acknowledge Kurdish ambitions for full political authority in the area.

Internal clashes weakened the Kurdish administration and deprived the Kurdish Federated Parliament of power. The general disunity which was manifested, not only between the Iraqi Kurdish parties but also by these parties toward the Kurdish parties of Iran and Turkey, played still further into the hands of the neighouring countries as well as the Western governments, all of whom remained opposed in principle to any form of Kurdish independence.

The only hope of salvaging 'free Kurdistan' – for which so many civilians had died in the course of the uprising – lay in negotiating a lasting political settlement among themselves. This was something Kurds everywhere recognised and understood; the word 'unity' (*yekîtî*) was on people's lips even as the Kurdish parties in south Kurdistan soaked themselves in one another's blood.

Western governments were loath to see either the religious movement or the Marxist-oriented PKK grow stronger in Kurdistan. They continued to back both the KDP and the PUK while tightening the noose on the PKK in Turkey, Kurdistan and across Europe. Neither a radical Islamic movement nor a powerful PKK active across both north and south Kurdistan promised to provide security for Western interests in the Middle East. These parties were outside the sphere of Western control.

Western statesmen have supported the supply of arms to the Middle East as 'good for protecting the jobs at home'. Western economies increasingly rely on maintaining high levels of military manufacture and supply. Human rights come a poor second to trade. But as the largest stateless people in the world the Kurds possess no single guarantee to ensure their survival, let alone any right to safeguard their own national and economic security or to arm themselves. The world's countries justify all manner of foreign military ecapades, political alliances and brutal internal repression at home on the grounds of 'national security' and economic preservation to achieve the same. Even the right of the Kurds to defend themselves on their own soil has never been acknowledged. How much longer before it is realised that the dilemma of the Kurds cannot be resolved at gunpoint?

A Kurdish revolution: MED TV

Following the inauguration in The Hague of the Kurdistan Parliament-in-Exile MED TV (short for *Medya* – the Medes are believed to be the ancestors of the Kurds), the first international Kurdish-language satellite television station, was officially opened in May 1995 under licence of the British Independent Television Commission (ITC).

The first ever broadcasts in Kurdish caused an uproar in Turkey as the Turkish government's ban on the use of the Kurdish language was torn apart overnight. Thousands of jubilant Kurds throughout Europe, the Middle East and North Africa tuned in to listen to the first six-hour special programme on MED TV on 20 April 1995.

The Turkish government condemned Britain and made protests 'at the highest levels' (*Daily Telegraph*, 24 May 1995) for having issued

MED TV with its licence to broadcast, and denounced those behind the scenes as PKK separatists. At the same time, police and soldiers in Turkey carried out raids on private homes and teahouses, seizing or destroying satellite dishes wherever possible throughout the Kurdish provinces in a desperate attempt to maintain censorship of all reporting of the Kurdish issue. But for the first time Kurds were able to speak openly to an international audience, apparently free of the threats of imprisonment and execution with which all previously televised attempts at open debate had been fraught.

From mid-May onwards, the station commenced transmission of a daily three-hour programme between 4 p.m. and 7 p.m. (GMT), beginning with children's cartoons dubbed into Kurdish and proceeding to international news, cultural programmes, talk shows, quiz shows and political debates in accordance with the terms of their licence. From October onwards this increased to six hours' broadcasting time.

Within a short period, the quality of programming, presentation skills and computer graphics began to demonstrate a confident new sophistication as MED TV employed those best able to carry it forward. The effects on the Kurdish populace both in Kurdistan and Europe were enormous. The lid was blown off hitherto forbidden subjects which could now be discussed in depth. Kurdish attitudes and outlook, the war in Kurdistan, internal rivalries spanning three hundred years, issues so long manipulated by the Turkish and other national media were at last made public.

Êhmedê Xanê, probably the most accomplished Kurdish writer of classical times, renowned for his Kurdish epic *Mem û Zin* (a Romeo and Juliet style tragedy) had recognised three hundred years ago the dilemma of Kurdish internal political division. The first carve-up of Kurdistan between the Persian Safavid Empire and the Ottoman Empire had taken effect a mere eleven years before his birth. Hence Xanê grew up with an intense awareness of its impact. The longing for Kurdish self-determination featured prominently in his work, despite this being an epoch when the peoples of the region were embroiled in religious conflicts and possessed little national self-awareness. The extract from Xanê's poem which follows is important because it underlines some of the most fundamental aspects of the Kurdish dilemma – how do you retain your sense of honour and preserve your national heritage when the outside world energetically attempts to prevent you from doing so?

Xanê's vision is offered at the conclusion of this chapter as it represents the Kurds' own voice of history. The poet evaluates the complex situation confronting the Kurdish tribes, as if they were blighted by fate to have found themselves living in so difficult a geographical region of the world. Incidentally, the Turkish government immediately banned the poem when the first Turkish translation was rendered by Kurdish scholar, Mohammed Emin Bozarslan, as late as 1968.

Extract from *Our Dilemma*

As if the Kurds held the keys to the border
every tribe as strong as a wall
whenever the seas of the Turks
lash the oceans of the Persians
rising and colliding
it is the Kurds who are washed in blood
and set one against the other

generosity, benevolence and chivalry
bravery, self possession and courage
are attributed to every Kurdish tribe
famed for their swords and their honour
brave as they are proud
in equal measure
they despise submission
spurn domination
and for this remain isolated
fighting one another, ever divided

had they once honoured an agreement
grown accustomed to standing together
then the Arabs, Turks and Persians
would be like our boy-servants
in that event we would perfect
the arts of government and religion
possess widsom and science
the true from the false would be evident
allowing the emergence
of those most rich in talent ...

Êhmedê Xanê (1651–1707?)[13]

Notes

1. Jochen Blaschke, 'Kurdische Gemeinschaften in Deutschland und Westeuropa: Ein Uberblick uber ihre soziale und kulturelle Situation', in R. Schneider (ed.), *Kurden Im Exil: Ein Handbuch*, Edition Parabolis /Berliner Institut für Vergleichende Sozial-

forschung, Berlin 1991; Ismet Cherif Vanly, 'Kurden im Exil', Introduction in R. Schneider (ed.), op. cit., pp. 1.3–10; updated in 1995 by Sheri Laizer in consultation with Kon-Kurd (Confederation of Kurdish Associations in Europe), Brussels.

2. Kon-Kurd (Confederation of Kurdish Associations in Europe), *Policy Programme towards the year 2000*, p. 10.

3. J. van Loon, *Kooerden in Den Haag. In de Marges van heet Migrantenbeleid*, Den Haag, RCB, 1992.

4. Martin van Bruinessen, R.K. Koopmans, W. Smit and L. van Velzen (eds), *Turkije in Crisis: ein sociale, politieke en economische analyse*, Bussum: het Wereldvenster, 1982.

5. See Alan Brooke, 'The Turkish Armed Forces and the Arms Trade', *Kurdistan Report, No. 18*, May /June 1994.

6. *Defend the Kurds: Defend Human and Civil Rights in Britain and Europe*, published by Defend the Kurds Campaign, London, 26 April 1995, p. 16.

7. KHRP (London)/Medico International (Frankfurt) *Final Resolution*. International Conference on North West Kurdistan (south-east Turkey), 12–13 March 1994, Brussels.

8. There is a very clear-cut distinction between supporters of the PKK and those who co-operate with the Turkish government, as for example, village guards (state militia) paid to bear arms against the 'rebels'. The village guards number around 50,000 Kurds (see Serdar Çelik in the bibliography) – a small percentage of the overall Kurdish population of around 15 million in Turkey.

9. Brooke, 'The Turkish Armed Forces', *Kurdistan Report, June/July 1994*, quoting *NATO's Sixteen Nations Special*; *Defence in Turkey*, Bonn, 1992; *Turkey Briefing* (CAAT, 1990 and 1992); Pax Christi International, *Security and Disarmament – the Turkey Connection: Military Build-up of a New Regional Power*, Brussels, 1993; *RUSI Journal* (June 1993); *Jane's Defence Weekly*, 14 August 1993; International Institute of Strategic Studies, *The Military Balance 1992–1993* and *1993–1994*.

10. CARDRI News, March 1995

11. See the full article by Stephen Long, 'MI5, Special Branch and the Criminalisation of the Kurds in Britain', *Kurdistan Report*, Jan/Feb 1995, pp. 4–5.

12. See the full article by MP John Austin-Walker, 'Hypocrisy of the British Government', *Kurdistan Report*, special issue, May/June 1995, pp. 28–30.

13. Êhmedê Xanê, excerpt from *Our Dilemma*, translated into English from a Turkish translation of the Old Kurdish by M. Emin Bozarslan (Turkish), 1968. Êhmedê Xanê's biographical dates supplied by Felat Dilgeş, a scholar and former director of the Mesopotamia Cultural Centre, Istanbul.

Postscript: beyond fratricide? 1996

Omnipresent portraits of Hafiz Asad, Syrian president for a quarter of a century, and his favourite son, Basil (groomed for succession, tragically killed in a car accident in February 1994) drape ten-storey municipal buildings, city walls, market stalls, restaurants, cafés and car windows, from where they gaze out over Syria's 16 million subjects. Of these, two million subjects are Kurds, 200,000 of whom are classed not as citizens but as 'foreigners', permitted neither Syrian nationality nor the identity cards, passports and work permits which this status confers.

The arabization of Kurdish areas in northern Syria, which began in 1962, ceased when Asad became president in 1970. Until that date, Syrian Kurds were deprived of the right to use the Kurdish language or possess Kurdish books and music cassettes. Although the situation is undeniably better today, many Kurds still feel that they live in an open prison. Thousands have joined the PKK's now 15,000-strong guerrilla forces to fight for the realisation of a free homeland. Scores languish in Syrian gaols for 'political' offences.

Syria remains a key player in the Middle East peace process, holding the cards to a number of regional issues in addition to that of the Golan Heights. Its other cards include dispute of Turkey's seizure in 1938 – and subsequent occupation – of the important Syrian coastal province of Antakaya, an area which geographically coheres with Syria and where resides a significant population of Alevi Arabs, the same religious colour as the Syrian president. The Alevi issue also links Hafiz Asad with the Turkish Kurds, discriminated against by the majority Sunni population of Turkey. Then there is the sensitive issue of water: Turkey has built dams across the Euphrates as part of the GAP (South Anatolia Project) affecting the river's flow into both Syria and Iraq. (The Turks did not negotiate this action with the government of either country beforehand.) The resulting lack of water also hinders the supply of available electricity, especially in the case of Syria. Turkey, chafed by Damascus having turned a blind eye to the presence of PKK training camps in the Syrian-controlled Bekaa valley and elsewhere, has consistently threatened to cut the flow of water to Syria. Recent reports obtained by the Syrian *Mukhabarat* allege that the Turks have been poisoning the Euphrates where it runs through Syrian territory – contaminating Kurdish villages.

On the eve of New Year 1996, fellow cameraman Tim Wise and myself were interviewing Kurdish families in Qamishli, northern Syria. Many had given fighters and martyrs to the PKK and the walls of their homes were decorated with their portraits and photos of PKK leader Abdullah Öcalan – not forbidden here. We had travelled to the region immediately following the fiasco of the national elections in Turkey – an event which clearly exhibited the deep divisions in the country and which resulted in a split vote with neither victor nor government on Christmas Day.

Necmettin Erbakan's Refah Party took a surprise lead, with 21.38 per cent of the vote, followed by Mesut Yilmaz's ANAP (19.65 per cent), Tansu Çiller's DYP (19.18 per cent) and Bülent Ecevit's DSP close on their tail (14.64 per cent) (source: *Turkish Daily News*, 7 January 1996). Other contenders, including Cem Boyner's YDP, Alparslan Turkes' far right-wing MHP, and the pro-Kurdish HADEP, led by Murat Bozlak, were constitutionally excluded from tendering MPs for the new cabinet, having failed to exceed the 10 per cent threshold. Although HADEP took more than 50 per cent of the vote in the Kurdish areas (despite there having been more than two million Kurds left unregistered after being forced from their villages), the 25 HADEP candidates who attained a regional majority could not officially be designated as MPs. HADEP accordingly declared that its elected representatives would form an alternative forum in Ankara to represent their constituents. Failing this the Kurdish sector of the population would have no voice at all. Meanwhile, in the ensuing confusion, Tansu Çiller and Mesut Yilmaz met with Bülent Ecevit to discuss the formation of a new coalition government, which would counterbalance the majority vote achieved by Refah and dilute the pro-Islamic vote. A mere week later President Süleyman Demirel would state that Refah was 'to form the next coalition government' (*Guardian*, 10 January 1996)

Abdullah Öcalan and the December 1995 ceasefires

The bilateral ceasefire between the PKK and the KDP announced on International Human Rights Day, 10 December 1995 still held good. There was intense discussion of the formation of a multi-party Kurdish National Congress, particularly on the part of the PKK, whose initiative it had been. The goal of unity between diverse Kurdish parties had been recognised as the most urgent of all political imperatives. Meanwhile, the PKK's unilateral ceasefire, announced on 14 December 1995, went ignored by the Turkish military. Air and land forces unhesitatingly pursued operations on both sides of the Turkish/Iraqi border in the first days of 1996.

This second ceasefire illustrated the PKK's positive response to the terms imposed by the European Parliament on Turkey for admittance into the European Customs Union earlier that month. Turkish membership had been agreed, subject to peaceful political negotiations taking place between representatives of the Ankara government and the PKK. Characteristically, Turkish government spokesmen vehemently condemned this condition.

Our programme in Kurdistan included a sought-after meeting and extensive filmed interview with the PKK leader to discuss the issues referred to above. Arrangements were made through the Party and before long, a driver materialised to convey us to a secret location. For security reasons we recevied no prior notification of either the time or the place.

A big, warm man with a fire in his eyes – certainly no feudal warlord – Abdullah Öcalan welcomed us and promised to place himself at our service for the rest of that day. Eloquent and down to earth, the PKK general secretary said we were at liberty to ask him whatever we wished to know, go wherever we would, and speak with anyone we chose – subject, of course, to their consent. He was as good as his word.

The interview began with a discussion of the situation of the Kurds in Europe and conditions pertaining to refugees. From there, the conversation naturally led to the topic of war and the issue of the two ceasefires currently in effect, and the human cost of the fighting, particularly to the younger generation in view of the unprecented numbers who desired to join the PKK and train as soldiers rather than obtain university qualifications or other skills vital to a balanced society.

Seated outside in the open air with us in the chill January sunlight, Abdullah Öcalan focused his thoughts and spoke without hesitation:

> This is a problem we fully recognise. We tell them [young people] that education is very important, that they should make every effort to study and learn things that are useful in these times. We do not believe that everybody should become a guerrilla. For example, in a family with two sons or daughters, let one become a guerrilla if he or she should so choose, but let the other pursue some equally useful path, political, diplomatic, whatever is appropriate to them.
>
> Here in the party's central schools, we also concentrate on education. The students do not simply learn the codes of war and peace, they learn how to live, how to think for themselves, to mature as people with deep feelings and true thoughts. They learn what humanity is, what freedom is,

what is true and straight in life. But we are living in a time of war where all these values are at stake because the Kurdish people's dispossession. The people are engaged in a struggle which is one of life or death (excerpt from a private interview, 3 January 1996).

As he spoke, his students and cadres stood to attention, hands clenched into fists at their sides, poised to catch the leader's every word. Öcalan, now aged 48, the most uncompromising of all the Kurdish leaders, passed slowly through their ranks like a commander inspecting his troops, or a father his children, pausing to question this one, to commend or correct that one, having genuine words for everyone. In the grey wintry light, assembled here during a short reprieve from the battlefield beneath a sky which promised storm, the faces of the students shone as 'Apo' walked among them.

Delil Andok, a cadre present there that afternoon, quoted PKK martyr Kemal Pir: 'It is because we *love* life so much that we are prepared to die for it.'

Appendix

Seventy years of military rule in Kurdistan authorised by Turkish Law

1. Martial Law, proclaimed in Sivas under decree No. 727, dated 12.12.1920.
2. Martial Law proclaimed in the counties of Mamuretulaziz, Erzincan, Divriği and Zara. No. 727, dated 10.3.1921.
3. Martial Law decree proclaimed for some of the Eastern Provinces (Elaziz, Genç, Muş, Ergani, Dersim, Diyarbakir, Mardin, Urfa, Siverek, Siirt, Bitlis, Van, Hakkari, Malatya, Kiği and Hinis), No. 114, Res. Gas. No. 85, dated 25.2.1925.
4. Martial Law proclaimed for some of the Eastern Provinces; decree for extension of one month, No. 121 R.G. No. 90, dated 23.3.1925.
5. Marital Law proclaimed for some of the Eastern Provinces, decree of extension for seven months. No. 163, dated 25.11.1925.
6. Extension of Martial Law, No. 163, dated 25.11.1925.
7. Decision to proclaim a one month interval of Martial Law, for the inclusion of Erzurum province, No. 167, dated 24.11.1925.
8. Proclamation for the region in revolt and adjoining provinces, of one year's further extension of Martial Law, No. 271, dated 22.11.1926.
9. Martial Law to be extended by a further period of one month in the provinces of Genç, Muş, Erzincan, Elaziz, Dersim, Diyarbakir, Mardin, Siverek, Urfa, Siirt, Bitlis, Van and Hakkari and in Erzurum's Kiği and Hinis counties. No. 11547, dated 23.2.1925.
10. Martial law to be extended for a further period of one month in the province of Malatya. No. 1640, dated 24.2.1925.
11. Extension of Martial Law under decrees 1547 and 1551 for the period of a further month. No. 1640, dated 23.3.1925.
12. Martial Law decree for an extension of one month in the entire province of Erzurum, No. 2754, dated 24.11.1925.
    Note: During the period between 1927-1947 the General (military) Inspectorate had supreme authority in the area.
13. In the administrative districts like Istanbul, and Kocaeli, where there

was a working class and Kurdish majority, military curfew (martial law) was imposed seven times between the years 1963 and 1970.

14. Martial law imposed on Istanbul, Kocaeli, Izmir, Ankara, Adana, Hatay, Diyarbakir and Siirt districts by Turkish Grand National Assembly/Parliamentary (TBMM) decree No. 250, dated 26.4.1971.

15. Extension of martial law in the above same districts passed under Turkish General Assembly/Parliamentary (TBMM) decree No. 251, dated 26.5.1971.

16. Extension of term of martial law for the same districts (to which was added Hakkari and Mardin) in 1975.

17. With only minor alterations, between 1927 and 1975 martial law was extended in the same provinces and districts 25 times by the Turkish Grand National Assembly/Parliamentary (TBMM) decree (adding Hakkari and Mardin in 1975).

18. Martial Law decree for the districts of Adana, Ankara, Bingöl, Elaziğ, Erzincan, Erzurum, Gaziantep, Istanbul, Kahramanmaraş, Kars, Malatya, Sivas and Urfa, TBMM decree No. 518, dated 26.12.1978.

19. Martial Law extended in the provinces of Adiyaman, Diyarbakir, Hakkari, Mardin, Siirt, and Tunceli eight times in 1978, 1979 and 1980.

20. Abolition of parliament and government and lifting the diplomatic immunity of MPs, with martial law for the entire country, National Security Council (MGK) proclamation notification dated 12 September 1980.

21. MGK martial law decree was extended 11 times at quarterly intervals between 1980 and 1986 and covered almost all the districts having a majority of Kurdish population.

22. After 1986, this was replaced by the Application of a State of Emergency in the Eastern Provinces, with the General Military Inspectorate being superseded by the State of Emergency Regional Governor (Super Vali or Super Governor) to oversee its implementation. It continues until the present day.

23. 1994. The parliamentary diplomatic immunity of a number of mainly Kurdish MPs was stripped and some of the MPs subsequently sentenced to as many as 15 years in prison by the Ankara State Security Court for having expressed their political views in public.

Source: Turkish Grand National Assembly (TBMM) Library-Documentation and Translation Administration/Research Service: Periods of Martial Law). Researched by Kurdish author and publisher, Mehmet Bayrak.

Select bibliography

Amnesty International, *Iraq – Human Rights Abuses in Iraqi Kurdistan since 1991*, AI International Secretariat, London, 28 Feburary 1995.

Balli, Rafet, *Kürt Dosyasi* (Kurdish File), Cem Yayinevi, Istanbul, 1991 (in Turkish).

Bedreddin, Salah, *Kurds in Syria*, Kawa Publications, Germany, 1993 (in Arabic).

British Medical Association, *Medicine Betrayed – the Participation of Doctors in Human Rights Abuses*, Zed Books, London, 1992.

Bulloch, John and Morris, Harvey, *The Gulf War: Its Origins, History and Consequences*, Methuen, London, 1989.

Bulloch, John and Morris, Harvey, *No Friends but the Mountains (The Tragic History of the Kurds)*, Viking, London, 1992.

Çelik, Serdar, *Türk Kontra-gerillasi -ölüm makinasi* (The Turkish Contra-guerrilla Death Machine) Ülkem Presse, Berlin, 1995.

Chaliand, Gérard (ed.), *People without a Country: The Kurds and Kurdistan*, Zed Books, revised and updated edition, London, 1993.

Chaliand, Gérard, *The Kurdish Tragedy*, Zed Books, London, 1994.

Chang, Jung, *Wild Swans – Three Daughters of China*, Flamingo, London, 1993.

Dağli, Faysal, *Birakuji – Kürtlerin İç Savaşi (Fratricide – The Kurds' Internal War)*, Belge Yayinlari, Istanbul, 1994.

Fraser, James Baillie, *Travels in Koordistan, Mesopotamia*, Richard Bentley, 1840.

Hamilton, A.M., *Road Through Kurdistan*, Faber and Faber, London, 1937.

Hawar, Mohammad Rassoul, *Shaikh Mahmoud and the Revolution of South Kurdistan*, Vols I and II, both in Kurdish; Jaf Press and M.R. Hawar, London, 1990 and 1991.

Hazleton, Fran (ed.), / CARDRI, *Iraq since the Gulf War*, Zed Books, London, 1994.

Human Rights Watch and Physicians for Human Rights, *The Anfal Campaign in Iraqi Kurdistan (the Destruction of Koreme)*, New York, January 1993.

Ignatieff, Michael, *Blood and Belonging – Journeys into the New Nationalism*, BBC/Chatto, London, 1993.

Keen, David, *The Kurds in Iraq – How Safe is their Haven Now?*, Save the Children Fund, London, 1993.

Koçtürk, Tahire, *A Matter of Honour – Experiences of Turkish Women Immigrants*, Zed Books, London, 1993.

Korn, David, *Sir Percy Cox and Sir Arnold Wilson, The Two Men Responsible for Iraq*, INC, Michigan, OH, 1993.

Kurdistan Democratic Party (KDP) Research Department, *What Happened in Iraqi Kurdistan May 1994 – A report on the internal conflict in May 1994*, London, June 1994.

Kurdistan Solidarity Committee–Kurdistan Information Centre, *Kurdistan Report*, KSC–KIC, monthly publications, London, 1991, 1992, 1993, 1994, 1995.

Laizer, Sheri, *Into Kurdistan – Frontiers Under Fire*, Zed Books, London, 1991.

Makiya, Kanan (Samir al-Khalil), *The Republic of Fear (Saddam's Iraq)*, Hutchinson, Radius, London, 1989.

Makiya, Kanan (Samir al Khalil),*The Monument – Art, Vulgarity and Responsibility in Iraq*, Andre Deutsch, London, 1991.

Makiya, Kanan (Samir al-Khalil), *Cruelty and Silence (War, Tyrany, Uprising, and the Arab World)*, Jonathan Cape, London, 1993.

McDowall, David, *The Kurds, a Nation Denied*, Minority Rights Group, London, 1992.

McDowall, David, *A Modern History of the Kurds*, I.B.Tauris, London, 1995.

Meiselas, Susan (ed.), *Kurdistan in the Shadow of History*, Random House, New York, 1996.

Middle East Watch (Human Rights Watch), *Genocide in Iraq: the Anfal Campaign against the Kurds*, New York, July 1993.

Parliamentary Human Rights Group Report, *A Desolation Called Peace, a Mission to Turkish Kurdistan, 12-17 October 1993*, Kurdistan Information Centre, London, November 1993.

Patriotic Union of Kurdistan (PUK), Foreign Relations Committee, *Iraqi Kurdistan: a situation report on recent events: The Context and Specifics of the infighting in Iraqi Kurdistan*, London, February 1995.

Simpson, John, *From the House of War*, Arrow Books, London, 1991.

Soane, E.B., *To Mesopotamia and Kurdistan in Disguise*, John Murrary, London, 1912; 2nd edn with introduction by A.T. Wilson, John Murray, London, 1924.

Select bibliography of specialist magazines and newspapers consulted

Berxwedan (Resistance) Kurmanji-language newspaper following PKK developments, published in Europe.

Denge Azadi (Voice of Freedom) – daily newspaper published in Turkey and Europe, now banned and closed.

Hengaw (Step) – Sorani-dialect newspaper published monthly by Kurdish Information Centre on issues throughout Kurdistan and cultural features. Caxton House, 129 St Johns Way, London N19 3RQ.

Hawkar (Helper) – English-language news and current events in Kurdistan newsletter published bi-monthly by Hawkarani Kurdistan, PO Box 3571, London NW6 4BN.

Kurdistan Report – English-language monthly magazine covering Kurdish issues, published by Kurdistan Solidarity Committee and Kurdistan Information Centre, 44 Ainger Road, London NW3 3AT and 10 Glasshouse Yard, London EC1.

Kurdish Life – published monthly in English by the Kurdish Library, 245 Park Place, Brooklyn, NY11238.

Medya Güneşi (Median Sun) – Turkish- and Kurmanji-language weekly newspaper of the Kurdistan Socialist Unity Platform, Istanbul.

Middle East Report (MERIP) – Suite 119, 1500 Mass. Ave. NW, Washington, DC 20005.

Özgür Gündem (Free Agenda) – now banned pro-Kurdish (Turkish-language) daily newspaper covering international news and Kurdish events, Turkey.

Özgür Ülke (Free Country) – daily (Turkish-language) now banned pro-Kurdish newspaper which succeeded *Özgür Gündem* after it was banned in Turkey.

Namah (Document) – quarterly in English. Badlisy Centre, 2413A Willow Ave., Tallahassee, Florida 32303.

Ronahi (Enlightenment) – daily (Turkish- and Kurdish-language) newspaper published in Turkey and Europe; succeeded *Denge Azadi*.

Serxwebun (Liberation) – newspaper (Turkish-language) updating developments in the struggle of the PKK. Published in Europe.

Sterka Rizgari (Star of Liberation) – daily newspaper (Turkish- and Kurmanji-language) featuring news and current affairs, published in Istanbul.

Yeni Politika (New Politics) – daily pro-Kurdish newspaper (Turkish-language) published in Turkey and Europe and succeeding *Özgür Gündem* and *Özgür Ülke*, itself finally banned in August 1995.

Index